The ESL Miscellany

the New 21st Century Edition

A Treasury of Cultural and Linguistic Information

Raymond C. Clark • Patrick R. Moran • Arthur A. Burrows

PRO LINGUA ⬤ ASSOCIATES

Pro Lingua Associates, Publishers

P.O. Box 1348
Brattleboro, Vermont 05302-1348 USA

Office: 802 257 7779
Orders: 800 366 4775
Fax: 802 257 5117
Webstore: www.ProLinguaAssociates.com
E-mail: prolingu@sover.net
SAN: 216-0579

At Pro Lingua
our objective is to foster
an approach to learning and teaching
that we call **interplay**, the **inter**action
of language learners and teachers with their materials,
with the language and culture,
and with each other in active,
creative and productive
play.

This book was designed and set in Century Schoolbook type by Arthur A. Burrows. It was printed and bound by Sheridan Books in Fredericksburg, Virginia.

Printed in the United States of America

Revised, third edition, second printing 2001.
26,500 copies in print.

Acknowledgements

"The first thing we should say is that a lot of people helped us and we appreciate their support." That is the way we began the acknowledgements in the first edition, and it is still true with this update for the year 2000 Third Edition, only more so. For ten years people have been coming to us with raves about this section or that, with suggestions about improvements, corrections, and additions, and with complaints. The complaint we have heard many times over is "I can't hold on to this book. Someone keeps stealing it. This is the fourth copy I've had to buy!" We have tried to take all the other suggestions for improvements into account in this complete revision, but we haven't got a solution to that most common problem.

Our acknowledgement for all this help must be made in a very general way. Of the hundred or so teachers who have made recommendations, three sat down and wrote us a letter. First and foremost of these has been the late Richard Yorkey of Saint Michael's College in Vermont. Dick sent us very useful ideas and resources on several occasions over the last several years. Both he and Terri Rapoport of the ELS Language Center at Wagner College, N.Y., recommended that we add the section on "Common Idioms and Collocations" based on specific words. Terri made several other good suggestions which we have included. Ding K. Lau of the Dekalb, Georgia, public schools wrote to tell us the proper term for a person from Singapore, and several other people gave us nationality and regional words more informally over the years. We decided that in revising we should make our resource list "complete," so we included every member country of the United Nations in our list and many regions (Middle East, Scotland) as well. We accepted the terms used by the U.S. State Department when we

could. In some cases, we called embassies in Washington and U.N. Missions in New York. To all the teachers who have used *The ESL Miscellany* and helped us with suggestions, thank you. Keep the ideas coming for the fourth edition which will reflect data from the 2000 census.

The original idea for this book came out of a project initiated for the U.S. Peace Corps at the School for International Training in 1977. A graduate student in the MAT program, Eleanor Boone, with assistance from Rick Gildea and with support and advice from Mike Jerald, Mary Clark, and Ray Clark, was contracted by the Peace Corps to develop a manual of practical suggestions for Peace Corps volunteers teaching English as a foreign language. Toward the end of the project Eleanor was joined by Pat Moran who, at Ray Clark's suggestion, compiled an appendix of information about the English language. The appendix was intended to be useful to the Peace Corps English teacher lost deep in the back country with no professional library to speak of, and nowhere to turn for such things as punctuation guidelines and metric conversion charts.

Two years later as Pro Lingua was being started, Ray, Pat, and Andy Burrows along with Mike Jerald, Peg Clement, Marilyn Funk, and John Croes began developing additional resource materials that might be useful to the ESL teacher. Pat's appendix has now become a book in its own right - a book that represents a collective effort by its three authors.

Peg Clement must be singled out among all those who added to the project for allowing us to use the pictures and classifications from her MAT thesis as the basis for the photographic study of American Gestures.

She in turn would like to acknowledge the help of George McFadden, who took the original pictures, and of Mike Jerald, who processed them and has since added three pictures and provided the basis for the intrepretations.

Mike Jerald has also contributed numerous editorial suggestions in all parts of the book.

Susannah Clark was our chief editorial assistant for the first edition. She spent hours in the Brooks Memorial Library producing the first draft of many of the Topics. For the second edition, she edited and added to the topics in the Cultural Aspect and put that section on her computer.

Mary Clark suggested the title for our wild array of information. We think it's a good one. She also gave permission to use and adapt her chart on modal verbs.

Diane Larsen-Freeman looked over the final draft of the Lingusitic Aspect in the first edition and made several suggestions that improved that section. Bonnie Mennell reviewed our list of communicative topics, added several words, and raised several good questions. Marty Fleischer, who with help from Lisa Cook, typed the first edition on one of the world's first word processors (just twenty years ago!), pointed out that our law topic didn't adequately cover crime and police work. So Topic # 49 came into being. Karen Kale also reviewed and made suggestions for some of the present topics. Susan McBean helped type some of the original manuscript.

And so we come back to ourselves for a final pat on the back. Pat contributed the illustrations including the Atlas in the new edition. He, Ray, and Andy wrote, edited, and revised the many lists so cooperatively that even they don't know who wrote what.

Pronouncement on Pronouns

In this book, we at Pro Lingua Associates are offering a solution to the vexing "he/she" pronoun problem. We have come to the conclusion that when a reference is made to a third person singular person, and that person is indefinite (and hence gender is unknown or unimportant), we will use the third person plural forms, they, them, their(s). We are fully aware that historically these forms represent grammatical plurality. However, there are clear instances in the English language where the third person plural form is used to refer to a preceding indefinite, grammatically singular pronoun. Examples:

Everyone says this, don't **they**?
Nobody agrees with us, but we will ignore **them**.

If you will accept the examples above, it is not a major step to find the following acceptable:

The user of this book should find this easier because **they** can avoid the confusion of *he* or *she*, the awkwardness of *he or she*, and the implicit sexism of using *he* for everybody.

So in this book, you will find statements such as, . . . *the teacher who is using this book to prepare **their** own lessons.* The reader of our text may disagree with our solution, but we ask them to consider that it is time to change the usage of gender-marked pronouns when they are clearly inappropriate. This is our solution, and we encourage you to try it out. And we invite your comments.

Contents

THE COMMUNICATIVE ASPECT

THE CULTURAL ASPECT

THE METALINGUSITIC ASPECT AND MISCELLANEOUS MATERIALS

Metalinguistic and Miscellaneous Materials: Checklist

The Paralinguistic Aspect

The ESL Miscellany

Introduction

The Purpose and Contents of the Miscellany

This book is a compendium of useful and interesting information for teachers and students of English as a Second Language. Although the book focuses on North American English, it will also be useful to teachers and students of other varieties of English. Teachers will find this book useful as a resource for developing material as they supplement, expand, replace, adapt, or develop a complete curriculum from scratch. This one book does not contain everything that the teacher/materials developer needs to know, but we believe it is the most comprehensive one-volume reference available to the lesson writer.

In addition to its usefulness in developing materials, this book offers another function as a guideline/checklist for teachers who teach "a little of this and a little of that." The problem with this kind of eclecticism, of course, is that it is not always easy to know if everything is being covered. This book will not be able to tell teachers everything they need to know about North American English, but it can serve as a comprehensive outline. By consulting the list of Situations, for example, the teacher can rather quickly review which conversational situations have been covered and what remains to be covered.

A third use for this book is that many of the lists can be copied and used as hand-outs. For example, the summary of religions in the U.S. and Canada could be copied and given to the students as the point of reference for a question-answer practice or discussion of religion. For that reason we encourage copying of these lists for classroom use.

We suggested earlier that students of North American English will also find this book useful, but it is likely that it will be especially valuable to advanced students of North American English who are in need of a one-volume guide that will help them determine what they already know and what they should focus their study on. We think this book will be of particular interest to advanced students who are preparing to be teachers of English as a Second Language.

The **Miscellany** is divided into five parts. Parts I and II contain information about the language itself. This information is classified as two major aspects: Linguistic and Communicative. The linguistic aspect contains information that in some way deals with what is commonly called the grammar of the language. However, this linguistic aspect is not a grammar, but rather a series of lists of words and forms that exemplify some grammar point. For example, under Phrasal Verbs, there will be no rules for the use of these verbs. Instead, there will be a list

1

of separable and inseparable phrasal verbs. In other words, it is assumed that the user will have some understanding of how phrasal verbs function in English.

The communicative aspect does not deal with linguistic forms such as "go, went, gone" but outlines ways in which the language is used to send and receive messages. We have included lists of *functions* such as asking, introducing, telling, etc. Also in the communicative aspect section, we have included vocabulary lists that outline potential *topics* of conversations and *situations,* the contexts in which communicative functions and topics of conversation are carried out.

In Part III we have compiled several lists that form an outline of North American culture. Each list can be used as the basic data upon which can be based a discussion or controlled conversation about some facet of North American culture. Part III can be used as the basis for an orientation to immigration and resettlement in the United States and Canada.

Part IV is a pot-pourri of information that is, in general, metalinguistic. In other words, the information in this part will help the teacher and the learner facilitate the teaching/learning process. But there is also information that does not fit neatly into any of the other categories and is best labeled as miscellaneous.

Part V needs little explanation. It contains some examples of communicative systems that parallel the language itself. Hence, we have called it the paralinguistic aspect. Of greatest interest is a photographic catalog of 50 gestures that are commonly recognized and understood in North America. We have provided titles and minimal explanations for the gestures, but otherwise we leave it up to you, the user of this book, to discuss, compare, practice, and even add to this listing.

We will be the first to admit that this volume is far from complete. The information is such that it changes almost as fast as it is updated. As we prepare for the next edition, we welcome your comments and suggestions.

PRO LINGUA ASSOCIATES
Brattleboro, 2000

The Interplay Lesson Plan

On the next page we offer a lesson plan that may be helpful to the teacher who is using material from this book to prepare their own lessons. For that matter, this lesson plan can be used for most teaching activities.

The plan is based on Pro Lingua's concept of **Interplay**: The **inter**action of the teacher and learner with the material, with the language and the culture, and with each other in active, creative, and productive **play**.

The basic format comprises three stages in the implementation of most lessons: **Before**, **During** and **After**. *Before* teaching, the typical lesson is based on the students (who), the context of the teaching (when and where), the objective of the lesson (why), and the lesson content (what). *During* is the time in which the teacher and the students are actively involved face-to-face in teaching and learning. *After* focuses on assessing the lesson and looking forward to review and future lessons.

A few brief definitions may be useful.

Students: Although it is usually unnecessary to state explicitly who the students are, it is, nevertheless, always useful to consider, as the lesson is planned, the age, proficiency level, and goals of the students.

Context: For purposes of maintaining a record of the lesson for future reference, it may be helpful to state the time and place of the teaching.

Objective(s): In simple terms, the objective is a statement of *what the students should be able to do* as a result of the lesson. There may be more than one objective, but unless there is at least one objective for the lesson, it may lack focus, and the assessment of the objective may be difficult to carry out.

Linguistic Content: The lesson may or may not have a specific linguistic content, but if it does, it will be in the area of *pronunciation, vocabulary,* or *grammar*.

Functional/Strategic Content: This aspect of the content is concerned with communicative competence. Typically, functional content involves "-ing words," such as *asking, demanding, explaining,* and strategic skills, such as *rejoindering, interrupting, confirming,* and *clarifying*.

Topical Content: This involves the "message," especially the vocabulary associated with topics, such as *clothing, restaurants, business, sports,* and *music*.

Cultural Content: There may be a cultural content to the lesson. For example, *a holiday, a folktale, family structure,* and *rites of passage, from birth to death.*

Presentation: Typically, this part of the lesson is teacher-centered as the teacher *introduces the material* to the students. The presentation of the new material is often preceded by review of old material or schema-building in which the teacher sets the stage for the introduction of the new material.

Practice: Once the material is presented, the teacher and students engage in relatively *controlled interaction* with error correction so that the students will gain skill in using the new material.

Production: The final part of the lesson features the students *using* the material with each other to accomplish a communicative task. Typically, the teacher stands aside and observes and encourages the students as they become more fluent at manipulating the material in real or realistic communication.

Assessment: At the end of the lesson, or shortly thereafter, the teacher looks back at the objective *to measure* the success of the lesson. This can be done formally as a quiz or informally as monitoring the students and noting successes and errors.

Assignment: The teacher may ask the students to do *homework* that is based on the content of the lesson.

Follow-up: The teacher notes how and when the lesson content can or should be *reviewed or recycled* in future lessons.

The Lesson Plan

Before

Students:

Teaching/Learning Context:

Objective:

Content

Linguistic:

Functional/Strategic:

Topical:

Cultural:

During

Presentation:

Practice:

Production:

After

Assessment:

Assignment:

Follow-up:

The Linguistic Aspect

For years, the teaching and learning of English has focused on texts, techniques, and exercises designed to enable students to manipulate the grammar of English with a minimum of grammatical errors, such as 'he go', and with clear pronunciation. Obviously, this is still an important part of teaching English; there will always be a time and place for the tried and true exercises and drills that help install grammatical accuracy. Practice still makes perfect.

On the following pages we have provided first a checklist of grammatical features that most teachers find it necessary to cover. This checklist is not intended to represent the best pedagogical sequence; it is only one possible sequence in which English grammar can be presented.

After the checklist are several selected lists that should prove helpful to the teacher or student who wants to work on a particular grammatical problem. It should be obvious that many syntactic features do not lend themselves to listing and so they will not be included in the lists.

Contents

7

A Grammar Sequence

The grammar sequence on the following pages is to be considered only a handy checklist for the person who wants to get a rough idea of what can or should be covered in an English course. We make no claims that it is complete or logical or carefully programmed in steps of equal difficulty or complexity. We have listed 139 steps, and we have placed them in a particular order. Some of the steps are big and some are small. Some steps can be omitted or placed elsewhere in the sequence, and some depend upon previous steps and should only be re-arranged with care. It will also be obvious that in some cases, two or more steps must be taken at the same time. In other words, please use this sequence with the understanding that it is not a grammar of English and it is not the best or the most natural sequence for proceeding through a grammatically-based English course.

The sequence does represent an attempt to proceed one step at a time through the grammar of English in a general progression of "easy and simple" points to "difficult and complex" points. It also represents a sequence that begins with useful and necessary points and leads to less useful and necessary points. At the very least, the sequence represents dozens of potential grammar lessons that nearly every teacher and student will need to struggle with in a basic English program. Mastery of what this sequence represents, along with commensurate progress in pronunciation and communicative skills, would probably mean that the student is capable of functioning independently in an English-speaking world.

❑ 1. Statement word order with *be*   I am here.

❑ 2. Forms of *be*   Am; are; is

❑ 3. Subject pronouns   I, you, he, she, it, we, they

❑ 4. Question word order with *be*   Is he here?

❑ 5. Negative of *be*   I am not; you are not

❑ 6. Plural of regular nouns   We are students.

❑ 7. Common irregular noun plurals   They are women.

❑ 8. Nationality words   I am Swedish. They are Swedish.

❑ 9. Indefinite article: *a/an*   I am an American.

❑ 10. Question word: *who*   Who is she?

❑ 11. *And* in compound sentences   He is a teacher, and she is a teacher.

❑ 12. *But* in compound sentences　　　He is a teacher, but she is a student.

❑ 13. Contractions of *be* and *not*　　　I'm not; he isn't

❑ 14. Main verbs in statements　　　I teach French. She teaches English

❑ 15. Yes/No questions with main verbs　　　Does she speak English? Do you see me?

❑ 16. Negatives of main verbs　　　I don't speak English. We don't see you.

❑ 17. Stative verbs: *have, need, want*　　　I have a dictionary.

❑ 18. Question word: *what*　　　What do you have?

❑ 19. Short Answers.　　　Yes, I do. No, he isn't.

❑ 20. Tag Questions　　　You have..., don't you?
　　　　You don't have..., do you?

❑ 21. Negative questions　　　Don't you have... ?

❑ 22. *Can, will.*　　　I can read English.

❑ 23. Positive imperative　　　Take a....

❑ 24. Negative imperative　　　Don't take a....

❑ 25. Colors　　　Take a red....

❑ 26. Definite and indefinite articles　　　...the yellow pencil. ...a yellow pencil.

❑ 27. Polite requests: *would, will, could*　　　Would you... ?

❑ 28. Demonstratives: *this/that these/those*　　　This is a ....
　　　　Those are ....

❑ 29. Count and non-count nouns　　　This is soup. This is a spoon.

❑ 30. Expletive *there is, there are*　　　There's a fly....

❑ 31. Expletive *here*　　　Here's a....

❑ 32. Expletive *it*　　　It's cold.

❑ 33. Form and position of modifiers　　　...green shoes.

❑ 34. Order of modifiers   ...small green tennis shoes.

❑ 35. Past tense of *be*   I was....

❑ 36. Past tense of regular verbs   I studied....

❑ 37. Use of *did*   Did you... ? No, I didn't....

❑ 38. Irregular past tense forms   I taught....

❑ 39. Question words as interrogative   Which book... ?
        adjectives: *what, which*

❑ 40. *Some, any* and *none*   I don't have any,....

❑ 41. Quantity expressions *(how)*   I have a few....
        much/many, few, little

❑ 42. Use of *quite* and *only*   I have quite a few....

❑ 43. *One* as a pronoun   ...the green one.

❑ 44. *One of/none of*   He needs one of the ....

❑ 45. *The other/another*   She likes the other ....

❑ 46. *Each/every/all of*   Each student has ....

❑ 47. Object pronouns   ...understand her.

❑ 48. Direct and indirect objects   ... give it to her.

❑ 49. Adverbs of frequency.   He always ....

❑ 50. *Ever*   Do you ever ... ?

❑ 51. Question words: *how often,*   How often do you ... ?
        where, where

❑ 52. Cardinal and ordinal numbers   The first five .... The fifth ....

❑ 53. Word order with place and time   ... here in the morning.
        adverbials

❑ 54. Prepositions with time expressions   ... at three o'clock on Monday.

❑ 55. Prepositions with places   ... on Main Street. In Brattleboro.

❑ 56. *Do* vs. *make*   Do the dishes and make the bed.

❑ 57. Form and position of adverbs of manner *(-ly)*   ... speak slowly.

❑ 58. Irregular adverbs of manner   ... talk fast.

❑ 59. Question word: *how*   How does she ... ?

❑ 60. *Say, tell, talk, speak*   Tell me about ....

❑ 61. Indirect object after *ask*   Ask her a question.

❑ 62. Indirect object with *to*   Explain it to her.

❑ 63. Indirect object with *for*   Do it for me.

❑ 64. Present progressive (continuous)   I am ...ing.

❑ 65. *Going to* future   I am going to ....

❑ 66. Question word: *why*   Why are you ... ?

❑ 67. Question word: *what ... for*   What are you... for?

❑ 68. Question word: *how come*   How come you ...?

❑ 69. Anticipatory *it*   It's easy to ....

❑ 70. *Let's*   Let's ....   Let's not....

❑ 71. Idioms with *go*   Let's go swimming.

❑ 72. Indefinite *you*   You can't go swimming there.

❑ 73. Question words: *who vs. who(m)*   Who sees Mary? Whom does Mary see?

❑ 74. Question word: *whose*   Whose ... is this?

❑ 75. Possessive adjectives   That's my ....

❑ 76. Possessive *'s*   Mary's ... is here.

❑ 77. Possessive *of*   The leg of my table.

❏ 78. Possessive pronouns   That's mine.

❏ 79. **Belongs to**   That belongs to ....

❏ 80. **Be about to** future   I am about to ....

❏ 81. Present tense for future time   I leave... next week.

❏ 82. Modals: **may, might, should, must**   We might go ....

❏ 83. Modals: **ought to**   We ought to go ....

❏ 84. **Have to, have got to**   We have to go ....

❏ 85. Modals in past time   We could have gone. We had to go.

❏ 86. Future tense with **will**   We'll go ....

❏ 87. Contractions of **will not**   We won't go ....

❏ 88. Future progressive   We will be going.

❏ 89. **Had better**   We'd better go....

❏ 90. **Would rather**   I'd rather be a ....

❏ 91. **Would like**   I'd like to be a ....

❏ 92. **Was going to ... but**   I was going to ..., but ...

❏ 93. **And ... too/either**   ... and she does too. ... and I won't either.

❏ 94. Separable/inseparable phrasal verbs   Let's call on them. Let's call them up.

❏ 95. Adverbials of purpose: **for** and **(in order) to**   He went for some books / to buy some books.

❏ 96. Adverbials of means and instrument: **by** and **with**   He went by bus. He went with a suitcase.

❏ 97. Verbs followed by an infinitive   I want to go.

❏ 98. Verbs followed by a gerund   I enjoy singing.

❏ 99. Verbs followed by an infinitive or a gerund   I like to read/reading.

❏ 100. Perception verbs followed by a simple verb instead of *-ing*   I saw him go.

❏ 101. *Very, too, enough*   That's too big

❏ 102. Comparison: *the same ... as, different from* and *like*   This is the same as that.

❏ 103. Comparison: *the same ... as, as... as*   Mine is the same color as yours.

❏ 104. Comparison: *-er than, more... than*   It's bigger than his and more useful than hers.

❏ 105. Superlative   It's the biggest and most useful.

❏ 106. Past habitual   I used to....

❏ 107. *Would* as past habitual   When we were young, we would ....

❏ 108. *Be used to*   I'm used to ....

❏ 109. Causatives: *let, have, help, make,* and *get*   We made him go.

❏ 110. Reflexive pronouns   He hurt himself.

❏ 111. Emphatic pronouns   He did it himself. He himself did it.

❏ 112. Embedded statements   I know (that) he's here.

❏ 113. Embedded question-word statements   I know where he is.

❏ 114. Relative clauses   I know the man who did it.

❏ 115. *Who/whatever*   Whoever has ....

❏ 116. *For* vs. *during*   ... during the afternoon for an hour.

❏ 117. Past Continuous   He was studying ....

❏ 118. *While* and *then* in clauses   ... while I was sleeping

❏ 119. *Before, until* and *after*   He studied before you arrived.

❏ 120. Present perfect   I have already studied.

❏ 121. Irregular past participles   She has gone.

❏ 122. Participles as modifiers   He is boring/bored.

❏ 123. *Still, anymore, already, yet*   He hasn't studied yet.

❏ 124. Present perfect progressive   They have been playing

❏ 125. Past perfect   They had gone.

❏ 126. Reported speech   He said she had gone.

❏ 127. Past perfect progressive   They had been working.

❏ 128. Passive voice   They were seen by ....

❏ 129. Adjective+preposition combinations   She is interested in....

❏ 130. Subjunctive   I suggested that she see....

❏ 131. *Wish* followed by a noun clause   I wish (that) you were here.

❏ 132. *Wish* and noun clause in past time   I wish (that) you had been here.

❏ 133. Conditionals   If you were here ....

❏ 134. Subordinators: *unless, because, although, whenever*   Unless I am mistaken ....

❏ 135. Future perfect   They will have gone ....

❏ 136. Future perfect progressive   They will have been working

❏ 137. *So ... that* vs. *such ... that*   He is so strong that ....

❏ 138. Nouns as complements   We elected him president.

❏ 139. Verb+preposition combinations   We agreed on that.

Grammar Lists

Grammar Checklist

1: Minimal Pairs

Vowels

/iy/	/i /
sheep	ship
leave	live
seat	sit
green	grin

/iy/	/ey/
eat	ate
see	say
week	wake
creep	crepe

/iy/	/e/
meet	met
mean	men
seeks	sex
beast	best

/i/	/ey /
it	ate
kick	cake
chin	chain
give	gave

/i/	/e/
pick	peck
did	dead
sit	set
knit	net

/i/	/æ/
big	bag
it	at
sit	sat
zig	zag

/i /	/ə/
big	bug
live	love
sick	suck
rib	rub

/ey/	/e/
wait	wet
date	debt
pain	pen
raid	red

/ey/	/æ/
snake	snack
ate	at
made	mad
hate	hat

/ey /	/ə /
ape	up
lake	luck
rain	run
came	come

/ey/	/ow/
taste	toast
say	so
break	broke
wake	woke

/e/	/æ/
dead	dad
said	sad
men	man
bed	bad

/e /	/ə /
beg	bug
ten	ton
many	money
net	nut

/e/	/a/
get	got
step	stop
red	rod
net	not

/æ/	/ə/
grab	grub
swam	swum
mad	mud
cap	cup

Vowels (Continued)

/æ/	/a/
an	on
map	mop
cat	cot
lack	lock

/æ/	/ay/
am	I'm
sad	side
dad	died
back	bike

/ə/	/a/
hug	hog
cup	cop
luck	lock
nut	not

/ə/	/u/
luck	look
buck	book
stud	stood
tuck	took

/ə/	/ow/
cut	coat
must	most
come	comb
but	boat

/ə/	/ɔ/
gun	gone
cut	caught
bus	boss
dug	dog

/a/	/u/
lock	look
pot	put
cod	could
shock	shook

/a/	/ow/
hop	hope
got	goat
want	won't
rod	road

/a/	/ɔ/
cot	caught
sod	sawed
are	or
tock	talk

/a/	/aw/
are	hour
shot	shout
dot	doubt
got	gout

/ɔ/	/oy/
all	oil
jaw	joy
ball	boil
bald	boiled

/u/	/uw/
full	fool
pull	pool
soot	suit
could	cooed

/u/	/ow/
bull	bowl
cook	coke
should	showed
brook	broke

/ow/	/oy/
toe	toy
old	oiled
bold	boiled
cone	coin

/aw/	/ay/
mouse	mice
tower	tire
proud	pride
found	find

/aw/	/oy/
owl	oil
vowed	void
sow	soy
bough	boy

/oy/	/ay/
toy	tie
boy	buy
voice	vice
alloy	ally

Consonants

/p/	/b/
pig	big
cap	cab
pie	buy
rapid	rabid

/b/	/v/
boat	vote
best	vest
curb	curve
cupboard	covered

/l/	/r/
light	right
bowl	boar
collect	correct
lead	read

/č/	/š/
cheap	sheep
catch	cash
watch	wash
cheese	she's

/ǰ/	/š/
jeep	sheep
jade	shade
jack	shack
gyp	ship

/ǰ/	/č/
gin	chin
joke	choke
jeer	cheer
junk	chunk

/ǰ/	/y/
juice	use
jet	yet
jam	yam
wage	weigh

/g/	/k/
bag	back
grape	crepe
glass	class
gap	cap

/ɵ/	/t/
death	debt
thigh	tie
thin	tin
three	tree

/ɵ/	/s/
think	sink
thing	sing
mouth	mouse
thin	sin

/ð/	/d/
they	day
lather	ladder
their	dare
breathe	breed

/f/	/v/
fine	vine
fail	veil
life	live
safe	save

/v/	/w/
vine	wine
veered	weird
veal	we'll
over	ower

2: Irregular Noun Plurals

A. Vowel change

man > men
woman > women

foot > feet
tooth > teeth

goose > geese
mouse > mice

B. *-en* Suffix

child > children

ox > oxen

C. f > v

thief > thieves
wife > wives
life > lives
knife > knives
calf > calves

half > halves
leaf > leaves
loaf > loaves
self > selves
sheaf > sheaves

shelf > shelves
wolf > wolves
hoof > hooves

D. Same

sheep > sheep
deer> deer
moose > moose
fish> fish
trout > trout

salmon > salmon
bass > bass
series > series
means > means
species > species

Chinese > Chinese
Japanese > Japanese
Swiss > Swiss

E. No singular

scissors
tweezers
tongs
trousers
slacks

shorts
pants
pajamas
 (eye) glasses
spectacles

binoculars
clothes
people

F. Borrowed Greek and Latin words

analysis > analyses
basis > bases
hypothesis > hypotheses
parenthesis > parentheses
synopsis > synopses
thesis > theses
crisis > crises

stimulus > stimuli
nucleus > nuclei
alumnus > alumni
radius > radii
syllabus > syllabi
medium > media
memorandum > memoranda

curriculum > curricula
phenomenon >phenomena
criterion > criteria
vortex > vortices
matrix > matrices
index > indices

3: Nationality and Place Words

Place	Person	Adjective
• Afghanistan	Afghan(s), Afghanistani	Afghan, Afghani
Africa	African(s)	African,
North, West, East Africa	North, West, East African(s)	North, West, East African
• Albania	Albanian(s)	Albanian
• Algeria	Algerian(s)	Algerian
America	American(s)	American
Americas, The	South American(s), North American(s)	North, South American
• Andorra	Andorran(s)	Andorran
• Angola	Angolan(s)	Angolan
• Antigua and Barbuda	Antiguan(s), Barbudan(s)	Antiguan, Barbudan
• Argentina	Argentine(s), Argentinean(s)	Argentine, Argentinean
• Armenia	Armenian(s)	Armenian
Asia	Asian(s)	Asian
• Australia	Australian(s), Aussie(s) (colloq.)	Australian
• Austria	Austrian(s)	Austrian
• Azerbaijan	Azerbaijani(s)	Azerbaijan, Azerbaijani
• Bahamas, The	Bahamian(s)	Bahamian
• Bahrain	Bahraini(s)	Bahraini
• Bangladesh	Bangladeshi(s)	Bangladeshi
• Barbados	Barbadian(s)	Barbadian
• Belarus	Belarussian(s)	Belarus
• Belgium	Belgian(s)	Belgian
• Belize	Belizean(s)	Belizean
• Benin	Beninese	Beninese
Bermuda	Bermudian(s)	Bermudian
• Bhutan	Bhutanese, Bhutani(s)	Bhutanese, Bhutani
• Bolivia	Bolivian(s)	Bolivian
• Bosnia	Bosnian(s)	Bosnian
• Botswana	Motswana (sing.), Batswana (pl.)	Motswana (sing.), Batswana (pl.) Setswana (lang.)
• Brazil	Brazilian(s)	Brazilian
• Brunei	Bruneian(s)	Bruneian
• Bulgaria	Bulgarian(s)	Bulgarian
• Burkina Faso (Upper Volta)	Burkinabe (Voltan(s))	Burkinabe (Voltan(s))
• Burma (Myanmar)	Burmese	Burmese
• Burundi	Murundi (sing.) Burundi(pl.)	Burundi, Kirundi (lang.)
• Cambodia (Kampuchea)	Cambodian(s)	Cambodian
• Cameroon/Cameroun	Cameroonian(s)	Cameroonian
• Canada	Canadian(s)	Canadian
• Cape Verde	Cape Verdean(s)	Cape Verdean
• Central African Republic	Central African(s), Centrafrican(s)	Central African, Centrafrican

This list includes all the members of the United Nations as of publication. They are indicated by "•" It also includes a number of places within nations (Wales for example) and regions which contain several nations (such as Southeast Asia). No political comments are implied. These are all terms in common English usage. The list could, of course, be endless, but the editors will appreciate corrections and additions.

Place	Person	Adjective
Central America	Central American(s)	Central American
Central Asia	Central Asian(s)	Central Asia
• Chad	Chadian(s)	Chadian
• Chile	Chilean(s)	Chilean
• China, Peoples Republic of	Chinese	Chinese
• Colombia	Colombian(s)	Colombian
• Comoros	Comorian(s)	Comoran
• Congo, Republic of	Congolese	Congolese, Congo
• Congo, Democratic Republic	Congolese	Congolese
• Costa Rica	Costa Rican(s)	Costa Rican
• Croatia	Croatians(s)	Croat(ian)
• Cuba	Cuban(s)	Cuban
• Cyprus	Cypriot(s)	Cypriot
• Czech Republic	Czech(s)	Czech
• Denmark	Dane(s)	Danish
• Djibouti	Djibouti(s)	Djibouti
• Dominica	Dominican(s)	Dominican
• Dominican Republic	Dominican(s)	Dominican
• Ecuador	Ecuadorean(s)	Ecuadorean
• Egypt	Egyptian(s)	Egyptian
• El Salvador	Salvadoran(s)	Salvadoran
England	Englishman/woman (men/women)	English
• Equitorial Guinea	Equitorial Guinean(s), Equitoguinean(s)	Equitorial Guinean, Equitoguinean
• Estonia	Estonian(s)	Estonian
• Ethiopia	Ethiopian(s)	Ethiopian
Europe	European(s)	European
Far East, East Asia	East Asian(s), Far Easterner(s)	East Asian, Far Eastern
• Fiji	Fijian(s), Fiji Islander(s)	Fijian
• Finland	Finn(s)	Finnish
• France	Frenchman/woman (men/women)	French
• Gabon	Gabonese	Gabonese
• Gambia, The	Gambian	Gambian
• Georgia	Georgians(s)	Georgian
• Germany	German(s)	German
• Ghana	Ghanaian(s)	Ghanaian
• Greece	Greek(s)	Greek
• Grenada	Grenadian(s)	Grenadian
• Guatemala	Guatemalan(s)	Guatemalan
• Guinea	Guinean(s)	Guinean
• Guinea-Bissau	Guinea Bissauan(s), Bissau Guinean(s)	Guinea Bissauan, Bissau Guinean
• Guyana	Guyanese	Guyanese
• Haiti	Haitian(s)	Haitian
• Honduras	Honduran(s)	Honduran
Hong Kong	Hong Kongese, Chinese	Hong Kong
• Hungary	Hungarian(s)	Hungarian
• Iceland	Icelander(s)	Icelandic

Place	Person	Adjective
• India	Indian(s)	Indian
Indochina	Indochinese	Indochinese
• Indonesia	Indonesian(s)	Indonesian
• Iran	Iranian(s)	Iranian
• Iraq	Iraqi(s)	Iraqi
• Ireland	Irishman (men, women)	Irish
• Israel	Israeli(s)	Israeli
• Italy	Italian(s)	Italian
• Ivory Coast (Côte d'Ivoire)	Ivorian(s)	Ivorian
• Jamaica	Jamaican(s)	Jamaican
• Japan	Japanese	Japanese
• Jordan	Jordanian(s)	Jordanian
Kashmir	Kashmiri(s)	Kashmir
• Kazakhstan	Kazakh(s)	Kazakh
• Kenya	Kenyan(s)	Kenyan
Kiribati (Gilbert Islands)	Kiribati(s)	Kiribati (Gilbertese)
• Korea, North	North Korean(s)	North Korean
• Korea, South	South Korean(s)	South Korean
Kosovo	Kosovar(s)	Kosovar
Kurdistan	Kurd(s)	Kurdish
• Kuwait	Kuwaiti(s)	Kuwaiti
• Kyrgyzstan	Kirgiz(es)	Kirgiz
• Laos	Lao(s), Laotian(s)	Lao, Laotian
Latin America	Latin American(s), Hispanic(s)	Latin American
• Latvia	Latvian(s)	Latvian
• Lebanon	Lebanese	Lebanese
• Lesotho	Mosotho (sing.), Basotho (pl.)	Basotho, Sesotho (lang.)
• Liberia	Liberian(s)	Liberian
• Libya	Libyan(s)	Libyan
• Liechtenstein	Liechtensteiner(s)	Liechtenstein
• Lithuania	Lithuanian(s)	Lithuanian
• Luxembourg	Luxembourger(s),Luxembourgian(s)	Luxembourgish, Luxembourgian
• Macedonia	Macedonian(s)	Macedonian
• Madagascar	Malagasy(ies)	Malagasy
• Malawi	Malawian(s)	Malawian
• Malaysia	Malaysian	Malaysian
• Maldives	Maldivian(s)	Maldivian
• Mali	Malian(s)	Malian
• Malta	Maltese	Maltese
• Marshall Islands	Marshall Islanders	Marshallese
• Mauritania	Mauritanian(s)	Mauritanian
• Mauritius	Mauritian(s)	Mauritian
• Mexico	Mexican(s)	Mexican
• Micronesia	Miocronesians	Mocronesian
Middle East, The (Mideast)	Middle Easterner(s)	Middle Eastern
• Moldova	Moldovan(s)	Moldovan
• Monaco	Monegasque(s)	Monegasque

Place	Person	Adjective
•Mongolia	Mongolian(s)	Mongolian
Montenegro	Montenegran(s)	Montenegran
•Morocco	Moroccan(s)	Moroccan
•Mozambique	Mozambican(s)	Mozambican
•Namibia	Namibian(s)	Namibian
Nauru	Nauruan(s)	Nauruan
•Nepal	Nepalese	Nepalese, Nepali
•Netherlands, The (Holland)	Dutchman (men, women)	Dutch
•New Zealand	New Zealander(s)	New Zealand
•Nicaragua	Nicaraguan(s)	Nicaraguan
•Niger	Nigerien(s)	Nigerien
•Nigeria	Nigerian(s)	Nigerian
North America	North American(s)	North American
Northern Cyprus	Turkish Cypriot(s)	Turkish Cypriot
•Norway	Norwegian(s)	Norwegian
•Oman	Omani(s)	Omani
Orient	Oriental(s)	Oriental
•Pakistan	Pakistani(s)	Pakistani
•Palau	Palauan(s)	Palauan
Palestine	Palestinian(s)	Palestinian
•Panama	Panamanian(s)	Panamanian
•Papua New Guinea	Papua New Guinean(s)	Papua New Guinean
•Paraguay	Paraguayan(s)	Paraguayan
•Peru	Peruvian(s)	Peruvian
•Philippines	Filipino(s)	Filipino
•Poland	Pole(s)	Polish
Polynesia	Polynesian(s)	Polynesian
•Portugal	Portuguese	Portuguese
Puerto Rico	Puerto Rican(s)	Puerto Rican
•Qatar	Qatari(s)	Qatari
•Romania, Rumania	Romanian(s)	Romanian
•Russia	Russian(s)	Russian
•Rwanda	Rwandan(s)	Rwandan
•St. Kitts and Nevis	Kittitian(s), Nevisian(s)	Kittitian, Nevisian
•St. Lucia	St. Lucian(s)	St. Lucian
•St. Vincent and the Grenadines	Vincentian(s)	Vincentian
•San Marino	Sammarinese (sing.), Sammarinesi (pl.)	Sammarinese
•Sao Tome and Principe	Sao Tomean(s)	Sao Tomean
•Saudi Arabia	Saudi(s)	Saudi, Saudi Arabian
Scotland	Scot(s), Scotsman	Scottish
•Senegal	Senegalese	Senegalese
•Seychelles	Seychellois	Seychellois
•Sierra Leone	Sierra Leonean(s)	Sierra Leonean
•Singapore	Singaporean(s)	Singaporean
•Slovakia	Slovakian(s)	Slovakian
•Slovenia	Slovenians(s)	Slovenian

Place	Person	Adjective
•Solomon Islands	Solomon Islander(s)	Solomon Island
•Somalia	Somali(s)	Somali
•South Africa	South African(s)	South African
South America	South American(s)	South American
Southeast Asia	Southeast Asian(s)	Southeast Asian
•Spain	Spaniard(s)	Spanish
•Sri Lanka (Ceylon)	Sri Lankan(s) (Ceylonese)	Sri Lankan (Ceylonese)
•Sudan	Sudanese	Sudanese
•Suriname	Surinamer(s)	Surinamese
•Swaziland	Swazi(s)	Swazi
•Sweden	Swede(s)	Swedish
•Switzerland	Swiss	Swiss
•Syria	Syrian(s)	Syrian
•Tajikistan	Tajik(s)	Tajik
Taiwan (Republic of China)	Taiwanese	Taiwanese
•Tanzania	Tanzanian(s), Zanzabari(s)	Tanzanian, Zanzabari
•Thailand	Thai(s)	Thai
Tibet	Tibetan(s)	Tibetan
•Togo	Togolese	Togolese
Tonga	Tongan(s)	Tongan
•Trinidad and Tobago	Trinidadian(s), Tobagonian(s)	Trinidadian, Tobagoan
•Tunisia	Tunisian(s)	Tunisian
•Turkey	Turk(s)	Turkish
Turkistan	Turkistani(s)	Turkistani
•Turkmenistan	Turkoman(s)	Turkmen, Turkoman
Tuvalu (Ellice Islands)	Tuvaluan(s)	Tuvaluan
•Uganda	Ugandan(s)	Ugandan
•Ukraine	Ukrainian(s)	Ukrainian
•United Arab Emirates	Emerian(s), Emeri(s)	U.A.E.
•United Kingdom of Great Britain	Briton(s), Brits	British
•United States of America	American(s)	American
•Uruguay	Uruguayan(s)	Uruguayan
•Uzbekistan	Uzbeki(s), Uzbek(s)	Uzbeki, Uzbek
•Vanuatu	ni-Vanuatu	ni-Vanuatu
Vatican City (The Holy See)	Roman Catholic(s)	Vatican
•Venezuela	Venezuelan(s)	Venezuelan
•Vietnam	Vietnamese	Vietnamese
Wales	Welshman/woman (men/ women)	Welsh
•Western Samoa	Samoan(s)	Western Samoan
•Yemen	Yemeni(s)	Yemeni
•Yugoslavia	Yugoslav(s), Serb(s)	Yugoslav
•Zaire (*now* Congo–DROC)	Zairian(s) (*now* Congolese)	Zairian (*now* Congolese)
•Zambia	Zambian(s)	Zambian
•Zimbabwe	Zimbabwean(s)	Zimbabwean

4: Prefixes and Suffixes

PREFIXES

Prefix	Meaning	Example
a-, an-	not	amoral, atypical, amorphous
ab-	away from	abnormal, abrupt, abstain
ad-	toward, to	administer, adhere, adapt
ante-	before, in front of	anteroom, antecedent, antedate
anti-	against, opposite	antidote, antipathy, antiseptic
arch-	chief, prime	archbishop, archangel, archenemy
auto-	self	automatic, automobile
be-	to cause, intensely	belittle, befriend, beware, bedecked, befuddled
bene-	well	benefactor, benefit, benevolent
bi-	two	bisect, bifocal, bigamy
circum-	around, on all sides	circumscribe, circumnavigate, circumvent
con-	with	conversation, confound, convoy
col-	with	collage, collateral, collapse
cor-	with	correlate, correspond, correct
co-	with	co-worker, co-exist, co-author
contra-	against, opposite	contradict, contraband, contravene
counter-	against, opposite	counteract, counterbalance, countermand
de-	not, away from, down from	descend, deflate, deviate
di-	apart, away, not	diverge, diminish, dilute, divorce
di-	twice fold, double	dichotomy, digraph, dilemma
dia-	through, completely	diameter, diaper, diaphanous, diaspora
dif-	apart, away, not	diffuse, differ, difficult
dis-	apart, away, not	distrust, disinterested, disorder
en-	make, create	engage, enact, entrust
epi-	above, around, additional	epicenter, epidemic, epidermis
equi-	equal	equivalent, equinox, equilibrium
ex-, e-	out from, former	exit, excavate, ex-governor, egress, exhale
extra-	outside, beyond	extraordinary, extrasensory, extravagant
hetero-	different	heterogeneous, heterosexual
homo-	same	homogeneous, homosexual
hyper-	extremely	hyperactive, hyperventilate, hyperbole
hypo-	below, beneath	hypodermic, hypocrisy, hypotenuse
in-	into, not	inhale, inept, innocent
im-	into, not	impel, imbalance, immoral
il-	into, not	illuminate, illiterate, illegal, illegible
ir-	into, not	irradiate, irregular, irresponsible, irresolute
inter-	between, at intervals	intersperse, intermittent, intervene
intra-	within	intracellular, intramural
intro-	motion inward	introduce, introspective, introvert
macro	large	macrocosm, macrobiotics, macro-organism
mal-	ill, badly, bad, wrong	malfunction, malnutrition, malevolent
mega-	big	megaphone, megaton, megalopolis, megabyte
micro-	small	microscope, microphone, micro-organism
mini-	small, little	minivan, miniskirt, minimal
mis-	wrong, wrongly, not	misunderstanding, misuse, mistrust

Prefix	Meaning	Example
mono-	single, one	monophonic, monologue, monomania
multi-	many	multisided, multiplex, multivitamin
neo-	new	neophyte, neoclassical, neonatal
non-	not	nonexistent, nonpayment, nonconformist
ob-	against	obstinate, obscure, object
pan-	all, whole, completely	Pan African, panorama, pandemic
para-	beyond, outside, near	parabola, paramilitary, paradox, paramedic
pen-	almost	peninsula, penultimate
per-	motion through, thoroughly	percolate, perfect, perceive
peri-	around, about, enclosing	perimeter, periscope, periphery
poly-	many	polygamy, polyglot, polychrome
post-	behind, after	posterity, posthumous, postscript
pre-	before, earlier, in front of	preconceived, premonition, predict
pro-	forward, before, in favor of	propulsion, prologue, project
proto-	earliest, first, original	prototype, proto-American, protocol
re-	back, again	reappear, recapture, reclaim, return
retro-	backwards	retrospect, retroactive, retroflex
se-	aside, apart	seclusion, secede, seduce
semi-	half, partly	semiannual, semicircle, semiprecious
sub-	under, below	subway, submarine, subnormal, submerge
super-	over, above, extra	superimpose, supernatural, superfluous
sur-	above, additional	survey, surtax, surface
syn-,sym-	together	synchronize, synthesis, sympathy
tele-	distant	telegraph, telepathy, television
trans-	across, over, through, beyond	transition, transcend, transgress
tri-	three	trimester, trilateral, trillion
ultra-	beyond, excessively	ultraliberal, ultramodern, ultraviolet
un-	not	unimportant, unflattering, unattractive
uni-	one	uniform, unicameral, unique
vice-	one who takes the place of another	vice-president, viceroy, vice-consul

NOUN SUFFIXES

Suffix	Meaning	Example
-ance,-ence	act of	attendance, precedence, reliance
-ancy, -ency	state of	hesitancy, presidency, consistency
-age	action, condition, collection	message, bondage, marriage, postage, baggage
-ant, -ent	one who, that which	stimulant, participant, student, president
-ar	one who	bursar, liar, beggar
-ary, -ory, -ery, -ry	one who, place where, study of	secretary, library, history, conservatory, winery, bakery, chemistry
-dom	domain, condition of	freedom, wisdom, kingdom
-ee	one who is	employee, refugee, absentee
-eer	one who	profiteer, racketeer, pamphleteer
-er	one who	painter, receiver, baker
-ess	one who (female)	actress, poetess, lioness
-hood	state of	boyhood, falsehood, manhood
-ian	one who	beautician, musician, librarian

Suffix	Meaning	Example
-ics	science, art, or practice of	graphics, mathematics, athletics, dramatics
-ion, -ation, -sion, -tion	state, action, institution	fixation, exploration, starvation, foundation, organization, preservation, suspension, competition
-ism	doctrine, point of view	mannerism, idealism, realism
-ist	one who, believer	segregationist, realist, cyclist
-ity	state, quality	sanity, rapidity, elasticity
-ment	state, quality, act of	amazement, payment, embodiment
-ness	state of	fullness, shyness, sickness
-ocracy	system, style of government	democracy, autocracy, plutocracy
-or	one who	actor, governor, inspector
-ship	state, condition	friendship, dictatorship, membership

ADJECTIVE SUFFIXES

Suffix	Meaning	Example
-able, -ible	capable of	capable, edible, visible
-al	like, pertaining to	criminal, practical, musical
-ary, -ory	connected with, engaged in	ordinary, budgetary, compensatory
-ed	covered with, affected by	wooded, clothed, blessed
-en	made of, resembling	wooden, ashen, silken
-ful	full of, having	useful, hopeful, successful
-ic	like, pertaining to	democratic, heroic, specific
-ish	like, pertaining to	foolish, childish, selfish
-ive	like, pertaining to	active, explosive, sensitive
-less	without	speechless, childless, harmless
-like	having the qualities of	childlike, cowlike, statesmanlike
-ly	having the qualities of	beastly, manly, worldly
-oid	like, resembling	spheroid, humanoid, paranoid
-ous	like, pertaining to	courageous, ambitious, grievous
-ward	manner, position	awkward, backward, forward

ADVERB SUFFIXES

Suffix	Meaning	Example
-ly	in a _ manner	happily, strangely, comically
-ward(s)	direction of movement	backward(s), earthward, homeward
-wise	in the manner of, as far as _ is concerned	crabwise, clockwise, corkscrew-wise education-wise, weather-wise

VERB SUFFIXES

Suffix	Meaning	Example
-ate	to cause, to make	placate, indicate, irritate
-en	to become, to make	deafen, ripen, widen
-ify	to cause, to make	beautify, diversify, simplify
-ize	to cause, to make	symbolize, hospitalize, publicize

5: Roots

Root	Meaning	Example
agr	field, farm	agriculture, agronomy
anthro	man	anthropoid, misanthrope
aqua	water	aquatic, aqueduct
astro	star	astrology, astronaut
aud	hear	auditorium, audience
biblio	book	bibliography, bibliophile
bio	life	biology, biography
celer	speed, hasten	accelerate, celerity
chronos	time	chronicle, chronology
cap, capt, cip	take	capture, reciprocate
cep, cept, ceive	take	reception, conceive
ced, cess, cede	go, move along	success, proceed
cid	kill	suicide, genocide
clud, clus	close, shut	seclusion, include
cosmo	world	cosmopolitan, cosmonaut
crat	power	democrat, autocrat
cred	believe, trust	credit, incredulous
cur, curr	run	incur, current
demo	people	democrat, demography
dict	say	diction, contradict
duc, duct	lead	induce, abduct, educate
fac, fact	make, do	manufacture, factory
fec, fect	make, do	infect, effect
fer	carry, bear	infer, conference
fic, fict	make, do	efficacious, fiction
flect	bend	inflection, deflect
frater	brother	fraternal, fratricide
fund, fus	pour	refund, effusive
gen, gener	birth, race	generation, regenerate
geo	earth	geology, geography
glot	tongue	polyglot, glottal
gram	written	telegram, grammar
graph	write	autograph, biography
gress, grad	go, step	progress, gradual
hydra	water	dehydrate, hydrant
ject, jact	throw	project, rejection
jud	judgement	judicial, judicious
lect, leg	read, choose	collect, legend, elect
logo, log, logy	study	anthropology, chronology
loq, loc	speak	eloquent, locution

28

Root	Meaning	Example
manu, mani	hand	manuscript, manicure
mar	sea	maritime, submarine
mater	mother	maternal, matriarch
med	middle	intermediary, medium
min	smaller, less	diminish, minute
mit, mis	send, let go	transmit, missile, missionary
mort	death	mortician, mortal
mot, mob, mo	move, start	motion, motivate
naut	sailor	astronaut, nautical
necro	death	necromancer, necropolis
neuro	nerve	neurology, neurotic
nom	name	nomenclature, nominal
nomo	knowledge, law	autonomy, astronomy
pater	father	paternal, patriotic
patho	suffering, ill	pathetic, pathology
ped, pod	foot	pedal, tripod
pend	hang, weigh	depend, ponderous
philo	love	philosophy, philanthropist
phobo	fear	hydrophobia, phobia
phone	sound, voice	phonology, telephone
photo	light	photography, photosynthesis
plex, pli, ply	fold	complexity, pliant, plywood
plic	fold	complicate, duplicate, implicate
poli	city	cosmopolitan, politician
port	carry	portable, import
pos, pon	place, put	postpone, position
psych	of the mind	psychic, psychology
reg, rect	rule, manage	direct, regulate
rupt	break	rupture, disrupt
scop	watch/look at	microscopic, telescope
scrib, scrip	write	inscribe, conscription
soph	wise	sophisticated, philosophy
spec, spic	see, watch	inspect, despicable
sta, stat	stand	stable, station
stit, sist	to set up, establish	constitution, insist
tact, tang	touch	tactile, tangible
ten, tain, tin	hold, keep	contain, tenacious
tend, tens, tent	stretch, weaken	extend, tenuous
typo	image	typical, typewriter
vacu	empty	vacuum, evacuate
ven	love	venerate, venereal
ven	come	prevent, convene, intervene
voca	call	vocal, invocation
vora	eat, devour	voracious, carnivorous

29

6: Verb Tenses

	SIMPLE	PROGRESSIVE	PERFECT	PERFECT PROGRESSIVE
FUTURE + ? –	I will walk. Will I walk? I won't walk.	You will be walking. Will you be walking? You won't be walking.	She will have walked. Will she have walked? She won't have walked.	We will have been walking. Will we have been walking? We won't have been walking.
PRESENT + ? –	I walk. He walks. Do I walk? Does he walk? I do not walk. He does not walk.	I am walking. You are walking. He is walking. Am I walking? Are you walking? Is he walking? I am not walking. You are not walking.	I have walked. He has walked. Have I walked? Has he walked? I have not walked. He has not walked.	I have been walking. He has been walking. Have I been walking? Has he been walking? I have not been walking. He has not been walking.
PAST + ? –	I walked. Did I walk? I didn't walk.	I was walking. You were walking. Was I walking? Were you walking? I was not walking. You were not walking.	I had walked. Had I walked? I had not walked.	I had been walking. Had I been walking? I hadn't been walking.

7: Stative Verbs

agree	doubt	look like	resemble
appear	dread	love	see
appreciate	fear	mean	seem
be	feel	need	smell
believe	forget	note	suppose
belong	equal	notice	taste
care	hate	owe	tend
consider	have	own	think
contain	guess	prefer	trust
cost	hear	realize	understand
depend	imagine	regret	want
desire	know	remember	weigh
dislike	like	require	wish

8: Frequency Adverbs

eternally	constantly	sometimes	rarely
forever	frequently	regularly	hardly ever
perpetually	habitually	periodically	scarcely ever
incessantly	generally	occasionally	almost never
always	commonly	irregularly	nearly never
almost always	normally	infrequently	never
nearly always	usually	seldom	never ever
invariably	ordinarily		
	often		

9: Non-Countable (Mass) Nouns*

A. Abstract	B. Matter, material	C. Generic terms
advice	air	business
age	beer	change
beauty	blood	equipment
capitalism	bread	fruit
communism	butter	furniture
democracy	cake	jewelry
energy	chalk	luggage
fun	cheese	machinery
happiness	coal	mail
help	coffee	money
honesty	electricity	news
information	fog	propaganda
justice	fish	scenery
kindness	gold	slang
knowledge	grass	stationery
laughter	hair	traffic
liberty	ice	vegetation
life	ink	weather
play	iron	
recreation	juice	
strength	lumber	
trouble	meat	
truth	milk	
virtue	oil	
wisdom	oxygen	
work	paper	
youth	rain	
	rice	
	smoke	
	snow	
	soap	
	soup	
	sugar	
	tea	
	water	
	wine	
	wood	

* This list is far from complete; it is intended only to be suggestive. We have tried to include high frequency nouns. Add your own to our lists.

D. Subject matter

architecture
art
chemistry
civics
economics
engineering
English
geology
grammar
history
literature
mathematics
music
philosophy
physics
science
technology
vocabulary

_____
_____
_____
_____
_____
_____
_____
_____
_____
_____
_____
_____
_____
_____
_____
_____
_____
_____
_____
_____

E. Sports and recreation

baseball
basketball
bridge
camping
dancing
drinking
football
golf
hiking
hockey
homework
hunting
opera
sailing
singing
softball
swimming
television
traveling
volleyball

_____
_____
_____
_____
_____
_____
_____
_____
_____
_____
_____
_____
_____
_____
_____
_____
_____
_____

F. Countable and noncountable nouns*

age
baseball (and other balls)
beer (and other drinks)
business
change
company
dope
glass
iron
paper
play
room
smoke
tape
tea (party)
work
youth

_____
_____
_____
_____
_____
_____
_____
_____
_____
_____
_____
_____
_____
_____
_____
_____
_____
_____

*This list(F) contains words that can have dual meanings: one countable meaning and a different non-countable meaning. Example: _The game of American **football** is played with an oddly shaped ball called a **football**."_

Many non-count nouns, if used to refer to items or units, can also be used as count nouns. Example: _We work at home and do a lot of business there. I run one business here and my wife runs two others._

10: Irregular Verbs
Past participle ends with *n:*

arise	arose	arisen	mow	mowed	mown/mowed
awake	awoke	awoken/awaked	prove	proved	proven
be	was/were	been	ride	rode	ridden
bear	bore	born	rise	rose	risen
beat	beat	beaten	run	ran	ran
begin	began	begun	see	saw	seen
bite	bit	bitten	sew	sewed	sewn/sewed
blow	blew	blown	shake	shook	shaken
break	broke	broken	shine	shone/shined	shone/shined
choose	chose	chosen	show	showed	shown
do	did	done	slay	slew	slain
draw	drew	drawn	sow	sowed	sown/sowed
drive	drove	driven	speak	spoke	spoken
eat	ate	eaten	spin	spun	spun
fall	fell	fallen	steal	stole	stolen
fly	flew	flown	stride	strode	stridden
forbid	forbid/forbade	forbidden	strike	struck	stricken/struck
forget	forgot	forgotten	strive	strove	striven
forgive	forgave	forgiven	swear	swore	sworn
forsake	forsook	forsaken	swell	swelled	swollen/swelled
freeze	froze	frozen	take	took	taken
get	got	gotten	tear	tore	torn
give	gave	given	throw	threw	thrown
go	went	gone	undertake	undertook	undertaken
grow	grew	grown	wake	woke	woken/waked
hide	hid	hidden	wear	wore	worn
know	knew	known	weave	wove	woven
lie	lay	lain	win	won	won
mistake	mistook	mistaken	write	wrote	written

Past participle ends with d:

bind	bound	bound	lead	led	led
bleed	bled	bled	make	made	made
breed	bred	bred	pay	paid	paid
dive	dove/dived	dove/dived	read	read	read
feed	fed	fed	say	said	said
flee	fled	fled	sell	sold	sold
find	found	found	slide	slid	slid
grind	ground	ground	speed	sped	sped
have	had	had	stand	stood	stood
hear	heard	heard	tell	told	told
hold	held	held	understand	understood	understood
lay	laid	laid	wind	wound	wound

Past participle ends with *t:*

bend	bent	bent	lose	lost	lost
bring	brought	brought	mean	meant	meant
build	built	built	meet	met	met
buy	bought	bought	seek	sought	sought
catch	caught	caught	send	sent	sent
creep	crept	crept	shoot	shot	shot
deal	dealt	dealt	sit	sat	sat
fight	fought	fought	sleep	slept	slept
feel	felt	felt	spend	spent	spent
keep	kept	kept	spit	spat	spat
kneel	knelt	knelt	sweep	swept	swept
leave	left	left	teach	taught	taught
lend	lent	lent	think	thought	thought
light	lit	lit	weep	wept	wept

Past participle ends with *d* or *t,*
but the verb does not change:

bet	bet	bet	quit	quit	quit
bid	bid	bid	rid	rid	rid
burst	burst	burst	set	set	set
cast	cast	cast	shed	shed	shed
cost	cost	cost	shut	shut	shut
cut	cut	cut	slit	slit	slit
fit	fit	fit	split	split	split
hit	hit	hit	spread	spread	spread
hurt	hurt	hurt	thrust	thrust	thrust
let	let	let	wet	wet	wet
put	put	put			

Past participle ends with *m, g,* or *k:*

become	became	become	sink	sank	sunk
come	came	come	sling	slung	slung
dig	dug	dug	spring	sprang	sprung
drink	drank	drunk	stink	stank/stunk	stunk
fling	flung	flung	strike	struck	struck
hang	hung/hanged*	hung/ hanged*	swim	swam	swum
ring	rang	rung	swing	swung	swung
shrink	shrank	shrunk	wring	wrung	wrung
sing	sang	sung			

*different meanings

35

11: Direct and Indirect Objects

A. Verbs that require the direct object before the indirect object

Verbs that usually require *to*

Example: *He admitted his mistake to his father*

admit	explain	prove	report
announce	introduce	recommend	say
describe	mention	remember	speak
			suggest

Verbs that usually require *for*

Example: *She answered the phone for me.*

answer	correct	keep	pronounce
cash	design	open	repeat
change	fill	prepare	sign
close	fix	prescribe	translate

B. Verbs that can have the indirect object before the direct object**

Verbs that usually require *to* or Ø

Example: *He brought the apple to Eve. He brought Eve the apple.*

bring	offer	sell	teach
deny	owe	send	tell
give	pass	show	throw
hand	pay	sign	write
lend	read	take	

Verbs that normally require *for* or Ø

Example: *She built a cage for her pet snake. She built her snake a cage.*

build	cook	get	order
buy	do	hire	save
call	draw	leave	type
catch	find	make	

*Some verbs can be used with either **to or for,** but note the difference in meaning.
  Example: *He brought the apple to Eve. He brought an apple for Eve.*

**The direct object is usually not a pronoun when it comes after the indirect object.
  Example: *He brought her the apple,* but not: *He brought Eve it.*

12: *Go* with "Recreational" Gerunds and Prepositional Phrases

Example: *He went to the beach.*

go biking	go for a bike ride	go birdwatching
go boating	go for a boat ride	go bowling
go canoeing	go for a canoe ride	go camping
go climbing	go for a climb	go to the beach
go diving	go for a drive	go to the movies
go picnicking	go for a picnic	go on a date
go riding	go for a ride	go cycling
go running	go for a run	go fishing
go sailing	go for a sail	go hang gliding
go drinking	go for a drink	go shopping
go hiking	go for a hike	go singing
go jogging	go for a jog	go skin diving
go swimming	go for a swim	go skating
go visiting	go for a visit	go skateboarding
go walking	go for a walk	go skiing
go dancing	go to a dance	go surfing
go partying	go to a party	go windsurfing

13. Modals

Meaning		Modal	Pre	Fut	Past	Expression	Examples
Obligation	unavoidable	**must**	✓	✓	had to	need to have to	We must pay our taxes by the 15th of April. You must be at school and at your desk before the bell rings.
	necessity	**must**	✓	✓	had to	need to have to	We had to drink brackish water in order to survive. The crops must have water or they will die.
	prohibition	**must not**	✓	✓	it was prohib-ited	be forbidden to	You must not smoke in an arsenal. You must not play in the streets.
	no obligation	**not have to**	✓	✓	didn't have to		She doesn't have to be at home before 10:00 p.m. They don't have to come to class.
	avoidable obligation	**should**	✓	✓	should have	be supposed to	You should do your homework every day. We should return these books to the library today.
		ought to	✓	✓	ought to have		
Advisability		**should**	✓	✓	should have		You look terrible, you should see a doctor. You ought to have knocked before entering.
		ought to	✓	✓	ought to have		
	obligation with implied consequences	**had better**	✓	✓	had better have		You had better pay me back before I leave. She'd better watch her language
	strong advisability, recom-mendation	**must not**	✓	✓	✗	should not	You mustn't go out alone. It's dangerous. She mustn't drive so fast. She'll have an accident.
Preference		**would rather**	✓	✓	would rather have	would perfer, would sooner	I'd rather do it myself. He'd rather have read the book.

✓ indicates that the modal is used in this time reference with no change in its form.

✗ indicates that the modal is not found in this time reference in any form.

Where the modal changes its form, the new form is indicated,

Ability	ability	can	✓	✓	could	be able to, know how to	I can speak Russian. He couldn't understand a word.
	former ability	could	✗	✗	could	used to be able to	He could run a 4-minute mile in those days. I couldn't express myself then.
Possibility	theoretical and/or factual	can	✓	✓	could have	it is possible, maybe, perhaps	Any citizen can become a senator. Could man have decended from apes? We could go to the movies tonight. The road may be blocked. He may buy a new car next year. He might have taken another road home.
		could	✓	✓	could have		
		may	✓	✓	may have		
		might	✓	✓	might have		
Probability	expectation	should	✓	✓	should have	expect	He should be here any minute now. They ought to have finished now.
		ought to	✓	✓	ought to have		
	inference	must	✓	✗	must have	have to. have got to	It's very muddy; it must have rained a lot.
		can't	✓	✗	can't have	it is not possible	She can't be hungry; she just ate.
		couldn't	✓	✓	couldn't have		He couldn't have flown a plane; he died in 1512.
Willingness		will	✓	✓	✗	not mind	Stay there, I'll do the dishes.
Invitation	you	could	✓	✓	✗	would like, can, will	Could you go to the dance with me? Would you come to dinner tonight?
		would	✓	✓	✗		
Request	he, she, we, they, I	may	✓	✓	✗	can. might	May I leave the room? Could Johnny stay overnight?
		could	✓	✓	✗		
	you	would	✓	✓	✗	can. will	Would you open the window? Could you please lower your voice?
		could	✓	✓	✗		
Permission		may	✓	✓	was allowed to, was permitted to	be allowed to, be permitted to	You may leave the room. She may marry whomever she likes. Johnny can't stay over.
		can	✓	✓			

39

14: Phrasal Verbs

A. SEPARABLE

Example: beat up *She beat up Freddy. She beat Freddy up.*

Verb	Meaning	Example
beat up	hurt physically	She beat Freddy up.
blow out	extinguish	The children wanted to blow the matches out.
break down	disassemble	Max broke his bike down into sixty parts.
bring up	raise children	Their parents brought the children up to respect the law.
call off	cancel	The umpire called the game off.
call up	telephone	Call me up tomorrow.
do over	do again	The teacher asked me to do the assignment over.
fill out	complete	Fill these forms out and come back tomorrow.
get up	arouse from bed	Jane gets her husband up by six every morning.
give back	return	The teacher gave the papers back.
give up	abandon	We had to give the puppy up to its real owner.
hand in	submit	The students handed their exams in late.
hang up	place on hook	He always hangs the phone up when I'm speaking.
keep up	maintain	It costs a lot to keep that car up.
leave out	omit	I've published; don't leave that out on my resume.
let down	lower	Let your hair down.
look over	review, examine	Look the test over before beginning.
look up	search for	I spent hours looking those words up.
make out	distinguish	The envelope was wet. He couldn't make her address out.
make up	compose, invent	They made a list up of people willing to contribute.
make up	use cosmetics	She made her daughter's face up for the party.
pack up	gather in a container	The carpenter packed his tools up at five o'clock sharp.
pass out	distribute	The captain passed aspirin tablets out to all of us.
pick out	choose	He picked a tie out to go with his shirt.
pick up	lift, collect	Someone picks the garbage up on Tuesday.
put away	put in the customary place	Put your toys away, children.
put off	postpone	Another meeting? Let's put it off.
put on	don	It's better to put your socks on before your shoes.
put out	extinguish	The fireman put the blaze out.
take back	return	My new radio doesn't work; I'm taking it back to the store.
take off	remove	They took their coats off when they entered.
take up	raise, discuss	Take that issue up with the manager.
talk over	discuss	The defendant talked his case over with lawyers.
throw away	discard	Don't throw those old magazines away.
try on	test the fit and appearance	She never tries clothes on when she shops.
try out	test	They tried the car out and decided not to buy it.
turn down	reject	The boss turned my request for a raise down.
turn down	lower the volume	Turn that television down! It's giving me a headache!
turn in	deliver, submit	The hub-cap thief turned himself in to the police.
turn off	stop power, shut off	Turn the lights off when you leave.
turn on	start power, put on	I turned the lights on to see better.
use up	finish	We've used all our sugar up.

B. NON-SEPARABLE

Example: break down *Luckily the plane broke down before it took off.*

Verb	Meaning	Example
break down	stop functioning	My car broke down just as I passed the service station.
break up with	end a relationship with	Betsy breaks up with all her boy friends after a month.
break into	enter forcibly	Sally broke into her piggy bank to get money for candy.
call on	ask to respond	That teacher enjoys calling on sleeping students.
come back	return	She never comes back from school on time.
come over	visit informally	Come over for lunch sometime.
come to	regain consciousness	She fainted from fright, but she soon came to.
find out	discover	I found out what was bothering her.
get along with	have a friendly relationship with	That fellow seems to get along with everyone.
get around	avoid	My daughter gets around every rule I set.
get by	succeed with a minimum effort	Do enough just to get by; that's his motto.
get over	recover	It took him weeks to get over the mumps.
get through	finish	I can never get through my exams in time.
get up	arise	He gets up early.
go along	agree	She goes along with every suggestion he makes.
go away	leave	Please go away; I'm busy now.
go over	review	Let's go over the battle plans again.
keep on	continue	He keeps on talking until everyone leaves.
keep up	continue	Keep up the good work, boys. You're doing fine!
look after	take care of someone	I need someone to look after the children on Tuesdays.
look into	investigate	Detectives are looking into the mysterious death.
look like	resemble	She looks like her grandmother.
look out	beware	Look out! The roof's caving in.
look up to	respect	Young boys often look up to famous athletes.
make out	succeed	She made out well on these investments.
pass out	faint	The heat was so intense that many people passed out.
put up with	tolerate	He can't put up with dishonesty.
run into	meet accidentally	Two old friends ran into each other on the street.
run across	find accidentally	She ran across an old love letter and wept.
run out of	exhaust a supply	They ran out of gas in the middle of the Bay Bridge.
show up	appear	His ex-wife showed up at the marriage ceremony.
take after	resemble	He takes after his father in everything he does.
take off	leave	I can't stand this concert! Let's take off.
talk back to	answer rudely	My children never talk back to me.
wait on	serve	He waits on tables for a living.

15: Common Idioms and Collocations
with *give, take, have, get, make, do, tell, say, come,* and *go*

Give

give your best	give authority	give notice
give ground	give permission	give as good as you get
give way	give offense	give and take
give up the ghost	give a whipping	
give a lot	give confidence	give away - a giveaway
give the world	give an idea	give back
give 'em hell	give time	give in
give it to 'em	give me the time	give into
give an account of yourself	give promise	give off
give rise to	give a promise	give out
give the benefit of a doubt	give a damn	give up

Take

take a nap	take advantage of	take courage
take a snooze	take amiss	take a break
take a rap	take someone's word	take a breather
take a fall	take me for a fool	take ten minutes
take a tumble	take possession	take effect
take the news	take my hand	take a shower
take messages	take unaware	take a beating
take notes	take a drink	
take dictation	take the blame	take after
take your medicine	take the train	take along
take a crack at	take shelter	take apart
take time	take a seat	take back
take care	take a picture	be taken by
take a try	take a bet	take down
take pains	take criticism	take for
take trouble	take to the cleaners	take in
take under your wing	take to task	take off
take home	take place	take on
take offense	take it from me	take out
take a back seat	take it for granted	take over
take out food	take it on the chin	undertake
take aback	take heart	take up

Have

have a ball	have chicken pox	have lots to do
have a good time	have an idea	have good weather
have a heart	have a seat	have a reason
have an advantage	have a job	have an excuse
have time	have an understanding	have under control
have the will	have an interest in	had enough
have a headache	have a drink	have nots

Get

get thin	get with it	get after
get fat	get pregnant	get ahead
get soft	get going	get along
get hard	get involved	get around
get lost	get under your skin	get away - a getaway
get sick	get into a fight	get away with
get well	get into trouble	get back
get tired	get out of trouble	get back at
get rested	get busy	get back to
get some rest	get down to business	get into
get mad	get dressed, undressed	get off on
get even	get dressed up	get on
get to bed	get together - a get-together	get on with
get to sleep	get up - a getup	get out
get some sleep		get over
get nowhere	get across	get through
get somewhere	get across to	get through to

Make

make do	make a decision	make a plane
make trouble	make a request	make room for
make peace	make an attempt	make progress
make war	make hay while the sun shines	make time
make love	make a bed	make up you mind
make a (phone) call	make a fire	on the make
make a copy	make a bet	clothes make the man
make friends	make book	
make money	make a date	make away with
make interest	make an appointment	make back
make a loan	make an agreement	make off with
make sense	make interesting	make out
make faces	make good	make over
make eyes at	make public	make up

Do

do your best	do the ironing	do the right thing
do your worst	do the vacuuming	do or die
do what's needed	do the cooking	do a drawing
do homework	do the shopping	do a portrait
do an assignment	do the cleaning	do a painting
do an excercise	do the laundry	do the artwork
do time	do the chores	do the editing
do a job	do housework	do away with
do a trick	do mischief	do in
do the trick	do rounds	do up
do a favor	do the driving	do over
do someone out of something	do evil	do out of
do the dishes	do good	do unto

Tell

tell the truth	tell time	time will tell
tell a lie	tell it like it is	tell about
tell a story	tell a fortune	tell apart
tell a secret		tell off
tell the weather	a telling detail	tell on
tell me what's on your mind	kiss and tell	all told

Say

say your piece	say your goodbyes	before you could say
say your prayers	goes without saying	Jack Robinson
say grace	I can't say	what do you have to say
say yes	say not a word	for yourself
say no	have a say in	say about
say what you have to say	that is to say	say against
say what's on your mind	say what you will	say of
say hello for me	never say die	say on
say goodbye	say it with flowers	say to

Come

come to an agreement	come along	come on to
come by it naturally	come around	come out
come to a stop	come away with	come out with
come and see	come back - a comeback	come over
come and get it	come between	overcome
come and go	come in for	come through
come off it	come into	come to
come about	come off	come upon
come across	come apart	come up against
come ahead	come on - a come on	come up with

Go

go crazy	go AWOL (absent without	go ahead of
go mad	leave)	go around with
go nuts	food to go	go at
go insane	go one better	go away
go batty	go from bad to worse	go back on
go wild	from the word go	go beyond
go on a spree	so it goes	go for
go over the edge	go bald	go in for
go into debt	go blind	go into
go all the way	go deaf	go off
go for broke	go lame	go off with
go one-on-one	go soft	go on
go head-to-head		go on about
go over the top	go about	go over
go in over your head	go after	go through
go behind your back	go along	go up against
go about your own business	go against	go with
go through hell	go ahead	go without

16: Verbs That Are Followed by an Infinitive

A. No object

Example: *He agrees to meet at noon.*

agree	deserve	learn	swear
appear	desire	manage	volunteer
arrange	fail	mean	offer
care	guarantee	tend	wait
claim	happen	promise	wish
consent	hesitate	refuse	
decide	hope	seem	
demand	know how	struggle	

B. With object

Example: *She advised the man to duck.*

advise	dare	instruct	request
allow	encourage	invite	require
authorize	forbid	oblige	teach
cause	force	order	tell
challenge	get	permit	train
command	help	persuade	urge
convince	hire	remind	warn

C. With or without object

Example: *He asks her to leave. He asks to be excused.*

ask	expect	prefer	want
beg	need	prepare	would like

45

17: Verbs Followed by Gerunds

Example: *She admits going to see the movie.*

admit	deny	keep on	recommend
anticipate	discuss	mention	resent
appreciate	dislike	mind	resist
avoid	enjoy	miss	risk
can't	finish	postpone	suggest
help	get through	practice	tolerate
complete	give up	quit	understand
consider	imagine	recall	
delay	keep	recollect	

18: Verbs Followed by Infinitives or Gerunds

Example: *He can afford to vacation in Italy. He can afford vacationing in Italy.*

(can)afford	forget*	love	remember*
attempt	go	neglect	start
(can) bear	hate	plan	(can) stand
begin	hesitate	prefer	stop*
choose	intend	pretend	threaten
dread	like	regret*	try*

19: Perception Verbs Followed by Simple Verbs**

Example: *She felt him approach.*

feel	overhear	remark	smell
hear	perceive	see	watch
observe	notice	sense	witness

*The meanings of these verbs are often slightly different when they are followed by an infinitive rather than a gerund.
  Example: *He stopped to listen to the speech. He stopped listening to the speech.*

**These verbs may also be followed by a gerund. Example: *She felt him approaching.*

20: Participles As Modifiers

Example: *She is amazing to him. He is amazed by her.*

absorbing	absorbed	fascinating	fascinated
amazing	amazed	frightening	frightened
amusing	amused	interesting	interested
annoying	annoyed	intriguing	intrigued
astonishing	astonished	irritating	irritated
boring	bored	pleasing	pleased
challenging	challenged	satisfying	satisfied
confusing	confused	shocking	shocked
convincing	convinced	surprising	surprised
disappointing	disappointed	terrifying	terrified
disgusting	disgusted	thrilling	thrilled
disturbing	disturbed	tiring	tired
embarrassing	embarrassed	touching	touched
exciting	excited		

21: Intransitive and Transitive Verbs

Most English verbs can be used in either an intransitive or transitive way.
(Transitive verbs take a direct object).

Example: (intransitive) *She writes every day.* (transitive) *She is writing a book.*

The verbs in the following lists are <u>usually</u> only intransitive or transitive.

Example: (intransitive) *He acted in Hamlet every night, and*
(transitive) *every night he accepted a standing ovation.*

However, some of them may be used either way.

Example: (intransitive) *She lived in Manhattan, but* (transitive) *she lived a good life.*

A. Intransitive Verbs

act	dream	live	sit
agree	fall	look	sleep
appear	go	matter	stand
arrive	happen	occur	step
belong	laugh	rain	talk
care	lie	remain	think
come	listen	rise	wait

B. Transitive Verbs

accept	cost	have	pick
admit	cover	hear	put
allow	demand	hold	raise
beat	destroy	include	realize
bring	discover	join	say
build	enjoy	kill	send
buy	expect	know	suppose
carry	express	lay	take
catch	feed	let	tell
cause	find	like	wear
consider	force	make	
contain	give	mean	

22: Adjective + Preposition Combinations

Example: *She is interested in becoming a judge.*

concerned about	slow at	conscious of	sure to
happy about	quick at	confident of	opposed to
angry about	lucky at	ashamed of	
enthusiastic about	surprised at	sure of	bored with
careful about	amazed at	afraid of	impressed with
excited about		certain of	involved with
glad about	interested in	sick of	annoyed with
worried about	involved in		delighted with
sorry about	disappointed in	upset over	satisfied with
disappointed about		disturbed over	pleased with
pleased about	fond of		disappointed with
	in favor of	accustomed to	
good at	tired of	slow to	
clever at	capable of	quick to	
bad at	aware of	resigned to	

23: Verbs and Adjectives Taking Subjunctive

Verbs

Example: *He **advises** that you **watch** the stock market very carefully.* Example: *It is **important** that you do this immediately.*

advise	propose	forbid	require
ask	recommend	desire	stipulate
beg	command	insist	suggest
demand	request	prefer	urge

Adjectives

advisable	essential	desirable	important
best	good	mandatory	urgent
better	imperative	necessary	vital
critical	crucial	required	requisite

24: Verb + Preposition Combinations

A. Verb + preposition + object

Example: *They agree on everything.*

agree on	care for	hear about	succeed in
agree with	complain about	hear from	talk to
approve of	consent to	laugh at	talk about
argue with	comment on	listen to	think about
arrive at	consist of	look at	vote for
arrive in	count on	object to	wait for
belong to	decide on	pay for	wish for
believe in	depend on	rely on	work for

B. Verb + object + prepostion + object

Example: *She adds fertilizer to her garden soil.*

add ___ to/with ___	explain ___ to ___	prefer ___ to ___
blame ___ for ___	excuse ___ for ___	remind ___ of ___
compare ___ with/to ___	introduce ___ to ___	thank ___ for ___
congratulate ___ on/for ___	keep ___ for ___	subtract ___ from ___

The Communicative Aspect

T he communicative aspect does not deal with linguistic forms, such as *go, went, gone*, the **medium** of communication. It outlines ways in which the language is used to send and receive **messages.** We have further analyzed this communicative aspect into three sub-aspects that are usually present when a message is being communicated. First, there is a **situational context** in which the message is exchanged, the *where*. The **topical content** is the subject matter of the message, the *what,* and the **communicative function** is the manner and purpose of the message, the *how* and *why*.

Contents

51

Situational Context

The situational context, in its simplest sense, is a definite, identifiable place or setting where communication happens *(a bank,* for example). However, some of the situations in the following pages are not specific places. There are events or chains of events that are common and recurrent in everyday life (for example, a *wedding* or *asking for prices).* There are also contexts which are topics for discussion and cultural exploration (such as *planning nutritious meals).*

In order to communicate effectively in these situations, students need appropriate topical vocabulary, cultural information, and functional language. The materials in the following sections will be helpful.

This section amounts to a series of lists of suggested communicative contexts that could be used in presenting and practicing communicative language and cultural insights. In many cases, vocabulary topics relevant to these contexts are given in the next section. When they are, cross-references are given.

A teacher using this section as a planning guide selects a situation appropriate to the interests and needs of their students and then plans a lesson using any of the topics which seem relevant. For example, looking over the list, the teacher settles on *restaurant* from List 1. The reference is to topic number 29, *restaurants,* but a quick review of the Topical Checklist at the beginning of the section suggests that the topics on *food, cooking,* and *eating* might also be helpful. In reading the topic on *restaurants,* the teacher finds that the vocabulary list suggests both vocabulary and cultural information students will need in a restaurant. They will need to know about *reservations, menus, waiters, orders, checks,* and *tips.* After teaching the lesson, the teacher may hand out photocopies of the relevant topic lists as further vocabulary enrichment.

Once the students have been given a handout, it can be used as the basis for pair work, writing assignments, situational role playing, and many other kinds of in-class and out-of-class activities.

The list of situations given in this section is in the form of an outline or checklist. It is intended to be suggestive rather than exhaustive. It is not intended as a situational sequence or syllabus, but it should help teachers develop sequences of their own appropriate for each class.

❏ 1. Basic Daily Needs 53
❏ 2. Transportation 53
❏ 3. Work 53
❏ 4. Health and Safety 54
❏ 5. Personal and Family Needs 54
❏ 6. Personal Finances 54
❏ 7. Education 55
❏ 8. Shopping & Service 55
❏ 9. Recreation 56
❏ 10. Citizenship 56

1: Basic Daily Needs

Food

kitchen
dining room
cooking
restaurant
using a recipe
planning nutritious meals
storing food safely
grocery shopping
weights and measures
planning to save money
serving meals
eating and drinking

See topics 1-3, 22, 29

Clothing

buying clothes, shoes
repairing clothes, sewing
using a washer, dryer
laundry/laundromat
cleaner

See topics 5, 6, 30

Shelter

types of housing
rooms, including:
  living room
  bedroom
  bathroom
  kitchen
housekeeping
maintenance
yard work

See topic 4

2: Transportation

asking directions
using maps
getting lost
walking—when,where
subway station, subway

See topics 9, 26

bus stop, city bus
bus station, intercity bus
railway station, trains
airport, plane
taxis

commuting
buying tickets, tokens
travel agent
customs/immigration
hitchhiking

3: Work

the work place
  home
  work shop/factory
  warehouse
  shipping/freight terminal
  store/department store/mall
  office
  studio
  school
  hospital/clinic/nursing home
  daycare/eldercare center
  hotel
  restaurant
  construction site
  outdoors
  farm
  travel/transportation
See topics 31, 43-47

work procedures
  housekeeping
  cooking/doing dishes
  gardening/groundskeeping
  cleaning and maintenance
  doing repairs
  using the telephone
  taking messages
  making/keeping appointments
  placing/taking orders
  writing receipts
  making change
  packing/shipping
  dictating/taking dictation
  typing
  filing
  using computers
  planning/following plans

scheduling/following schedules
getting paid
cashing pay checks
supervising/being supervised
following instructions
scheduling staff meetings
following safety regulations
asking for help
dealing with mistakes
changing jobs
applying for work
employment office
job training
health insurance/benefits
social security
compensation insurance
labor unions/union dues
health and safety regulations

4: Health and Safety

advice on a healthy diet	dentist's office	hospital
advice on getting exercise	emergency services	emergency
gym, athletics	police	visiting
taking vitamins	fire	medical insurance
taking medicine	ambulance	personal hygiene
drug store	medical center	sex and contraception
doctor's office	health clinic	personal safety

See topics 1-3, 25, 38, 39 and 42)

5: Personal and Family Needs

interpersonal relationships, roles	adult education, training	family activities
work	elderly people	family trips
school	relatives	record keeping
sports	spiritual	retirement
friendship	wedding	elder care
romance	ceremony	death, burial
family relationships	wedding party	places of worship
family planning	bridal dinner	community organizations
family counseling	wedding gown, dress	ethnic
children	bachelor party	religious
siblings	marriage	civic
discipline	anniversary	service
child care	counseling	political
babysitting	separation, divorce	cultural
schooling	living together	social life, entertaining
afterschool activities	as roommates	dating
birthdays/holidays	out of wedlock	caring for pets
camp	commonlaw partners	veterinarian

See topics 7, 8,24, 53-55, 60

6: Personal Finances

spending money	bank, savings and loan	savings bonds
cash	planning a family budget getting/	retirement accounts
checks, cashing checks	making a loan	buying stock, bonds
charging	getting a mortgage	insurance
charge accounts	getting a second mortgage	social security
credit cards	home equity loan	work benefits
interest costs	educational loans, financial aid	taxes
loan payments	planning investments	gambling
	savings accounts	retirement

See topic 33

7: Education

Expectations, routines

classroom
schedules
being on time
assignments, homework re-
searching, writing papers
library
tests, quizzes
final exams
standardized tests
grades, records
tuition, room and board schol-
arships
neatness
honesty/cheating

See t0pics 50, 54, and 55

At school, on campus

registration
dean's office
adviser's office
   scheduling
   course change
teacher's office hours
   getting help
   planning a research paper
housing office
bursar's office
dormitory life
   rooms, roommates
   dorm rules
   laundry
off campus housing

campus post office
book store
student center
cafeteria, dining hall
fraternity, sorority
chapel, chaplain's office
student health service
foreign student adviser
computer center
library
other campus services
gymnasium
team, coach
team spirit
locker room
drugs and sports

8: Shopping and Services

planning
making a shopping list using
the yellow pages newspaper/
magazine ads, junk mail
sales, come on's
coupons, bargains
internet shopping
finding products in big stores
kinds of stores
   department store
   supermarket
   mall
   specialty shops
   main street
   boutiques
   copy center
getting advice about products
   from consumer services
   in specialty shops
    bakery
    optician
    book store
    camera store
asking for prices
fixed prices/bargaining

unit pricing
ordering from catalogues
paying for purchases
   cash
   charge
   credit cards
   time payments
   layaway plans
   lease-purchase
   rental
   getting change
   tipping
returning merchandise
choosing and getting services
   mechanic
   barber/hair dresser
   plumber
   electrician
   carpenter
   car mechanic
   doctor
   dentist
   lawyer
   accountant
   tax preparation service

insurance agent
pastor/priest
real estate agent
getting help/public services
   police department
   court
   public defender/legal aid
   emergency services
   ambulance service
   hospital/emergency room
   fire department
   town offices/city hall
   local town officials
   extension agent
   post office
   state and congressional
    representatives
   school board
   IRS - internal revenue service
   INS - immigration and
    naturalization service
   public library
   adult center
   teen center
   YMCA

*See topics 30 and 31

9: Recreation

Athletics
local team sports - seasonal
children's and adult leagues
    finding a team
    signing up
    schedules
exercising – working out
    walking, running
    swimming
games – tennis, golf
children's games
    capture the flag
    jumping rope
    dodge ball
    marbles/jacks
    hide and seek
    tag
    three legged races

See topics 34-37

Social
dinner parties
cocktail/beer parties
dances
community events, socials
restaurants

Entertainment
movies
theater
opera, musicals
popular music concerts
classical music concerts
rock concerts
professional sports events
night clubs
coffee houses

Arts and crafts
art classes
music lessons

art studios
galleries
craft shows
gift shops
museums

At home
TV, radio
games - cards, board games
parties
    children's parties
    family parties
    holiday parties
special meals –
    barbecue
    picnic
    brunch
    potluck
    buffet
hobbies

10: Citizenship

town/city offices
police department
court
contacting government officials
    local and national
    getting help
    expressing opinions
election campaigns
voter registration
voting
discussing taxes
discussing immigration status
discussing work permits
discussing civil rights
discussing civil obligations
discussing national holidays
discussing historic landmarks
discussing corruption
    bribery
    protection money

See topics 31,48,49,51,56

honor codes
organized crime
codes of conduct
truth in advertising
civic responsibility
discussing
    national anthem
    other patriotic songs
    Gettysburg address
    Dr. King's "I have a dream"
American history
  explaining important events
    leaders
    movements
    the constitution
    functions of government
      local
      state
      national
      international

discussing the importance of
    dissent
    getting involved
    an informed electorate
    bill of rights
discussing what makes a
  community
    a good place to live
    a good place to work
    a good place to raise children
discussing the roles of
  organizations –
    civic
    political
    special interest
    religious
    cultural
local, state, federal taxes
volunteer work

56

Topical Content

The topics of human conversation are virtually endless, but it is possible to predict a general list of topics that virtually every language learner will encounter at some time or other. The following lists are an attempt at a comprehensive list of **basic** topics. Each topic is outlined as a vocabulary list of the words, phrases, and idioms that might be encountered in a general conversation about the topic. In the case of the idioms, they are included not because they might appear in the context of a conversation, but rather because they have some semantic relationship to the topic, usually at the literal level, rather than the figurative.

It will again be obvious that the vocabulary collected under each topic is influenced by the cultural context of contemporary North America.

Finally, please bear in mind that these lists are far from complete. They should be seen as basic words of fairly high frequency. You will want to add your own discoveries to our lists, and once again we welcome your additions and comments.

Topic checklist

1: Food

Vegetables

bean	cucumber	radish
beet	lettuce	spinach
broccoli	onion	squash
cabbage	peas	tomato
carrot	pepper	turnip
celery	potato	
corn	pumpkin	

Fruit

apple	lemon	prune
banana	lime	raspberry
berry	melon	raisin
blueberry	orange	strawberry
cantaloupe	peach	tangerine
cherry	pear	watermelon
grape	pineapple	
grapefruit	plum	

Bread and Cereal

bread	grain	roll
biscuit	muffin	toast
cold	oatmeal	waffle
cereal	pancake	
doughnut	rice	

Meat

bacon	fish	meat
beef	hamburger	loaf
chicken	hot dog	pork
duck	lamb	turkey
egg	meatball	

Dairy

butter	cream	skim milk
cottage cheese	half and half	sour cream
cheese	margarine	yoghurt
ice cream	milk	

Desserts

brownie	ice cream	cookies
cake	pie	sundae
cupcake	pudding	

Spice and Flavoring

cinnamon	ginger	oregano
chili	herb	pepper
clove	honey	salt
cocoa	mustard	syrup
curry	nutmeg	sugar

Beverages

ale	lemonade	soft drink
beer	liquor	tea
brandy	punch	water
coffee	Sanka	whiskey
coke	soda	wine
juice		

Idioms and Expressions

baker's dozen	to not know beans	cup of tea
baloney	to pepper with questions	to egg on
to beef about	proof of the pudding	fishy
to beef up	to put one's eggs in one basket	sour grapes
to bring home the bacon	food fit for the gods	to spill the beans
corny	to know which side one's	square meal
cream of the crop	bread is buttered on	to take the cake
to cry over spilled milk	like two peas in a pod	upper crust
to have one's cake and eat it	Variety is the spice of life.	hot dog!

2: Cooking

Equipment

baking pan	cookbook	kettle	pan	sifter
blender	colander	ladle	pot	skillet
bowl	cover	lid	potato masher	spatula
bread pan	double boiler	measuring cup	pressure cooker	stove
broiler	eggbeater	mixer	recipe	strainer
burner	food processor	mixing spoon	rolling pin	thermometer
casserole dish	frying pan	oven	saucepan	whip

Processes

add	combine	grate	parboil	simmer
bake	cook	grease	peel	slice
beat	cover	grind	pour	spread
blend	deep fry	knead	refrigerate	sprinkle
boil	dice	mash	roast	stir
braise	drain	measure	sauce	stir-fry
brown	fold in	melt	season	toast
chill	freeze	mince	salt	toss
chop	fry	mix	sift	turn
coat				whip

Ingredients, Dishes, Measures

baking soda	cornstarch	flour	salad	stick of butter
batter	crust	lard	salad dressing	stuffing
broth	cup	loaf	sauce	syrup
casserole	dash	leftover	seasoning	tablespoon
chops	dough	molasses	shell	teaspoon
cocktail	dressing	oil	soup	vinegar
condiments	filling	pinch	steak	(egg) whites
corn meal	flavor	roast	stew	(egg) yolks

Adjectives

boiled	fresh	medium	raw	slow (oven)
broiled	fried	moderate (oven)	ripe	steamed
crisp	ground	rare	scalloped	tender
curdled				thickened
				well-done

Idioms and Expressions

a flash in the pan	half-baked	pot calling the kettle black
take with a grain of salt	hard-boiled	watered down

3: Eating

Dishes and Utensils

carving knife	gravy boat	saucer
dessert dish	knife	serving dish
cup	napkin	spoon
fork	plate	soup bowl
glass	platter	soup spoon
goblet	salad bowl	tureen

Meals

appetizer	course	picnic
breakfast	dessert	smorgasbord
brunch	dinner	snack
buffet	lunch	supper

Verbs

bite	drink	nibble
chew	eat	sip
diet	gobble	swallow
dine	munch	taste

Adjectives

bitter	moist	tart
delicious	rich	thick
dry	sour	thin
famished	starved	thirsty
full	succulent	tough
hungry	sweet	

Misc

baker	natural food	seconds
chef	nutritious	vegetarian
cook	organic	whole food
gourmet	potluck	

Idioms

to eat like a bird	to pig out	to eat for two
a picky eater	to wolf down one's food	to bite off more than
to eat like a pig		one can chew

4: Housing/Housekeeping

General

building	farm	development	suburb
city	ghetto	neighborhood	town
community	home	quarter	village
country	house	residence	
development	housing	subdivision	

Types

adobe	high-rise	mobile home	tenement
A-frame	houseboat	palace	tent
apartment	hut	ranch house	tepee
cape	igloo	salt-box	trailer
condominium	log cabin	skyscraper	tree house
chalet	manor	split-level	wigwam
flat			

Construction Materials

brick	concrete	log	steel
cement	glass	shingles	stone
clapboard	linoleum	siding	wood

Parts

addition	dormer	frame	sill
bay	drive(way)	fuse box	stairs
breezeway	electric outlets	garage	steps
bulkhead	ell	light switch	walk
ceiling	fireplace	picture window	wall
chimney	floor	plumbing	window
door	foundation	rafters	wiring

Places

attic	den	lawn	porch
basement	dining room	living room	store room
bath(room)	family room	mud room	study
bedroom	garage	nursery	sun room
breakfast room/nook	hall	pantry	toilet
cellar	kitchen	patio	utility room
closet	laundry room	play room	yard

63

Events and Activities

visitors	mail carrier	TV watching	light repair work
house guests	cooking	doing the laundry	babysitting
delivery person	house cleaning	yard work	home improvement

Furnishings and Equipment

ashtray	counter	hutch	shelf
basin	crib	iron	sheets
bathtub	cupboard	ironing board	shower
bed	curtains	kitchen table	sideboard
double	desk	lamp	sink
twin	dining room table	laundry basket	sofa
bunk	dishwasher	light	stereo
queen-size	draperies	linen	stove
king-size	dresser	linoleum	table
blanket	dryer	love seat	television
bookshelves/case	easy chair	mircrowave oven	TV/ VCR stand
cabinet	end table	oven	toaster
carpet	electric outlet	radio	toilet bowl
chair	entertainment center	record player	towel
coffee table	fireplace	refrigerator	vacuum cleaner
computer	freezer	rug	washing machine
cot	furnace	shades	water heater

Activities

change (the linen/ sheets)	do the ironing	straighten (up)	lease
clean (up)	make the bed	sweep	let
do the dishes	paint	vacuum	mortgage
do the laundry	pick up	wash	move
dust	polish	wax	own
fix	put away	buy	renovate
fold the laundry	repair	build	remodel
hang out the laundry	scrub	furnish	rent
	set the table	insure	sub-let

Idioms and Expressions

to hit home	to hit the sack	to make a clean sweep of
on the house	spick and span	to ride a broomstick
to raise the roof	to whitewash	handwriting on the wall
wet blanket	to turn the tables on	to keep up with the Joneses
on the carpet	up/down one's alley	A new broom sweeps clean.
to pull up stakes	blind alley	A house is not a home.

5: Clothes
General

bathing suit
bathrobe
belt
blazer
blouse
bow tie
boxer shorts
bra
briefs
buckle
cap
cape
cardigan
coat
cocktail dress
dinner jacket
dress
dungarees
earmuffs
garter
girdle
gloves
gown
hat
jacket

(blue)jeans
leotard
jumpsuit
mittens
muffler
nightgown
nylons
overalls
overcoat
pajamas
panties
pants
pantsuit
pantyhose
parka
raincoat
running shorts
scarf
shirt
   dress
   sport
shorts
ski jacket
   pants
skirt

slacks
slicker
slip
snowsuit
sport coat/jacket
stole
suit
suspenders
sweater
sweat pants
sweat suit
sweatshirt
(neck)tie
tank top
tights
trench coat
trousers
t-shirt
turtleneck
tuxedo
underclothes
underpants
undershirt
vest
wig

Footwear

boots
   cowboy
   dress
   riding
clogs
flats
high heels

galoshes
gym shoes
moccasins
knee socks
overshoes
peds
rubbers

running shoes
shoes
shoelaces/strings
slippers
sneakers
socks
stockings

Sewing and Parts

bobbin
button
buttonhole
cloth
collar
cuff
darn

elastic
fabric
fringe
knit
hem
hemline
hood

material
mend
nap
neckline
needle
notch
patch

Sewing and Parts, continued

pattern	sewing machine	thread
pins	size	threader
pocket	sleeve	tack down
ruffle	snap	tape measure
scissors	stitch	tuck
seam	thimble	yarn
		zipper

Adjectives

brand new	knit	second-hand
checkered	large (sized)	silk
corduroy	loose	small (sized)
cotton	machine washable	striped
dress	medium (sized)	tight
dry	nylon	torn
cleanable	permanent press	velvet
flannel	plaid	washable
frayed	polka dot	worn out
hand-me-down	polyester	wool
hand washable	rayon	woven

Verbs

baste	hem	take in
cut (out)	knit	take off
darn	pin up	take up
dress	put on	tear (out)
fit	rip (out)	thread
gather	sew (up)	trace
get dressed	stitch	wear
grow out of (into)	tack	wear out

Idioms and Expressions

all dressed up	to handle with kid gloves	on a shoestring
to be in someone's shoes	to hit below the belt	on pins and needles
to burn a hole in one's pocket	if the shoe fits	the shoe's on the other foot
to buttonhole someone	to keep one's shirt on	to spin a yarn
to collar someone	to look for a needle in the	spit and polish
clothes make the man	haystack	stuffed shirt
dolled up	to lose one's shirt	tied to someone's apron strings
		wear and tear

6: Paraphernalia
Nouns

address book

bag

barrette

beads

beeper

billfold

bobby pin

bracelet

briefcase

brooch

calling/business card case

calculator

cane

cell phone

change purse

checkbook

chewing tobacco

choker

cigar

cigarette

coin

coin purse

comb

contact lens

credit card case

crutches

cufflinks

date book

diskman CD player

earring

(eye) glasses

  bifocal

  sun

  reading

glasses case

hair pin

hair brush

hair pull

handbag

handheld PC

handkerchief

hanging bag

identification

ID bracelet

jack knife

kerchief

key chain

key ring

keys

laptop computer

lighter

locket

mace

marker

matches

minidisk player

mp3 player

nail clippers

nail file

necklace

notebook

notebook PC

organizer, pocket or palm

overnight bag

pager

pen

  ball point pen

  fountain pen

pencil

pencil sharpener

penknife

pen light

pillbox

pin

pipe

playing cards

pocketbook

pocket calendar

pocket computer

pocketknife

pocket watch

purse

ring

  engagement

  school

  signet

  wedding

shoulder bag

snuff

tie clip

tie pin

tissues

tobacco pouch

umbrella

wallet

walking stick

wristwatch

Idioms and Expressions

to flip a coin

to make heads or tails of

key to the city

little black book

to pick someone's pocket

pipe dream

purse snatcher

to put that in one's pipe and smoke it

rose colored glasses

up to snuff

well groomed

7: Family

adopted child
adoptive parent
aunt
baby brother/sister
big brother/sister
biological parent
bride
brother
cousin
dad
daddy
daughter
dependent
family dog
folks
father
fiance(e)
first husband/wife
foster parent
foster child
genealogy

godparents
gram
gramp
grandchild(ren)
granddaughter
grandfather
grandma
grandmother
grandpa
grandson
great aunt/uncle
great grandchild(ren)
groom
guardian
half-brother/sister
husband
in-laws
kin, kin folks
kindred
ma
maternal

middle child
mom
mommy
mother
(mother)-in-law
niece
nephew
orphan
pa
paternal
pop
relative
sibling
sis
sister
son
spouse
uncle
widow
widower
wife

Idioms and Expressions

all in the family
better half
blood brother
blood is thicker than water
chip off the old block
close/distant relations
to come by it naturally

extended/nuclear family
kissing cousins
family feud
family tree
favorite son
runs in the family
sibling rivalry

spitting image
to take after
son of a gun
wicked stepmother
wife (to be)
one's old (man)
like father, like son

8: Human Relationships, Qualities, and Stages

Nouns

admiration	antagonism	competition	envy	hatred	love	rivalry
affection	cooperation	friendship	hate	intimacy	marriage	sex
						teamwork

Verbs

admire	cooperate	dislike	envy	have sex	like	make love
befriend	compete	distrust	hate	ignore	love	share
						trust

People

acquaintance	colleague	crony	fiance/	girlfriend	mate	party
antagonist	companion	crowd	fiancee	guest	mistress	playmate
associate	company	date	follower	host	mob	relative
boyfriend	comrade	disciple	friend	leader	pal	roommate
buddy	counselor	enemy	gang	lover	partner	team
						teammate

Qualities

aloof	cooperative	fresh	insane	pretty	sexy
artistic	courageous	friendly	intelligent	quiet	shy
attractive	courteous	funny	jealous	reserved	spiteful
bashful	cowardly	gorgeous	kind	romantic	stand-offish
beautiful	crazy	greedy	lazy	rude	strong
bold	cruel	gullible	loud	ruthless	stuck up
brave	dependable	handsome	lovely	sane	studious
brazen	determined	hard-working	lovable	self-conscious	stupid
cheerful	diligent	helpful	mean	selfish	trustworthy
conceited	disciplined	humorous	plain	sensitive	ugly
cold	dumb	ill-mannered	pleasant	sentimental	up-tight
complacent	foolish	impolite	polite	serious	well-mannered

Stages

adolescent	childhood	immature	juvenile	pre-teen	teenager
age	childish	infant	mature	retired	toddler
aged	elderly	infantile	middle-age	senior citizen	young
baby	grownup	kid	old	senile	young adult
child					youth

Idioms and Expressions

to have an affair	to flip one's lid	to have a crush on	side-kick
blind date	to gang up on	living together	to sponge off
to break up	to go through the motions	old man (lady)	steady date
fair sex	to hang in there	to pull no punches	to take someone down a peg
fall-guy	to hang it all out	ringleader	every Tom, Dick and Harry

69

9: Travel

Places

airport	dining car	parking lot
auto rental agency	garage	parking place/space
baggage check in	gas station/service station	passing lane
baggage claim area	hotel	repair shop
baggage office	immigration	rest area
bed and breakfast	inn	restaurant
berth	information booth	terminal
bus station	intersection	train station
Chamber of Commerce	Interstate Highway	ticket office
check-in counter	junction	toll booth
club car	lobby	tourist office
coach (car)	motel	travel agency
customs	parking garage	waiting room

Some Events

arrival	departure	layover
auto accident	flat tire	packing
boarding	flight cancellation	parking ticket
checking in	go through security	passing
checking out	hitch-hiking	speeding ticket
delay	hailing a cab	traffic violation

Idioms and Expressions

to bump into	to hang around	to go through customs
to car pool	to hit the road	life in the fast lane
to get a move on	to catch the (bus)	jet lag
to split	to take the (bus)	to hitch a ride
to take off	to travel light	to bum a ride

10: Time

Daily

dawn	forenoon	p.m.	dusk
sunrise	noon	sunset	evening
sunup	midday	sundown	night
morning	afternoon	twilight	midnight
a.m.			middle of the night

Instruments

alarm clock	chronometer	metronome	sun dial
almanac	clock	stop watch	watch
calendar			wristwatch

Measures

second	day	month	decade
minute	week	year	century
half-hour	fortnight	leap year	millennium
hour			

General measures

instant	era	every day	yearly
moment	eon	weekly	past
period	split-second	bi-weekly	present
age	daily	monthly	future
epoch			

Seasons

spring	summer	fall	winter
		autumn	

Idioms and Expressions

behind the times	the time is right	time out	to make a night of it
for the time being	to lose time	time-honored	to get along in years
in the nick of time	behind the times	from the first	
in time	it's high time	in the beginning	ASAP - as soon as
to kill time	time zones	in the wink of an eye	possible
to pass the time	time-and-a-half	in a jiffy	PDQ - pretty darn
on time	the time of one's life	the crack of doom	(or damn) quick
once upon a time	time will tell	doomsday	B.C. - before Christ
overtime	double time	to call it a day	A.D. - *anno Domini*
to keep time	to two-time	all the live long day	in the year of our
to make time	at no time	fly-by-night	Lord

11: Weather and Climate

Nouns

air	snow	thunder
breeze	air mass	thunderstorm
cyclone	front	cloud
gale	high	cumulus
gust	low	thunderhead
hurricane	bolt	humidity
tornado	downpour	pressure
wind	drought	temperature
blizzard	drizzle	velocity
drift	fog	barometer
freezing	lightning	hygrometer
rain	mist	thermometer
frost	rain	forecast
hail	shower	weather report
ice	smog	el niño
sleet	squall	la niña

Verbs

blow	hail	rain
cloud up	lift	shine
drift	mist	snow
drizzle	pour	thunder

Adjectives

breezy	freezing	partly (sunny/cloudy)
chilly	frigid	polar
cloudy	frosty	rainy
cold	hazardous	severe
dreary	hot	snowy
dusty	humid	sunny
dry	inclement	temperate
foggy	mild	tropical
		wet

Idioms & Expressions

bolt from the blue	hot air	to take the wind out of
to break the ice	to make hay while	one's sails
castles in the air	the sun shines	three sheets to the wind
cats and dogs	to rain on one's parade	up in the air
cold snap	to shoot the breeze	weather the storm
heat wave	silver lining	windfall

12: Geography

Space

asteroid	meteor	nebula	ring	solar wind
comet	meteorite	orbit	satellite	star
constellation	meteor shower	outer space	shooting star	sun
falling star	moon	planet	space	sun spot
galaxy				universe

Solar System

Earth	Mars	Neptune	Saturn	Venus
Jupiter	Mercury	Pluto	Uranus	

Earth

Antarctic Circle	cliff	fault	isthmus	plain	strait
Arctic Circle	coastline	field	lake	plateau	stream
area	continent	fiord	lagoon	pole	surf
atoll	crater	forest	latitude	pond	swamp
bay	current	geyser	ledge	prairie	tide
beach	dam	glacier	longitude	range	Tropic of Cancer
bog	dale	globe	marsh	ravine	Tropic of Capricorn
brook	delta	gorge	meadow	reef	undertow
canal	desert	gulf	mountain	reservoir	valley
canyon	ditch	gully	north	rift	volcano
cape	east	hedge	ocean	river	wave
cascade	equator	hill	peak	sea	waterfall
channel	estuary	island	peninsula	south	west
chasm					woods

Material

dirt	mud	rock	soil	turf
earth	pebble	sod	stone	

Events

after shock	earthquake	erosion	flow	landslide
avalanche	ebb	eruption	flood	tremor

Idioms and Expressions

a stone's throw	East is East and West is West	over the hill
babes in the woods	high and dry	to sell down the river
to bog down	to leave no stone unturned	spaced out
dirt cheap	to make a mountain of a mole hill	to stem the tide
down-to-earth	once in a blue moon	a stick in the mud
earthy	out of the woods	true grit
	out of this world	under the sun
	over hill and dale	to win by a landslide

13: Animals
Rodents

bat	guinea pig	hamster	prairie dog	rat
gerbil	hare	mouse	rabbit	squirrel

Domestic animals

cat	donkey	horse	ox	sheep
cow	elephant	llama	pig	horse
dog	goat	mule	pony	mule

Wild Animals

badger	cougar	fox	porcupine	skunk
bear	coyote	moose	porpoise	squirrel
beaver	deer	mountain lion	possum	whale
bobcat	dolphin	lynx	raccoon	wildcat
chipmunk	elk	otter	sea cow	wolf

Reptiles and Amphibians

frog	newt	snake	toad	turtle
lizard	salamander	tadpole	tortoise	

Fish

bass	cod	guppy	perch	sturgeon
bluegill	eel	herring	pike	sunfish
catfish	goldfish	monk(fish)	shark	trout

Shellfish and Crustaceans. etc

clam	oyster	snail	mussel	shrimp
lobster	sea urchin	crab	scallop	starfish

Insects, etc

ant	butterfly	cricket	millipede	spider
aphid	caterpillar	dragonfly	praying mantis	termite
bee	centipede	grasshopper	scorpion	water strider
bug	cockroach	lady bug	silverfish	worm

Zoo animals

alligator	crocodile	gorilla	leopard	rhinoceros
bear	elephant	hippopotamus	lion	tiger
buffalo	giraffe	hyena	monkey	zebra

Body parts

abdomen	fur	legs	snout	teeth
antennae	hair	neck	spine	thorax
claw	head	paw	spot	whiskers
fangs	hoof	scale	stripe	wings
feelers	horns	shell	tail	wool

Dwellings

aquarium	burrow	cave	nest	pen
barn	cage	hutch	pasture	tank
				trap

Groupings

band (gorillas)	colony (ants)	herd (elephants)	pod (whales)	team (horses)
bed (clams)	flock (sheep)	herd (horses)	pride (lions)	tribe (goats)
brood (hens)	flock (birds)	nest (snakes)	school (fish)	troop (monkeys)
cloud (gnats)	gaggle (geese)	pack (dogs)	swarm (bees)	yoke (oxen)

Young Animals

bunny - rabbit	cygnet - swan	fingerling - fish	kid - goat, man
calf - cattle, elephant, whale	duckling - duck	fledgling - birds	kitten - cat
chick - chicken, other fowl	eaglet - eagle	foal - horse, zebra	lamb - sheep
colt - horse (male)	fawn - deer	fry - fish	piglet - pig
cub - fox, bear, lion, whale	filly - horse (female)	gosling - goose	polliwog/tadpole - frog
			puppy- dog

Comparative Expressions

big as a whale	fast as a jackrabbit	slow as a turtle	eats like a horse
blind as a bat	happy as a clam	sly as a fox	eats like a bird
brave as a lion	proud as a peacock	strong as an ox	runs like a deer
busy as a bee	quiet as a mouse	stubborn as a mule	swims like a fish
crazy as a loon	silly as a goose	wise as an owl	climbs like a monkey
dumb as an ox	slippery as an eel	drinks like a fish	

Idioms and Expressions

to back the wrong horse	to get one's goat	pig-headed
black sheep	to look a gift horse in the mouth	to play possum
bull session	to go to the dogs	road hog
bum steer	to hold one's horses	to shoot fish in a barrel
to let the cat out of the bag	to horse around	to smell a rat
cock and bull story	horse of another color	snake in the grass
copycat	in the doghouse	straight from the horse's mouth
crocodile tears	to make a beeline for	to take the bull by the horns
cry wolf	to make a monkey out of	to throw the bull
darkhorse	to monkey around with	white elephant
fish out of water	monkey business	wolf in sheep's clothing

75

List 14: Birds

albatross	grackle	penguin	beak
blackbird	grosbeak	pheasant	breast
bluebird	grouse	phoebe	claw
bobwhite	gull	pigeon	crest
boobie	hawk	puffin	egg
cardinal	heron	quail	feather
catbird	hummingbird	raven	flock
chickadee	jay	roadrunner	fly
chicken	kingbird	robin	nest
condor	kingfisher	sandpiper	peck
cormorant	kite	snipe	shell
cowbird	kiwi	sparrow	tail
crane	lark	starling	talon
crow	loon	stork	wing
cuckoo	magpie	swallow	
duck	meadowlark	swan	
eagle	nighthawk	tern	
egret	nuthatch	thrasher	
emu	oriole	thrush	
falcon	osprey	titmouse	
finch	ostrich	turkey	
flamingo	owl	vulture	
flycatcher	parrot	warbler	
frigate bird	partridge	whippoorwill	
goldfinch	peacock	woodpecker	
goose	pelican	wren	

Idioms and Expressions

bird in the hand	early bird	swan song
birds of a feather flock together	to eat crow	to talk turkey
the bluebird of happiness	feather in one's cap	ugly duckling
chicken	to kill two birds with one stone	water off a duck's back
to cook one's goose	nest egg	wild goose chase

15: Plants and Trees

Types, etc.

arbor	field	garden	hedge	park	wilderness
bush	forest	grove	orchard	woods	

Trees

ash	cedar	dogwood	lilac	oak	spruce
beech	chestnut	elm	maple	palm	sumac
birch				pine	willow

Fruit trees

apple	avocado	grapefruit	lemon	orange	pear
apricot	cherry	kiwi	lime	peach	plum

Tree parts

acorn	graft	needle	ring	sap	stump
bark	bud	pine cone	root	seed	trunk
branch	leaf				twig

Plants, Weeds, etc.

blueberry	cattails	fern	grass	milkweed	reeds
burdock	crabgrass			poison ivy	water lily

Wildflowers, etc.

clover	daisy	goldenrod	Indian paintbrush	sunflower
columbine	dandelion	lady's slipper	Queen Anne's lace	violets

Garden flowers

alyssum	daffodil	iris	lily of the valley	poppy	sunflower
chrysanthemum	geranium	lily	marigold	rose	tulip
crocus	impatiens			snapdragon	zinnia

Flower parts

anther	petal	pollen	seed	stamen	stigma
ovary	pistil			stem	style

Idioms and Expressions

Adam's apple	to hit the hay	to rest on one's laurels
against the grain	in a nutshell	to reap what one sows
to beat around the bush	that's just peachy	to sow one's wild oats
bed of roses	the last straw	to turn over a new leaf
grapevine	out on a limb	wallflower

16: Language

Nouns

adjective	etymology	narrative	recitation
adverb	fiction	noun	semantics
article	grammar	paragraph	sentence
autograph	idiom	paraphrase	signature
comma	interview	period	slang
comprehension	jargon	phonology	speech
conversation	journalism	poetry	spiel
definition	linguistics	prayer	style
dialect	literature	pronoun	syntax
dialogue	meaning	pronunciation	title
diction	monologue	punctuation	usage
drama	narration	quotation	verb
essay			verbiage

Verbs

abridge	edit	print	stammer
call	encode	pronounce	stutter
censor	erase	punctuate	swear
chat	explain	quote	symbolize
communicate	explicate	read	talk
comprehend	express	recite	tell
converse	gossip	relate	title
cry	interpret	report	transcribe
curse	interview	respond	translate
debate	mean	say	transliterate
decode	misspell	scrawl	type
define	mutter	sign	utter
dictate	narrate	speak	vow
discuss	paraphrase	spell	whisper
drawl	pray	sputter	write

Idioms and Expressions

to call a spade a spade	double talk	to swear on a stack of Bibles
to call to order	gobbledygook	neither rhyme nor reason
a close call	to read between the lines	talk of the town
far cry	to sign on the dotted line	tall story

17: Thinking

Nouns

analysis	decision	intention	reason
attitude	deduction	judgement	reflection
belief	deliberation	knowledge	speculation
brains	experience	logic	stupidity
certainty	fantasy	meditation	thinking
cogitation	feeling	mind	thought
comprehension	idea	notion	truth
conception	image	observation	understanding
conclusion	impression	perception	view
contemplation	intellect	rationale	wisdom
conviction	intelligence	realization	wit

Verbs

analyze	decide	learn	retain
appreciate	deliberate	meditate	ruminate
apprehend	distinguish	memorize	see
believe	experience	note	sense
brood	fantasize	notice	speculate
comprehend	feel	observe	think
conceive	figure out	perceive	trust
conclude	imagine	ponder	understand
consider	judge	realize	view
contemplate	know	reflect	

Adjectives

analytical	cognizant	intellectual	smart
appreciative	convinced	intelligent	stupid
aware of	crafty	irrational	thoughtful
brainy	decisive	knowing	trusting
brilliant	deliberate	observant	truthful
certain	dull	perceptive	understanding
clever	experiential	pensive	vague
conclusive	imaginative	rational	wise
cognitive	indecisive	reasonable	witty

Idioms and Expressions

absent minded	level-headed	pipe dream
fat headed	literal minded	narrow minded
to know the ropes	to make head or tail	neither rhyme nor reason

18: Numbers and Math

Nouns

addition	equation	product
algebra	figure	proof
analysis	formula	radius
angle	fraction	rate
arithmetic	function	relativity
average	geometry	remainder
axiom	plane	root
calculation	solid	set
calculator	infinity	sequence
calculus	integral	solution
cipher	logarithm	square root
circumference	long division	statistics
computation	mathematics	straight line
computer	median	subtraction
cube	multiplication	sum
decimal	numeral	theorem
decimal point	percentage	theory
difference	pi	topology
diameter	postulate	trigonometry
dimension	probability	value
division	problem	variable

Verbs

add	divide	multiply
average	double	solve
calculate	equal	square
compute	figure	subtract
count	formulate	triple

Idioms and Expressions

face value	math facts	second-rate
fifty-fifty	multiplication tables	to see double
lump sum	to put two and two together	sixes and sevens

19: Colors

Primary

red	green	violet/purple
orange	blue	
yellow	indigo	

Secondary

aquamarine	emerald	pink
beige	gold	rose
black	gray	ruby
bronze	ivory	silver
brown	khaki	slate
buff	lavender	tan
chestnut	maroon	teal
chocolate	off white	turquoise
coffee	olive	umber
copper	olive drab	white

Adjectives

bright	earth	metallic
brilliant	fluorescent	mottled
cool	glossy	pale
dark	hot	pied
dull	light	rich
flat	lurid	vivid

Miscellaneous

rainbow	camouflage	spectrum

Paints

acrylic	latex	tempera
enamel	oil	water
finger	pastel	

Idioms and Expressions

black and blue	in black and white	red herring
black hearted	in the pink	red letter day
blue, the blues	in the red	red tape
dyed in the wool	to paint the town red	rose colored glasses
greenhorn	red carpet	silver lining
green with envy	red cent	yellow (cowardly)

20: Shapes

Adjectives

angular	globular	round
arched	hexagonal	rectangular
blunt	horizontal	regular
circular	irregular	sharp
concave	linear	slender
conical	long	slim
curved	narrow	square
crooked	octagonal	smooth
cylindrical	oval	straight
elliptical	parallel	triangular
elongated	perpendicular	twisted
flat	pointed	warped
flattened	ragged	wide

Nouns

arc	dome	pentagon
arch	globe	point
block	helix	pyramid
blob	heptagon	rectangle
circle	hexagon	sphere
cone	horseshoe	spiral
cube	mound	square
cylinder	octagon	surface
diamond	oval	tip
disc	peak	triangle

Idioms and Expressions

round peg in a square hole	odds and ends	to run circles around someone
domestic triangle	sharp as a tack	the Pentagon
vicious circle	square	point of an argument
a crooked person	straight as an arrow	tip of an iceberg

21: Substances and Materials

Nouns

acid	flint	plastic
air	gas	plywood
aluminum	gasoline	powder
ashes	glue	rock
asphalt	goo	rubber
base	grease	sand
brass	gunk	sheet
bronze	kerosene	rock
cement	lubricant	smoke
cloth	moisture	soil
cloud	mud	steam
concrete	oil	steel
copper	ointment	stuff
dirt	paste	tar
dust	petroleum	water
earth	plaster	wood

Adjectives

abrasive	impermeable	slippery
corroded	invisible	slimy
corrosive	liquid	soft
crumbly	metallic	solid
dull	pliable	soluble
durable	resilient	spongy
dusty	rough	sticky
flammable	rubbery	strong
gaseous	rusty	thick
gooey	sharp	thin
gritty	shiny	tough
hard	slick	wet

Idioms and Expressions

to blow off steam	to go up in smoke	to scratch the surface
brass tacks	to lay it on thick	to throw cold water on
a fly in the ointment	to take a powder	to knock on wood
slick operator	greaseball	powder keg
to grease the wheel	to grease one's palm	to cement a deal
to cast in concrete	to be plastered	dull as dishwater

22: Containers

bag	canteen	demijohn	mug	sack
barrel	carafe	dish	pack	snifter
basket	carton	file folder	package	thermos
bottle	case	flask	pail	tin
bowl	container	glass	pitcher	tray
box	crate	jar	portfolio	tub
bucket	cup	jug	pot	tube
can	demitasse	keg	rack	vase
canister				vessel

Idioms and Expressions

in the bag	boxed in	lock, stock and barrel
to have someone over a barrel	a drop in the bucket	soapbox
bottleneck	left holding the bag	windbag
barrel of monkeys	jug wine	ugly mug
bag lady	on the bottle	a real dish

23: Manipulations

aim	fill	mold	screw	tip
arrange	flatten	move	scratch	trip
assemble	flex	open	seal	turn
attach	flick	pick up	set	turn off
bash	flip	pick out	set down	turn on
beat	flop	pick over	slam	turn over
bend	fold	pluck	spin	turn under
bolt	hammer	plug in	start	turn around
break	hang (up)	plug up	stop	twist
close	heat	pound	strike	undo
cool off, down	hook	press	strip	unfold
crack	ignite	pull	take apart	unhook
crumble	insert	punch	take out	unplug
crush	knead	push	take up	unlatch
cut	latch	put in	take down	unlock
deposit	level	reverse	tap	unscrew
depress	light	rap	tear	untie
disassemble	load	rip	thread	unzip
detach	lock	roll	throw	weave
drain	loop	rub	thrust	wipe
drive	maneuver	sand	tie	work
empty	mix	scrape	tilt	zip

Idioms and Expressions

flop house	to put the screws to someone	spin doctor
to pull a fast one	to put a spin on information	to strike while the iron's hot

24: Emotions

Nouns

affection	bravery	fatigue	joy	rage
aggravation	cheer	fear	joviality	regret
amusement	courage	feeling	laughter	restlessness
anger	craziness	fright	love	sadness
anguish	dejection	gladness	mood	sorrow
annoyance	delight	glee	nervousness	tears
anxiety	depression	greed	pain	temper
awe	disappointment	happiness	passion	terror
belligerence	disgust	hope	pity	tiredness
bitterness	embarrassment	horror	pleasure	trouble
bliss	enthusiasm	indifference	prejudice	weariness
boredom	envy	jealousy	pride	zest

Verbs

abhor	bother	disgust	hate	rejoice
aggravate	burn up	embarrass	hope	sadden
agitate	calm	envy	laugh	shake up
amuse	cheer up	excite	lament	stir
anger	console	fatigue	like	tire
annoy	cry	fear	love	tremble
antagonize	delight in	feel	mope	trouble
bewilder	depress	frighten	mourn	weep
blush	detest	fume	pain	
bore	disappoint	gladden	please	

Adjectives

abhorrent	bitter	disgusted	happy	painful
abject	blissful	embarrassed	hopeful	passionate
affectionate	bored	enthusiastic	insane	pleased
afraid	bothered	envious	irritated	restless
aggravated	brave	excited	jealous	sad
amorous	calm	fatigued	jolly	sexy
amused	cheerful	fearful	joyful	shy
angry	cheery	flustered	jovial	sorrowful
annoyed	crazy	forlorn	loving	tearful
anxious	dejected	frightened	melancholy	timid
apprehensive	delighted	gay	merry	tired
belligerent	depressed	glad	moody	troubled
berserk	disappointed	gleeful	mournful	upset
bewildered	disconsolate	grouchy	nervous	weary

Idioms and Expressions

at wit's end	happy as a clam	method in one's madness	a heart breaker
to blow one's top	hot and bothered	love will find a way	tear jerker
fit to be tied	in a dither	out of sorts	troubled waters
to go to pieces	to make a scene	standoffish	at the end of one's rope

25: The Body and its Function

External

head	fist	fingernail	penis	shin
hair	hand	chest	foreskin	ankle
shoulders	palm	breast	testes	heel
neck	thumb	nipple	testicles	instep
arm	finger	stomach	anus	sole
armpit	index	abdomen	leg	foot
forearm	middle	waist	knee	toe
elbow	ring	hip	thigh	big toe
wrist	little	buttocks	calf	little toe

Face

forehead	eye	eyelid	mouth	lip
eyebrow	pupil	cheek	jaw	chin
temple	white	nose	tongue	dimple
ear	eyeball	nostril	tooth	mustache
earlobe	eyelash	bridge	gums	beard
eardrum				sideburns

Bones

skull	spine	shoulder blade	pelvis	thigh bone
backbone	collarbone	ribs	hipbone	kneecap
vertebrae				skeleton

Insides

brain	liver	appendix	muscle	tonsils
windpipe	pancreas	bladder	blood	larynx
heart	kidney	vein	nerves	vagina
lung	intestines	artery	throat	rectum

Body products

urine	saliva/	perspiration/	tears	sperm
feces	spit	sweat	oil	eggs

Adjectives

pregnant	fat	healthy	strong	supple
tall	muscular	sick	athletic	lithe
short	skinny	robust	tight	
thin	plump	weak	loose	

86

Verbs

sit	flex	eat	digest	cry
stand	creep	bite	fornicate	weep
jump	belch	chew	copulate	sob
leap	burp	nibble	menstruate	sniffle
hop	breathe	spit	smile	moan
skip	gasp	defecate	grin	groan
run	see	urinate	laugh	scowl
twist	hear	swallow	giggle	
bend	smell	taste	titter	

Idioms and Expressions

after one's own heart
all ears
apple of one's eye
to give one's right arm
at arm's length
with open arms
to turn one's back on
bad blood
to beat one's brains out
to beat one's head against a
   stone wall
to bend over backwards
to bite off more than one
   can chew
in cold blood
brainstorm
to waste one's breath
to save one's breath
to take away one's breath
to breathe freely
cold feet
to cool one's heels
to cut off one's nose to
   spite one's face
to eat one's heart out
to eat one's words
to rub elbows with
elbow grease
to keep an eye on
to see eye to eye
to make eyes at
to keep a straight face
to keep one's fingers crossed

first-hand
to foot the bill
to put one's foot down
to put one's best foot forward
to put one's foot in one's mouth
on all fours
funny bone
to get on one's nerves
to get something off
   one's chest
guts
potbelly
to let down one's hair
to split hairs
hard-hearted
hard-headed
head and shoulders above
over one's head
heart-to-heart
by heart
to have a heart
a heel
to keep a stiff upper lip
to knock one's block off
lowbrow, highbrow
to make no bones about
by word of mouth
to shoot one's mouth off
foul-mouthed
narrow-minded
neck and neck
up to one's neck
nosey

to pay lip service to
to pay through the nose
to pick a bone with
to pull one's leg
to pull the wool over
   one's eyes
to shake a leg
straight from the shoulder
a cold shoulder
a chip on one's shoulder
by the skin of one's teeth
to get under one's skin
a slap in the face
a pain in the neck
a slip of the tongue
sweet tooth
to take a load off one's feet
to set one's teeth on edge
under one's thumb
all thumbs
to toe the mark
to be on one's toes
tooth and nail
tongue in cheek
tongue tied
tongue twister
on the tip of one's tongue
to turn the other cheek
to turn up one's nose at
to turn one's back on
to watch one's step
to make one's mouth water
to wet one's whistle

Vulgarities*

"Proper" term	Acceptable euphemism	Vulgarity
anus		ass hole, bung hole
breasts		boobs, knockers, tits
buttocks	backsides, butt, cheeks, fanny, rear end	ass, buns, tail
copulate, (have) intercourse	make love	fuck, screw, lay
defecate	go to the bathroom go to the john	shit, (take a) dump (take a) crap
ejaculate		come
expectorate	spit	clam
(to be) flatulent	pass gas, break wind	cut the cheese, fart
masturbate		jack off, jerk off
menstruation	period, time of the month	on the rag
orgasm	climax	come
penis		cock, dick, dong, pecker, prick, shaft
testicles		balls, nuts
vagina, labia		cunt, pussy, snatch, twat
clitoris		clit
vomit	spit up, throw up	barf, up chuck, toss (snap) one's cookies

*** IMPORTANT –**

To the student: These vulgarities must be used very carefully since many people find them offensive. They are included here because you may hear them. Be careful. It is best not to use them.

To the teacher: These vulgarities should be taught, if at all, with warnings and care. They are included here because students often hear them and misuse them, and it is important that they know when and how to use them and, more important, when not to use them.

88

26: Transportation

Land

ATV	chariot	rickshaw	subway
(all-terrain vehicle)	coach	RV	tanker
automobile, auto	convertible	(recreational vehicle)	tank
bus	el, elevated railway	scooter	truck
bicycle,	jeep	sedan	taxicab, taxi, cab
bike	litter	skateboard	train
cable car	locomotive	skimobile	tricycle
camper	moped	sled	trolley
car	motorcycle	sleigh	truck
carriage	pick-up	sports car	van
cart	railroad, railway	stagecoach	wagon

Animals

burro	dog (sled)	horse	pony
camel	donkey	llama	oxen
cow	elephant	mule	water buffalo

People

bus driver	driver	taxi cab driver	co-pilot
chauffeur	engineer	teamster	flight attendant
coachman	guide	truck driver	pilot
conductor	mechanic	aviator	steward/stewardess

General

alley	engine	path	thruway
bridge	gasoline	rest area	timetable
burden	highway	road	trail
cargo	interstate	schedule	tire
coal	lane	steam	turnpike
diesel	oil	street	vehicle
			wheel

Air

aircraft	boarding pass	helicopter	seat
airliner	concourse	jet	seat assignment
airplane	control tower	light plane	spacecraft, ship
airport	dirigible	luggage	space shuttle
baggage check	engine	propeller	ticket
baggage claim area	gate	reservation	ticket counter
balloon (hot air)	glider	rocket	window
blimp	hangar	runway	wings

Water

ark	harbor	ocean	sailboat
barge	helm	ocean liner	ship
boat	hovercraft	paddlewheel	steamship/steamboat
canal	hull	pond	steering wheel
canoe	kayak	port	stream
channel	keel	propeller	submarine
cruise ship	lake	rapids	tugboat
dinghy	lifeboat	riverraft	vessel
ferry/ferryboat	lighthouse	rowboat	warship
fleet	mast	rudder	yacht
freighter	motorboat	runabout	sea
galley	oars	sail	white water

Verbs

arrive	drive	paddle	take off
check in	embark, disembark	ride	tow
depart	fly	sail	travel
disembark	land	steer	walk

Idioms and Expressions

to back-fire	to miss the boat
to get on the bandwagon	to pave the way for
on the (water) wagon	water under the bridge/ over the dam
in the same boat	to fall asleep at the wheel
off the beaten track	to take a back seat to
to burn one's bridges behind one	to run around in circles
to know the ropes	slow boat to China
to lose one's way	shipshape
to make way for someone or something	up the creek without a paddle
to meet someone half-way	backseat driver

27: Community
Places and Organizations

arts council
chamber of commerce
sidewalk
park
park bench
civic center
community center
public library
Catholic church

mosque
Protestant church
Jewish synagogue
Grange
VFW - Veterans of
    Foreign Wars
DAR - Daughters
    of the American
    Revolution

Elks
Eagles
Knights of Columbus
Lions Club
Shriners
Masons
Boy/Girl Scouts
4-H Club
playground

FFA - Future Farmers
    of America
American Legion
PTA - Parent-Teachers
    Association
school board
senior center
garden club
union hall
university club

Events

wedding reception
wake
funeral
memorial service
church bazaar
church supper
bingo

strike
picket line
demonstration
walk-a-thon
parade
band concert

county fair
farmers' market
hoedown
rodeo
auction
flea market

scouting jamboree
tag, yard, lawn sale
Town Meeting
political rally
voting
rummage sale
beauty contest

28: Hotels

airport limousine,
    limo
baggage
ball room
bar
bath
bed
bellhop
bill
bureau
bed and breakfast
boarding house
call (wake-up)
cashier
currency exchange
chair
chambermaid

coffee shop
convention desk
concierge
clerk
dining room
doorman
elevator
elevator operator
fitness center
flop house
gardener
guest
guest house
health club
hospitality center
housekeeper
hostel

hotel
ice machine
information desk
inn, innkeeper
key/ room key
laundry
lobby
lounge
luggage
maid
manager
meeting
motel
operator
organization
party
reservation

residential hotel
resort
room
    single
    double
room clerk
room service
restaurant
safety deposit box
security guard
suite
table
tourist
tourist cabins
tourist court
tour guide
travel desk

Verbs

call (roomservice)
check in

check out
disturb (do not)

pack
register

reserve
stay

Idioms and Expressions

bag and baggage
room and board

it's the Ritz
stop for the night

overnight guest
overnight stay

home away from home
weekend rates

29: Restaurants

Nouns

appetizer	course	main course	refill (of coffee)
ashtray	cup	meal	salad bar
bar	dessert	menu	salt
bowl	dish	mug	serving spoon
booth	fork	napkin	table
buffet	glass	order	tablecloth
chair	gourmet	plate	tax
check	gratuity	platter	tip
cocktail	knife	reservation	wine cellar
		round (of drinks)	wine list

Verbs

dine	order	prepare	tip
eat out	pay	reserve	take out

Types

automat	deli(catessen)	gourmet	pizza parlor
cafe	diner	luncheonette	snack bar
cafeteria	drive-in	natural foods	soda fountain
coffee shop	fast-food	pizzeria	vending machine

Personnel

baker	chef	headwaiter	manager
bartender	cook	host	waiter
busboy	dishwasher	hostess	waitress
cashier	guest	maitre d'	

Adjectives

a la carte	fresh	rare	succulent
baked	fried	raw	take-out
bland	grilled	salty	tasteless
boiled	hot	scrumptious	tasty
broiled	mashed	sliced	to go
cold	medium	spicy	vegan
delicious	overdone	steamed	vegetarian
dry			well-done

Idioms and Expressions

to wine and dine	doggy bag	to go dutch	to foot the bill
bill of fare	dutch treat	pick up the check	dine and dance
bottomless cup	room and meals tax	to take the check	

30: Stores and Shops

General

downtown	neighborhood	specialty shops	shopping center
main street	variety store	department store	shopping district
window shopping	mall	browsing	one-stop shopping
			outlet center

Specific

roadside	drug store	flea market	Salvation Army store
vegetable stand	pharmacy	furniture store	sporting goods store
grocery store	optician	appliance store	arts and crafts store
supermarket	department store	hardware store	toy store
delicatessen	discount store	fabric/draperies store	used furniture store
bakery	outlet store	sewing center	used clothing store
health food store	printing/copy center	carpets & flooring	gift shop
restaurant	clothing store	store	pet shop
cafeteria	shoe store	paint store	hobby shop
camera shop	thrift shop	stationery store	antique shop
snack bar	country store	bookstore	jewelry store
coffee shop	mail-order	art gallery	photography store
fast-food chain	minimart	newsstand	florist
pizza parlor	service center	tobacconist	farmers' market
candy store	electronics store	music store	car dealership
dollar store	fix it shop	TV-radio store	computer store

List 31: Agencies and Services

bank	advertising agency	appliance repair
post office	auto rental agency	auto parts store
town/city offices	copy center	electrician
loan association	counseling office	plumber
insurance agency	shipping center	welding shop
real estate agency	newspaper office	auto repair shop
military recruiting office	beauty parlor	service station
travel agency	barber shop	carpenter
law firm	tanning salon	moving company
police department	health center	storage warehouse
fire department	martial arts studio	employment agency
Internal Revenue Service	dance studio	day-care center
certified public	funeral parlor	senior citizen's center
accountant office	dry cleaners	welfare office
stockbroker	laundry	Planned Parenthood
telephone company	laundromat	Women's Crisis Center
business office	shoe repair service	homeless shelter
TV cable company office	radio-TV repair	charities

32: Post Office

Personnel

carrier	mail carrier	postmaster/mistress
clerk	post office worker	sorter

Nouns and Adjectives

address	general delivery	postage stamp
aerogram	insured mail	post card
airmail	international	post office (P. O.) box
book of stamps	mail	priority mail
book rate	junk mail	registered mail
box	letter	return address
bulk mail	lobby	return receipt
cancellation	magazine rate	self-addressed envelope
certified mail	mail box	self-adhesive stamp
C.O.D.	money order	service window
coil of stamps	next day	special delivery
commemorative stamp	newspaper	special handling
customs form	overnight	stamp
dead letter	package	stamp collecting
envelope	parcel post	surface mail
express mail	philatelic window	U.S.P.S
fee	postage	ZIP Code
first class/second, third.	postage due	plus four
franking privileges	postage meter	Zone (shipping)

Verbs

address	insure	register
cancel	lick	return
certify	mail	seal
deliver	post	send
fill out	pick up	ship
forward	receive	stamp

33: Banks and Money

Verbs

apply for	change	deposit	overdraw
authorize	charge	endorse	pay
balance	close out	insure	put in
borrow	convert	justify	save
cancel	count	loan	stop payment
call in a loan	credit	lend	take out
cash	debit	make change	withdraw

Nouns

asset	check stub	frozen assets	record book
automatic payment	coin	line of credit	safe
ATM - automatic	commercial loan	loan	safe deposit box
teller machine	credit card	loan agreement	savings account
balance	currency	loan payment	savings bond
bank	debit card	money	second mortgage
bank account	deposit	mortgage	secured loan
bank book	deposit slip	nickel	silver dollar
bill	deposit	paycheck	statement
cash	receipt	payment book	traveler's check
CD - certificate of	dime	penny	total
deposit	dollar	piggy bank	vault
check	half dollar, 50¢ piece	principal	window
checking account	interest	quarter	withdrawal
check register	invoice	receipt	withdrawal slip

Personnel

drive-up teller	loan officer	president	secretary
executive officer	messenger	safe deposit clerk	security guard
			teller

Idioms and Expression

to bank on something	to take a rain check	to make both ends meet
to bounce a check	rubber check	I.O.U.
bottom dollar	a run on the bank	a man of means
cheapskate	bank holiday	a panhandler
to get one's money's worth	flat broke	penny wise and pound foolish
layaway plan	in the money	to nickel and dime to death
to pass the buck	to corner the market	Waste not, want not.
pretty penny	to make or break	A penny saved is a penny earned.
queer as a three-dollar bill	to make a buck	A fool and his money are soon parted.

34: Recreation

Games (also see 35)

backgammon
board games
bridge
canasta
cards
charades
checkers
chess

Chinese checkers
cribbage
crossword puzzle
computer games
hearts
jig saw puzzle
mahjong
mankala

Monopoly
poker
role playing games
rummy
solitaire
Scrabble
twenty questions
video games

Hobbies

aquariums/ tropical fish
butterfly collecting
coin collecting
collecting antiques, etc.
canning
ceramics
cooking
dolls/ doll houses

embroidery
flower arranging
gardening
gun collecting
house plants
miniatures
model building
model railroading

painting
pottery
rock collecting
sewing
terrariums
stamp collecting
Sports (see List 35)
Music (see List 36)

Amusements & Shows

amusement park
carnival
circus
concert hall
dinner theater/ summer stock

disco
ice show
magic show
movies
pool hall

night club
radio
television
theater
video game arcade

Arts

ballet
concert
dance
drama

exhibition
martial arts
music
painting

photography
recital
sculpture
theater

Crafts

batik
carpentry
crewel
crocheting

embroidery
knitting
needlepoint
pottery

quilting
sewing
weaving

Places

museum	sports stadium	nightclub
concert hall	health club	discotheque
historical site	country club	bar
zoo	racquet/racket club	cocktail lounge
aquarium	tennis club	marina
botanical garden	social club	swimming pool
circus	ski resort	teen center
campground	theatre	amusement park
beach	movie theatre	national park, forest

Activities

concert	pottery making	baseball
ballet	fishing	softball
opera	hunting	basketball
board game	hiking	football
playing cards	camping	volleyball
watching TV	mountain climbing	croquet
listening to radio, stereo	horseback riding	tennis
reading	bicycling/ cycling	badminton
gourmet cooking	roller skating	squash
gardening	hockey	racquetball
birdwatching	skating	handball
jogging	skate boarding	golf
body building	in-line skating	minature golf
weight lifting	skiing	gymnastics
martial arts	surfing	track and field
wrestling	water skiing	bowling
flying	motor boating	frisbee
kite flying	canoeing	horse race
sky diving	sailing	dog race
bungee jumping	swimming	car race
paragliding	diving	rally
sewing	surfing	long-distance running
painting	soccer	extreme sports

Idioms and Expressions

to put one's cards on the table	drawing card	to steal the show
to put one's money on the line	to flip over something	up one's sleeve
to put up or shut up	go fly a kite	surfing the net
no dice	a flop	do not pass Go
dicey	to hit the jackpot	to win by a nose
an ace up one's sleeve	on the wrong track	nip and tuck

97

35: Sports and Games

archery	canoeing	hiking	racquetball	speedskating
badminton	climbing	hockey	roller	surfing
baseball	curling	horseback riding	skating	swimming
basketball	diving	hunting	running	tennis
billiards	fencing	jogging	skiing	track
bowling	figure skating	mountaineering	downhill	volleyball
boxing	fishing	pingpong	cross-country	water polo
bicycling	golf	pool	soccer	weight lifting
bronco busting	gymnastics	polo	softball	wrestling

Equipment

arrow	fishing rod	mat	puck	soccerball
balance beam	flying rings	net	racket/racquet	softball
baseball bat	glove	paddle	racquetball	surfboard
birdie	golfball	parallel bars	reins	target
bow	golf clubs	ping pong	saddle	tee
bicycle	hockey stick	ball	skates	tennis ball
canoe	horse	pole	ski pole	tennis racket
fishing lure	indian clubs	pool cue	skis	trampoline

Areas

arena	course	green	pool	rollerdrome
coliseum	court	gymnasium	ring	stadium
country club	field	lane	rink	track
				trail

Verbs

aim	defend	kick	play	serve
attack	hike	lose	punt	tackle
catch	hit	participate	run	take part in
club	hurl	pitch	save	tie
coach	jog	place	score	throw
defeat				win

Idioms and Expressions

all part of the game	hook, line, and sinker	last lap
batting average	to keep the ball rolling	for keeps
below par	to make a hit	long shot
behind the eight ball	in the rough	to be punchy
to break the record	to rate a ten	to pull one's punches
come-back	right off the bat	to know what the score is
double-header	to pinch hit	second wind
to get on the ball	rain check	to have a score to settle
to get to first base	free-for-all	seventh inning stretch
to go to bat for	hit or miss	a shot in the dark
to have a lot on the ball	to jump the gun	to win hands down

36: Music

Nouns

album	composition	jazz	rhythm
alto	concert	lyrics	singer
artist	conductor	measure	solo
ballad	concerto	melody	sonata
band	disc	note	song
bar	disc jockey (DJ)	piece	soprano
bass	folk song	program	symphony
beat	group	recital	tape
cassette	hit	record	tenor
compact disc (CD)	hymn	release	tune

Verbs

accompany	harmonize	play	sing
compose	hum	pluck	strum
conduct	interpret	read (music)	toot
croon	pick	record	whistle
finger			write

Types

acoustic	classical	jazz	popular, pop
background	contemporary	light classical	rap
band	country & western	modern	religious
baroque	dance	mood music	rock and roll, rock
bebop	electronic	muscial	rhythm and blues
bluegrass	folk	new age, space	spirituals
chamber	hard rock	opera	soul
church	hip hop	operetta	symphonic

Instruments

banjo	drums	oboe	tambourine
bass	dulcimer	organ	trombone
bassoon	electric guitar	mandolin	trumpet
cello	fiddle	piano	tuba
clarinet	guitar	saxophone	viola
cornet	harp	strings	violin
cymbals	horn	synthesizer	

Idioms and Expressions

to blow your own horn	to play second fiddle	song and dance	music to one's ears
to face the music	to soft-pedal	for a song	the blues
to fiddle around with	to pipe down	to sing for one's supper	to beat the band

37: Photography, Video, and Cinema

Photography

accessory	dodge	matte	screen
album	double exposure	mug shot	setting
aperture	double prints	negative	shutter
automatic	duplicate	out-of-focus	slide
battery	enlargement	over-exposed	snapshot
black and white	exposure	photo(graph)	speed
blow up	film	pixel	strap
camera	filter	Polaroid	studio
canister	flash	portrait	take (a picture)
cartridge	focal length	pose	telephoto
case	focus	positive	time lapse
color	frame	process	tripod
come out	glossy	projector	under-exposed
composition	instamatic	print	viewer
darkroom	lens	reduce	viewfinder
definition	light meter	rewind	washed out
developer	load	roll (of film)	wide-angle lens
digital	mailer	rez, resolution	zoom lens

Video and Cinema

action	feature	rating	tear-jerker
actor/actress	film festival	reel	thriller
adult	film studio	release	ticket
adventure	format(ted)	rent	tracking
animation	freeze	restricted	trailer
camcorder	home video	reverse	VCR (video tape
cartoon	independent film	rewind	recorder)
cassette	letter-box	romance	video
classic	matinee	running time	camera
closed captioned	mature	score	disc
critic	movie	screen	game
director	musical	sequel	player
documentary	mystery	short subject	rental
drama	Oscar	show	store
dubbed	playback	sound track	tape
DVD (digital video disc)	porno(graphy)	star	x-rated
entertainment	preview	sub-titled	western
fast forward	producer	supporting actor/ress	wide-screen

100

38: Medicine and Health

Places and Areas

admitting
ambulance
birthing room
clinic
check in
delivery room
emergency room

hospital
HMO (health
    maintenance org.)
insane asylum
intensive care unit
    (ICU)

labor room
laboratory
maternity ward
mental hospital
nursing home
operating room

out-patient clinic
pediatric ward
private room
recovery room
sanitarium
waiting room
ward

Equipment

adhesive tape
band-aid
bandage
bed
bed pan
cane
cast

crutches
gauze
heating pad
hot water bottle
operating table
oxygen tent
Q-tip (swab)

sanitary
napkins
scalpel
stethoscope
thermometer
    oral
    rectal

tongue
depressor
toothpaste
tweezers
vaporizer
walker
wheelchair
x-ray machine

People

anesthetist
candy striper
chiropractor
dermatologist
doctor (M.D.)
general practitioner
    (G.P.)
gynecologist
intern

lab technician
neurologist
nurse
nurse practitioner
obstetrician
ophthalmologist
orthopedic surgeon
out-patient

pathologist
patient
pediatrician
pharmacist
physician
podiatrist
practical nurse
psychiatrist

psychoanalyst
psychologist
radiologist
receptionist
registered nurse (R.N.)
specialist
surgeon
undertaker
urologist

Verbs

ache
admit
bleed
cough
deliver

diagnose
discharge
examine
faint
give birth
gargle

hurt
irritate
nurse
operate
pain
prescribe

recover
recuperate
relapse
set
swell
throw up
vomit

Processes

appendectomy
blood pressure
Caesarean section
D&C
delivery (of a baby)
diagnosis
EKG

examination
heart beat
hysterectomy
injection
inoculation
intensive care

MRI
observation
prognosis
pulse
sample
shot

specimen
surgery
temperature
tonsillectomy
transplant
vaccination
x-ray

101

Medicine

antacid	aspirin	eyedrops	penicillin	sedative
antidote	capsules	laxative	pill	suppository
antihistamine	contraceptive	nasal spray	the Pill	tablet
antiseptic	decongestant	ointment	prescription	vitamins

Problems

abscess	constipation	exhaustion	injury	sore
accident	cough	fever	infection	sprain
ache	cut	the flu	inflammation	stiff
allergy	deaf	fracture	nausea	strain
blind	diarrhea	hemmorhoids	pain	swollen
burn	dislocation	(piles)	rash	virus
chills	dumb	indigestion	runny nose	vomit
a cold				wound

Diseases and Conditions

AIDS	chicken pox	herpes	mononucleosis	scarlet fever
allergy	cholera	high blood pressure	(mono)	schizophrenia
alcoholism	diabetes	HIV positive	multiple sclerosis	skin cancer
Alzheimer's	diarrhea	immunity	mumps	smallpox
angina	drug addiction	influenza (flu)	neurosis	stroke
arteriosclerosis	emphysema	leukemia	paranoia	syndrome
arthritis	fetal alcohol	malaria	pneumonia	syphilis
asthma	syndrome	measles	polio	tuberculosis (T.B.)
autism	gonorrhea	meningitis	psychosis	tumor
bronchitis	heart attack	mental	rheumatic fever	ulcer
bursitis	hepatitis	retardation	rubella (German	V.D. (venereal
cancer	hernia		measles)	disease)

Idioms and Expressions

on call	over the hill	a shiner
office hours	to kick the bucket	a black eye
say "ah"	a new lease on life	a shot in the arm
turn your head and cough	to give someone a dose	a sight for sore eyes
born with a silver spoon	of their own medicine	to turn one's stomach
in one's mouth	to take one's medicine	under the weather
to cough up	nuts, nutty as a fruitcake	on the wagon
chain smoker	to go off the deep end	"break a leg"
dead as a doornail	a bitter pill to swallow	an apple a day
dead to the world	in the pink	keeps the doctor away
over one's dead body	safe and sound	skin and bones
one foot in the grave	to have a screw loose	sick and tired of
to croak	hooked on drugs	to catch a cold
to give up the ghost	monkey on your back	to come down with
hard of hearing	horrors (withdrawal)	

102

39: Dentistry

Places

clinic	office	waiting room

Equipment

air compressor	dentist's chair	toothbrush
cleaning tools	drill	toothpaste
dental floss	mirror	x-ray machine

People

dentist	hygienist	orthodontist
dental assistant	oral surgeon	receptionist
dental		

Verbs

ache	extract	pull out
cap	fill	repair
clean	hurt	seal
drill		x-ray

Miscellaneous

abscess	decay	incisor
bicuspid	dentures	jaw
braces	dog tooth	molar nerve
bridge	eye tooth	novocaine
buck teeth	false teeth	pain
cavity	front tooth	root
checkup	filling	root canal
crown	gap toothed	wisdom tooth
canines		

Idioms and Expressions

baby teeth	to knock your teeth out
one's bark is worse than one's bite	like pulling teeth
to bite the hand that feeds one	long in the tooth
to bite off more than one can chew	toothy grin
to cut one's teeth on	winning smile
to give one's eye tooth for	the tooth fairy

List 40: Barber and Beautician

Nouns

Afro	cream rinse	hair net	razor cut
appointment	crew-cut	hair oil	razor blade
bangs	curl	hairpiece	receding hairline
barber	curler	hairpins	redhead
barrette	DA (duck tail)	hair style	rollers
beard	dandruff	hair stylist	scissors
beautician	depilatory	handlebar moustache	shampoo
blond,blonde	drier	highlight	shave
bobby pin	dye	manicure	setting lotion
bowl cut	fashion	mancurist	sideburns
braid	flat top	Mohawk	split ends
brunette	goatee (beard)	mousse	streak
brush	hairbrush	moustache	tint
butch	haircut	page boy	towhead
carrot top	hairdo	pedicure	toupee
clippers	hairdresser	permanent	wave
comb	hair drier	pigtails	whiskers
conditioner	hair grease	ponytail	wig
cosmetics	hairline	razor	

Verbs

bleach	curl	dye	shampoo
blow dry	cut	massage	shave
brush	design	rinse	tint
clip	dry	set	trim
comb			wave

Adjectives

bushy	frizzy	normal	straight
close	hairless	oily	thick
curly	hairy	over the ear	thin
dry	kinky	scraggly (beard)	unisex
dyed	long	short	wavy

Hair colors

auburn	brown	honey blonde	gray
black	brunette	flaxen blond	red
blond, blonde	dishwater blonde	strawberry blond	white

Idioms and Expressions

to get in one's hair	hairline crack	not a hair out of place	Handsome is as handsome
hairbreadth escape	long hair	one's hair stands on end	does.
hairpin turn	to put one's hair up	tall, dark, and handsome	Beauty is in the eye of the
let one's hair down	hairy	blonds have more fun	beholder.

41: Cosmetics and Toiletries

Nouns

after-shave lotion	solid	hair rinse	razor blade
baby shampoo	spray	lip balm	rouge
bath oil	stick	lip gloss	scent
bath salts	dental floss	lipstick	septic stick
bath soap	depilatory	make up	shampoo
beauty cream	emery board	mascara	shaver (electric)
beauty lotion	eyebrow pencil	moisturizer	shaving brush
blush	eye drops	mouth wash	shaving cream
body lotion	eye-liner	mud pack	shaving mug
body cream	eye-shadow	nail clippers	shaving soap
bubble bath	eye wash	nail file	skin cream
cold cream	facial cleanser	nail polish	soap
cologne	facial mask	nail polish remover	sun block
comb	facial soap	ointment	sun screen
compact	hand cream	oral rinse	suntan lotion
cosmetic base	hand cleanser	perfume	tissues
cotton balls	hand lotion	powder	toilet water
cotton swabs/ Q-tips	hand soap	razor	toothbrush
cuticle remover	hair brush	disposable	toothpaste
deodorant	hair color	one-track	toothpaste gel
roll-on	hair dye	safety	tooth powder
soap	hair remover	two-track	tweezers
			witch hazel

Verbs

apply	cleanse	deodorize	put on
beautify	clip	manicure	shave
blend	cut	moisten	trim
brush	dab	perfume	touch up

Idioms and Common Sayings

Beauty is in the eye of the beholder.

Beauty is only skin deep.

B.O. (body odor)

Cleanliness is next to Godliness.

a close shave

five o'clock shadow

a greaser

the great unwashed

Handsome is as handsome does.

a little shaver

to look oily

a painted woman

to smell of trouble

to wash one's mouth out with soap

42: Hygiene and Contraception

Hygiene

breast shields	feminine syringe	panty shields
deodorant	feminine napkins	sanitary belt
diuretic tablets	fountain syringe	sanitary napkins
douche	fungicide	shower
concentrate	mini (maxi) pads	tampons
fluid	nursing pads	vaginal cream
powder	panty liners	water pills

Contraception
contraceptive methods and information

contraceptive implant	contraceptive creams	oral contraceptives
norplant	foam	"the pill"
cervical cap	gel	the rhythm method
condom	insert	vaginal spermicides
prophylactic	jelly	vasectomy/tubal ligation
rubber	suppository	withdrawal
safe	vaginal tablets	*coitus interruptus*
sheath	diaphragm with spermicide	abstinence
shield	emergency contraceptive pill (ECP)	"just say no"
	hormone injection/ depoprovera	self-constraint
	intrauterine device (IUD)	self-control

People

gynecologist	obstetrician	fertility counselor

Organizations and Expressions

abortion	free choice	right to life
abortion clinic	Planned Parenthood	reproductive rights
abortion rights	population bomb	Roe versus Wade
anti-abortion	pro-choice	women's rights
family planning	pro-life	zero population growth

43: Jobs and Work

accountant	elevator operator	longshoreman	rubbish collector
advertising agent	employment officer	machine operator	sailor
artist	engineer	mail carrier	sales clerk
assembly line worker	entertainer	maintenance worker	scientist
automotive engineer	factory worker	manager	school administrator
babysitter	farmer	mason	secretary
baggage handler	farm hand	masseur, masseuse	security officer
baker	field hand	mechanic	service station
banker	file clerk	merchant marine	attendant
bank teller	fireman, firefighter	messenger	shipping clerk
barber	fisherman	meter reader	shoemaker
beautician	flight attendant	mother/father	soldier
bookkeeper	food handler	mover	spy
building contractor	garbage collector	musician	stenographer
bureaucrat	gardener	news reporter	steward(ess)
bus driver	glazier	nurse	store clerk
business consultant	guard	office boy	street cleaner
businessman/woman	groundskeeper	ombudsman	student
butcher	heating contractor	optician	surgeon
carpenter	hotel/motel clerk	optometrist	surveyor
car washer	house detective	painter (house)	swimming pool
cashier	housekeeper	parking lot attendant	contractor
chambermaid	housewife/ -husband	pest exterminator	tailor
chef	insurance agent	pharmacist	tax consultant
chiropractor	insurance claims	photographer	taxidermist
civil engineer	adjustor	piano tuner	taxi driver
cleaningman/ woman	insurance	pilot	teacher, professor
cobbler	investigator	plumber	technician
con artist	interpreter	podiatrist	telephone lineman
commercial artist	illustrator	police officer	telephone operator
computer programmer	interior decorator	politician	teller
construction worker	jack of all trades	pollster	translator
cook	janitor	post office clerk	travel agent
courier	jeweler	potter	traveling salesman
cowboy/ cowgirl	journalist	priest, minister,	tree surgeon
crossing guard	judge	rabbi, evangelist	trucker, truck driver
delivery person	junk dealer	nun, imam	TV/radio repairman/
dental hygienist	lab technician	press spokesperson	woman
dentist	landscape architect	printer	typesetter
detective	laundry worker	psychiatrist	typist
diplomat	lawyer	psychologist	undertaker
dishwasher	legislator	publicist	upholsterer
doctor	librarian	publisher	veterinarian
dog walker	life guard	receptionist	volunteer
doorman/woman	lighting contractor	real estate agent	waiter, waitress
editor	loan shark	red cap	window washer
electrical engineer	lobbyist	repairman/woman	writer
electrician	logger	roustabout	zoo keeper

44: Office

Nouns

adding machine	dictaphone	postage meter
appointment	dictation	postage scales
business	disc storage	printer
calculator	duplicate	records
carbon copy	envelope	shorthand
computer	equipment	shredder
hard disc	FAX machine	stapler
hardware	file cabinet	stationery
mainframe	files	supplies
network	information backup	supply cabinet
personal (PC)	intercom	switchboard
program	letter	swivel chair
software	letterhead	telephone
conference	mail	telephone answering machine
copier	meeting	tape dispenser
department	modem	typewriter
desk	paper clip	word processor
desk chair	pencil sharpener	work station

Verbs

copy	file	staple
dictate	mail	take dictation
input	manage	transmit
fax	program	type

Personnel

accountant	chief financial officer (CFO)	personnel officer
assistant	director	president
boss	employee	receptionist
board of directors	employer	secretary
bookkeeper	executive	supervisor
bursar	executive secretary	treasurer
chairman/woman	manager	typist
clerk	office manager	vice-president (VP)
chief executive officer (CEO)	officer	

Idioms and Expressions

to take a letter	to be called on the carpet	business is business
secretarial/typing pool	right-hand man/woman	office politics

45: Business

Nouns

account
accounting software
accounts payable
accounts receivable
advertisement,
ad, advertising
annual report
asset
audit
bad debt
balance
balance sheet
benefit, benefits
  package
bid
bill
bill of lading
bond
books
bottom line
buy out
capital
capital gains
cash
cash flow
commercial
commission
common stock
computer

computer support
contract
corporate seal
corporate secretary
corporate officers
cost benefit analysis
cost of sales
credit
credit check
debit
debt
deduction
deficit
department
depletion
depreciation
Dow-Jones Average
(the) economy
equipment
equity
estimate
excise tax
expenditure
expense
expense account
fee
fiscal year
financial statement
fringe benefit

income
income tax
interest
inventory
investment
invoice
labor
labor union
labor contract
lease
ledger
leverage
liability
license
loss
maintenance
management
margin
(the) market
merger
mortgage
negotiations
offer
operations
overhead
payroll
petty cash
president
profit

pro forma invoice
purchase order
quotation (quote)
research and
  development (R&D)
receipt
rent
rental
retained earnings
royalty
sales
sales tax
securities
share (of stock)
social security
spread sheet
supplies
statement
stock
stock exchange
stock market
takeover
tax
value added tax
wage
wage scale
Wall Street
worksheet
write off

People

accountant
administrative
  assistant
agent
analyst
bookkeeper
broker
certified public
  accountant (CPA)
chairman of the board
chief executive
  officer (CEO)

chief financial
  officer (CFO)
clerk
communications
  specialist
comptroller
consultant
dealer
director
employee
employer
executive

foreman
investor
lawyer
legal counsel
manager
operator
owner
partner
part-time employee
proprietor
salesman/woman
secretary

specialist
supervisor
stenographer
stockholder
telemarketer
temporary worker
trader
treasurer
trustee
typist
vice president
worker

Types

agency	corporation	industry	non-governmental
chain	dealership	monopoly	organization (NGO)
company	franchise	non-profit	partnership
conglomerate	holding company	organization	service
			trust

Verbs

balance	finance	liquidate	merge
borrow	invest	lease	sell
buy	lend	loan	tender an offer

Adjectives

commercial	incorporated (Inc.)	limited (Ltd.)	non-commercial
fiscal	industrial	net	private
gross			public

Idioms and Expressions

in the black	monkey business	"There's no business	industrial wasteland
bullish	profit motive	like show business.."	It's none of your
in the red	good repute	funny business	business.
bearish	"The business of	good morale	
the bottom line	America is business."	employee relations	

Employment: Getting a Job

apply for a job	work permit/	workman's	competency testing
application	Green Card	compensation	work evaluation
employment forms	probationary period	benefit packages	performance review
employment record	wages, pay, salary	reimbursement	discrimination
former employer	hours, work week	vacation	affirmative action
interview	payroll deduction	child care	classified ads
reference	W-4 form	civic duties (jury, etc.)	help wanted ads
resume	W-2 form	union membership	employment office,
skills	I9 eligibility	union dues	agency
training	verification	drug screening	

46: Agriculture

Nouns

acreage	farmers' market	kitchen garden	seed
agronomy	feed	manure	shepherd
aqua culture	fence	market	sheep farm
baler	field	milking equipment	silage
barn	fish	milk	silo
bulk tank	farm	processing plant	spreader
combine	fodder	mowing	staple crops
commodity	garden	gardening	subsidy
contour plowing	harrow	orchard	ranch
crop	harvest	pasture	thresher
crop-dusting	herb garden	pesticides	tiller
cultivation	horticulture	pitchfork	tractor
cultivator	horticulturist	plow	truck
dairy	hydroponics	produce	truck farming
earth	insecticide	product	veterinarian (vet)
fallow ground	irrigation	rotation	wagon
farm	implements	reaper	well
farmer			yield

Verbs

breed	graze	hoe	mulch	sow
clone	grow	inseminate	plant	thresh
cultivate	harvest	irrigate	plow	water
fertilize	harrow	mow	raise	weed
graft	hay		reap	winnow

Livestock

bull	cow	goose	lamb	poultry
calf	duck	hog	ox	rabbits
cattle	goat	horse	pig	sheep
chicken				steer
				turkey

Crops and Products

berries	dairy	grains	milk	sugar beets
citrus	eggs	legumes	organic produce	vegetables
cotton	fruit	livestock	silage	wool

Idioms and Expressions

cut and dried	40 acres and a mule	one reaps what one sows
to farm something out	The grass is always greener on	to sow one's wild oats
to make hay while the	the other side of the fence.	to separate the wheat from the
sun shines	genetically altered	chaff

47: Shops and Tools

Names of tools

ax, axe	hatchet	square
bit	level	straight edge
blow torch	mallet	staple gun
brace	plane	tape measure
calipers	pliers	tin snips
chisel	router	vise
clamp	sander	wedge
drill	saw	wire cutters
hammer	screwdriver	wrench

Verbs

bolt	nail	scribe
build	paint	solder
clamp	plane	staple
cut	pound	turn
glue	sand	varnish
hammer	saw	weld
measure	screw	wire

Miscellaneous

apprentice	paint	stain
bolt	plumber	staple
brad	plywood	steel
carpenter	polyurethane	wool
coat (of paint)	primer	tack
electrician	sandpaper	tubing
helper	screw	varnish
nail	shellac	welder
nut	spike	wire

Idioms and Expressions

to get the axe	jack of all trades	handyman
to have an axe to grind	live wire	on the level
to hit the nail on the head	nuts and bolts	to measure up
many irons in the fire		

48: Law

People

attorney
bailiff
clerk
coroner
counsel
court
court reporter
defendant
defense attorney
district attorney

expert witness
Grand Jury
investigating officer
judge
juror
jury
jury foreman
law office
lawyer

minor
offender
parole officer
plaintiff
probation officer
prosecutor
prosecuting attorney
public defender
state's attorney
witness

Places and Things

bar
bench
civil trial
court
courthouse
Court of Appeals
courtroom

criminal trial
Family Court
Federal District Court
gavel
jury box
judge's chambers
legal aid service

probate court
public defender
session (of the court)
Small Claims Court
State District Court
Supreme Court
witness stand

Adjectives

alleged
hanged (criminal)
hung (jury)
guilty

innocent
judicial
legal
liable

no contest; *nolo contendre*
(objection) over-ruled
(objection) sustained
pre-trial

Verbs

accuse
acquit
allege
appeal
argue
award
call (a witness)
charge
charge the jury
commute
convict

defend
deliberate
dissent
enter a plea
find
hear a case
indict
instruct
jump bail
overturn
plead

post bail
prosecute
reverse a decision
sentence
serve a sentence
sue
swear
testify
throw out a case
try
uphold

113

Events and Processes

accusation	deposition	parole
aquittal	evidence	perjury
alimony	exhibit	probation
allegation	findings	prosecution
appeal	fraud	recess
bail	grievance	retrial
case	hearing	right(s)
charge	indictment	ruling
claim	injunction	sentence
conviction	inquiry	sequester
court order	inquest	settlement
crime	law	suit
cross-examination	libel	summons
damages	litigation	testimony
death penalty	manslaughter	trial
decision	mistrial	verdict
defense	opinion	writ

Idioms and Expressions

to bail out	to lay down the law	to take the fifth amendment
death row	of age	third degree
to do time	open and shut case	to throw the book at
to get away with murder	to take the law into one's own hands	under age
jailbird	to take the stand	

49: Police, Crime, and Emergencies

Good Guys

chief of police	investigator	private eye	SWAT team
constable	meter maid	private investigator	traffic cop
cop	narcotics officer (narco)	riot police	undercoverman/woman
detective	patrolman	sergeant	U.S. Marshal
deputy	plainclothesman	sheriff	vice squad
F. B. I.	policeman/woman	state trooper	victim
game warden			warden

Bad Guys

arsonist	hit man	mobster	second-story man
burglar	hood	mole	serial killer
call girl	juvenile delinquent	mugger	street walker
con artist	Ku Klux Klan (KKK)	petty thief	swindler
con man	killer	pickpocket	thief
crook	loan shark	prostitute	thug
deadbeat dad/mom	lynch mob	pusher	tough
felon	madam	rapist	underworld
fence	Mafia	rioter	vandal
gang	mob	robber	whore

Crimes

armed robbery	hold-up	laundering money	robbery
arson	homicide	manslaughter	sexual molestation
assault (and battery)	embezzlement	mugging	skimming profits
assassination	forgery	murder	smuggling
blackmail	fraud	narcotics smuggling	speeding
breaking and entering	gambling	premeditated murder	stalking
break in	gun running	prostitution	statutory rape
bribery	harassment	protection racket	stick up
burglary	kickback	purse snatching	theft
con game	kidnapping	pushing dope	treason
drunk driving	larceny	rape	vandalism
extortion			wilding
			white collar crime

Places

beat	jail	rounds
betting parlor	lock-up	station
cell	precinct	whorehouse

Events

apprehension
arrest
chase
conviction
frame up

get away
investigation
line up
mug shot
pay off

raid
reading one's rights
round up
speed trap
traffic violation

Emergencies

accident
ambulance
blood bank
civil defense
clinic
CPR - cardiopulmonary
  resuscitation
dentist
doctor
doctor's office
drowning
drug overdose
drug store
Emergency Broadcasting
  System
emergency entrance

emergency room
emergency vehicle
evacuation
explosion
fire
fire department
fire drill
fire engine
fire horn
fireman
flashing lights
jaws of life
loud speaker
megaphone
monitor
mouth-to-mouth

natural disaster
neck brace
nuclear alert
pharmacist
pharmacy
public alarm signal
rescue
robbery
shock
siren
stretcher
tourniquet
training
transfusion
veterinarian's office
911

Things

assault weapon
badge
billy club
gun
handcuffs
knife

mace
manacles
night stick
paddy wagon
pistol

police gazette
revolver
siren
squad car
wanted posters

Idioms and Expressions

cement overshoes
cops and robbers
Cosa Nostra
crime boss
crime doesn't pay
deadly weapon
fuzz

the godfather
by hook or by crook
inside job
in the name of the law
the mob
organized crime

police protection
the rackets
to rub someone out
Smoky the Bear
the syndicate
victimless crime

116

50: Communication Technology

Computers

application	floppy disk	operating system
back-up	freeze	printer
break in	hack	printout
cable	hard disk	program
CD-ROM	hardware	save
chat room	icon	scanner, to scan
chip	input	screen saver
click on	internet	search engine
CPU	ISP (internet service provider)	server
crash	keyboard	software
cyberspace	laptop	spam
delete	link	surf
disk	megabyte	trash
display	memory	undo
distance learning	minidisk	upgrade
download	modem	virus
e-commerce	monitor	web site
EFT (electronic funds transfer)	mouse	word processor
email	network	WWW (world wide web)

Telephone

800 line	dial	pound
answering machine	extension	prepaid phone card
answering service	fund raising	pulse
call	hang up	redial
call forwarding	information	speakerphone
caller ID	local	star
car phone	long distance	toll free
cell phone	pay phone	touchtone
collect	phonathon	trace
conference call	phone booth	voice mail

Other

CB (citizen's band radio)	intercom	radar
communication tower	network	sonar
fax	pager	walkie-talkie
		satellite

Idioms and Expressions

The computer is down.	Sorry, wrong number.
computer freak, whiz	Your call cannot be completed as dialed.
to crash	Your call is important to us.
to cut and paste	
to surf the net	

51: Politics and Government

See topics on Government in the Cultural Aspect section.

People

aide	congressperson	representative
alderperson	delegate	secretary of state
assemblyperson	governor	selectperson
attorney general	incumbent	senator
candidate	mayor	sheriff
city council person	member of congress	speaker
columnist	pollster	vice president
commentator	president	voter

Places, etc.

apportionment	hearing	minority
bill	inauguration	negotiation
cabinet	independent	Pentagon
campaign	investigation	petition
capitol	INS (Immigration and	polling place
congress	Naturalization Service)	precinct
conressional district	IRS (Internal Revenue	primary
Congressional Record	Service)	Republican
conservative	legislation	State House
district	liberal	voter check list
Democrat	majority	ward
election		

Adjectives

city	judicial	national
county	legislative	state
executive	local	town
federal		

Verbs

campaign	govern	propose
debate	impeach	re-elect
elect	lobby	reform
enact	pass	veto
filibuster	preside	vote

Idioms, Expressions, and Issues

abortion rights	equal rights	minority representation
affirmative action	fiscal responsibility	minority rights
balanced budget	graft and corruption	one person, one vote
campaign contribution	international security	political action committee (PAC)
civil rights	lame-duck	pork barrel
discrimination	machine politics	rights and obligations
environmental protection	military expenditures	terrorism
equality before the law	military-industrial complex	undue influence

52: The Media

Print

ad(vertisement)
by-line
classifieds
columnist
copy editor
correspondent
daily
edition
editor
editorial
headline
journal

journalist
lead story
magazine
monthly
news
news magazine
newspaper
newsprint
press
print
publish
publisher

quarterly
reader
reporter
review
scandal sheet
scoop
subscribe
subscription
(newspaper) syndicate
tabloid
weekly
writer

Television

anchorman/woman
antenna
audience
broadcast
bulletin
cable
cameraman/woman
channel
commercial
coverage
game show

host
interview
live
network
news
newscaster
panelist
pay-per-view
prime time
producer
program

ratings
reception
satellite dish
sit-com
sponsor
studio
talk show
taped
televise
transmitter
viewer

Radio

air wave
AM (amplitude modulation)
antenna
band
broadcast
bug

call letters
CB (Citizen's Band Radio)
commercial
dial
DJ (disc jockey)
FM (frequency modulation)

frequency
fund raising
ham operator
NPR (National Public Radio)
short-wave
station

Idioms and Expressions

"All the news that's fit to print"
No news is good news.
Stop the presses!
Don't touch that dial.
We'll be right back.

the cable, cable news
the comics/ funny papers
hard news
hot tip
investigative reporting

late breaking story
letter to the editor
theater section
top of the hour
top story

53: Religion

See the topic on Religion in the Cultural Aspect section.

Nouns

altar	hymnal	pew
baptismal font	meeting house	prayer book
belfry	mission	pulpit
cathedral	mosque	Star of David
chapel	nave	steeple
church	synagogue	temple
confessional	organ	transept
cross	parish	under croft

People

altar boy	congregation	monk
alter guild	deacon	nun
acolyte	elder	organist
archbishop	evangelist	pastor
bishop	imam	Pope
cantor	laity	priest
cardinal	lay brother/ sister/ man/ woman	rabbi
choir	minister	reader
cleric/ clergy	missionary	usher
crucifer		

Sacraments, Rituals, and Scriptures

baptism	Haj	pilgrimmage
Bible	hymn	Ramadan
bar mitzvah	Koran	ritual
call to prayer	last rites	scroll
catechism	marriage	seder
christening	mass	sermon
circumcision	New Testament	Sunday school
confirmation	offering	Talmud
confession	Old Testament	Torah
cross	prayer	Veda
funeral	psalm	vestments
Gospel		

Verbs

believe	meditate	preach
be saved, to save	persecute	shun
celebrate	pray	sing hymns
convert		worship

Major Religions and Denominations

Baha'i Faith
Baptist Churches
Brethren (German Baptist)
Buddhism
(Roman) Catholic Church
Churches of God
Congregationalist Churches
Christianity
Eastern Orthodox Churches
Episcopal Church

Hinduism
Islam
Jehovah's Witnesses
Judaism
Lutheran Churches
Mennonite Churches
Methodist Churches
Mormon Churches (Church of
    the Latter Day Saints)

Pentecostal Churches
Presbyterian
Protestant
Quaker (Society of Friends)
Seventh Day Adventist
Shi'ah Moslem
Sufism (Islamic Mysticism)
Sunni Moslem
Unitarian Universalist

Adjectives

agnostic
atheist
Buddhist
Christian
conservative
fundamentalist
Hindu

holy
Jewish
kosher
liberal
Moslem
Orthodox

reformed
religious
reverend
reverent
sacred
spiritual
strict

Important days

Ash Wednesday
Christmas
Easter Sunday
Good Friday

Hannukah
holy week
Kwanza
Lent

Palm Sunday
Passover
Ramadan
Rosh Hashana
Yom Kippur

Idioms, Expressions, and Concepts

act of God
Amen!
apocalypse
between the devil and the deep
    blue sea
Bible belt
born again
damnation,
to damn
diaspora
charity
crucifixion
end of the world is at hand
epiphany
eye for an eye
faith

fire and brimstone
good heavens
goodness gracious
God bless you
God willing
go to hell
Hallelujah!
heaven
heavens to Betsy
hell fire
Holy City
holy Moses!
holy roller
judgment day
kismet

matter of faith
messiah
month of Sundays
next year in Jerusalem
paradise
pass the hat
pass the plate
redemption
reincarnation
resurrection
revelation
to raise Cain
salvation
seventh heaven
straight and narrow
vengeance

54: Elementary, Secondary Education

Types of school

preschool programs	primary school	secondary school	parochial school
day care	elementary school	high school	specialized schools for:
nursery school	grade school	senior high	the blind,
toddler program	day school	preparatory (prep)	the deaf
head start program	middle school	school	children with learning
kindergarten	junior high school	public school	disabilities
		private school	competitive athletes

Nouns

assignment	desk work	science laboratory	school
auditorium	detention	language lab	semester
blackboard	exam	learning center	study hall
bulletin board	grade	lunch room	teachers' room
cafeteria	grading period	photocopier	test
chalk	gymnasium, gym	playground	textbook
classroom	high honor roll	quiz	vacation
computer center	homework	recess	workbook
desk	honor roll	report card	worksheets

People

instructor	pupil	student	teacher
principal	secretary	superintendent	teacher's aide

Verbs

cram	fail, flunk	learn	study
enroll	grade	pass	take a course
evaluate	graduate	register	teach

Subjects

Elementary:	reading	**Secondary,**	foreign language
art	science	**the elementary**	history
arithmetic, math	social studies	**subjects plus:**	home economics
geography	spelling	chemistry	physics
music	writing	English	shop

Classroom Activities

manipulating objects	using a tape recorder	spelling bee	games
moving furniture	using a typewriter	taking attendance	pencil and paper work
operating equipment	using a computer	operating a language lab	cutting and pasting
using the blackboard	taking dictation	body movements	map work

Idioms and Expressions

to play hooky	teacher's pet	apple polishing	tardy

122

55: College Education

Types of schools

training schools
junior college
community college
college

university
graduate school
business school
medical school

law school
divinity school

Places

administration building
assembly hall
auditorium
boat house
book store
cafeteria
campus police
class room
chapel
computer center

dining hall
dormitory
field house
fraternity house
gym
housing office
lab
language lab
lecture hall

library
locker room
mail room
playing field
seminar room
sorority house
stadium
student union
theater

Offices

academic dean
academic departments
accounting
athletic department
bursar
campus dean

chancellor
counseling
dean
foreign student adviser
health
housing

physical education
president
registrar
R.O.T.C. headquarters
student activities
treasurer

Events

baccalaureate
convocation
examination
exam week
faculty tea
faculty meeting
fraternity/sorority rush

games
  home
  away
  championship
graduation
hell week
homecoming

open house
orientation
party
prom
registration
reunion
vacation

People

counselor
chaplain
coach
dean

department head/chair
dorm head
instructor
librarian

professor
psychologist
tutor

Academic activities

lecture
lab
class discussion
comprehensive exams
field work
final exams

GRE (Graduate Records Exam)
grades
Law Boards
quiz
scheduling
semester/study abroad
seminar

research paper
SAT (Scholastic Achievement
   Test)
standardized test
thesis
TOEFL
workshop

Miscellaneous

academia
academic credit
academic freedom
academic gown
campus newspaper
campus radio station
cheerleader
co-education
co-ed
deadline
diploma

disciplinary action
excuse
expulsion
grading periods
grind
humor magazine
homecoming queen
liberal arts
literary magazine
major

marking period
minor
mortar board
pass-fail grading
plagiarism
social life
suspension
student political organizations
undergraduate
year book

Idioms and Expressions

to bone up on
to burn the midnight oil

to cram
to hit the books

sheepskin

56: History

Periods

AD	CE	era	pre-historic
age	episode	geological time	Stone Age
BC	epoch	millennium	time
century	eon	period	

People

admiral	explorer	peon	seer
adventurer	founder	philosopher	serf
anthropologist	frontiersman	political boss	scholar
archaeologist	general	politician	secret agent
artist	geographer	pope	senator
assassin	hero	president	slave
bishop	high priest	prime minister	spy
builder	historian	prince	statesman
businessman	innovator	princess	teacher
captive	inventor	promoter	terrorist
chief	judge	prophet	trader
common man	king	queen	tradesman
counselor	knight	rabble rouser	traitor
creative genius	labor leader	rebel	tycoon
dictator	leader	representative	usurper
duke	orator	saint	warlord
engineer	peasant	scout	warrior
emperor			

Events

assassination	defeat	exploration	invention
coronation	depression	famine	massacre
coup d'etat	discovery	genocide	natural disasters
battle	election	holocaust	overthrow
breakthrough	epidemic	inflation	plague
			rebellion

Miscellaneous

agreement	constitution	historical research	social unrest
alliance	economic growth	mob	social upheaval
biography	enemy	pact	starvation
chronicle	historical novel	saga	treaty

Idioms and Expressions

chronicle of events	history is bunk	milestone of history
history is yesterday's news	lessons of history	since the dawn of time

Those who ignore history are condemned to repeat it.
Y2K

57: Disasters

Nouns

accidents	epidemic	plane crash
aftershock	eruption	pollution
airplane crash	evacuation	richter scale
ambulance	explosion	relief
atomic/nuclear disaster	ethnic cleansing	rescue
avalanche	famine	riot
blizzard	fatality	shelter
bomb	fire	shipwreck
carnage	fire storm	sinking
catastrophe	first aid	starvaion
civil war	flash flood	state of emergency
collision	flood	storm
conflagration	genocide	terrorism
cyclone	global warming	tidal wave
death	hurricane	tornado
deforestation	injury	tropical storm
desertification	loss of life	tsunami
devestation	mud slide	twister
disaster relief	nuclear meltdown	typhoon
drought	oil slick	victim
earthquake	oil spill	war
emergency	pestulence	wild fire
environmental destruction	plague	wreckage

Verbs

blow up	damage	freeze
blow down	destroy	injure
burn	devastate	massacre
bury	drown	rescue
collapse	evacuate	ruin
collide	explode	smash
crash	flatten	starve
crush	flood	suffocate

Idioms and Expressions

an act of God	better safe than sorry	death toll
any port in a storm	calm before the storm	loss of life

58: The Military and War

Nouns

aircraft carrier
air force
airplane
air defense
air raid
alliance
allies
armed forces
armor
armored division
armory
army
artillery
attack
battle
battleship
base
biological weapon
blackout
bomber
bomb
bomb blast
boot camp
briefing
brigade
bullet
bunker
cannon
cease fire
chain of command
civil defence
cluster bomb
coalition
coast guard
command
cruiser
defeat
defense

depot
destroyer
disinformation
division
draft
field of battle
field command
field hospital
field promotion
fighter
fire storm
fleet
foot soldier
foxhole
germ warfare
grenade
gun
headquarters
helicopter
information
infantry
jeep
jet
logistical support
land mine
map room
marines
materiel
morale
mine
mine sweeper
missile
national guard
navy
offense
offensive
officer
peace

peacekeeper
personnel
planning session
platoon
poison gas
propaganda
promotion
reconnaissance
radioactive cloud
recruit
regiment
reserves
retreat
rocket
seabees (CB - Construction Battalion)
shell
smart bomb
squad
staff
strategy
submarine
superior officer
surrender
tactics
tank
target
target practice
torpedo
training camp
trench
victory
volunteer
volunteer army
warfare
war games
weapon
weaponry

People

admiral	deserter	lieutenant	petty officer
bombardier	draft dodger	liaison	private
captain	foot soldier	major	pilot
cavalry	general	marine	sailor
chaplain	G.I.(government issue)	military adviser	sergeant
chief of staff	guerrilla	military police (MP)	sniper
colonel	gunner	navigator	soldier
corporal	hostage	officer	terrorist

Events and actions

advance	cut off	make war	sink
ambush	defeat	offensive	sortie
battle	deploy	order	skirmish
break through	dissent	overrun	surround
bombardment	infiltrate	retreat	strafe
casualty	interrogation	shell(ing)	torpedo
court marshal	invasion	shoot	wound

Peace

appeasement	defeat	peace conference	peace treaty
armistice	disengagement	peace initiative	reconciliation
cease fire	make peace	peacekeeping force	surrender
concessions	mediation	peacemaker	truce
conciliation	negotiation	peace settlement	United Nations
conscientious objector	pacification	peace talks	victory

Idioms and Expressions

all's fair in love and war	marked man	under the gun
an army lives on its stomach	MIA (missing in action)	USO
AWOL (absent without leave)	mutual assured destruction	War and Peace
balance of power	Nobel Peace Prize	war criminal
balance or terror	peace at any cost	the war to end all war
battle hardened	"peace in our time"	win the war but lose the peace
to bear arms	peace with honor	world war
camp follower	POW (prisoner of war)	yeoman service
concentration camp	to pull rank	Symbols:
cowards die twice	point blank	flags
deterrence	on the warpath	flags flown at half mast
Geneva Convention	R and R (rest and recreation)	flags in a graveyard
isolationist	scorched earth policy	hands raised over the head
4F	shell shock	white flag
a just and lasting peace	to stick to one's guns	red cross
a just war	turncoat	red poppy
make love, not war	to turn tail	yellow ribbon

128

59: Energy and Environment

Nouns

acid rain	filter	oil well
atomic wastes	fire	ozone
barrel of oil	fission	petroleum
battery	fossil fuel	pipeline
catalytic converter	fuel	pollution
coal	fuel efficiency	power
combustion	fusion	propane
conservation	gas pump	reactor
consumable resources	gasoline, gas	recycling
consumption	gasoline taxes	refinery
dam	generator	regulations
depletion	heat	renewable energy sources
drilling rig	hydro-electric power	resources
electricity	insulation	scrubbers
endangered species	kinetic	smog
energy costs	land fill	smoke
energy efficiency	light	solar power
energy (in)dependence	mass transit	solar cell
energy loss	motor	source
energy taxes	natural gas	steam
engine	nuclear power	super conductors
environmentalist	nuclear reactor	tidal
environmental cleanup	oil	turbine
environmental law	oil drilling	utilities
environmental policy	oil field	water power
environmental science	oil production	wildcat operator
ethanol	oil slick	windmill
extinct	oil spill	wind power

Adjectives

active	hydro-	petro-
chemical	mechanical	passive
electric(al)	nuclear	radioactive
extinct	off-shore	solar
geothermal		wood-burning

Idioms and Expressions

to burn the candle at both ends	gas guzzler	OPEC
to carry coals to Newcastle	greenhouse effect	R factor
energy czar	to hold a candle to	unbridled consumption
environmental catastrophe	limits to growth	where there's smoke there's
environmental impact statement	sustainable growth	fire

60: Death
Nouns

ashes	death	gravestone	mourner
autopsy	demise	graveyard	mourning
body	dissection	inscription	murder
burial	effigy	lamentation	necropolis
cadaver	elegy	last rites	obituary
capital punishment	epitaph	last words	pall bearer
casket	eulogy	mausoleum	pit
catacomb	euphemism	medical examiner	plot
cemetery	euthanasia	memorial	(the) remains
churchyard	funeral	memorial contribution	sepulcher
coffin	funeral director	memorial service	service
coroner	funeral home	mercy killing	tomb
corpse	funeral parlor	moaning	undertaker
cremation	funeral procession	monument	urn
crypt	grave	morgue	vault
(the) deceased	grave digger	mortician	wake
(the) dead	graveside	mortuary	widow
			widower

Verbs

bereave	die	eulogize	grieve
bury	elegize	expire	inter
cremate			mourn

Idioms and Expressions

ashes to ashes, dust to dust	to give up the ghost	open-casket funeral
to cash in one's chips	in deep mourning	living will
cause of death	Irish wake	right to die
deader than a door nail	to kick the bucket	to wake the dead
dearly departed	to pass away	RIP (rest in peace)

Of the Living Dead

ashen	gallows	hideous	shade
apparition	ghastly	horrible	specter
to appall	ghost	horror story	spell
banshee	ghost story	loathsome	spider web
bat	ghoul	mummy	spirit
body snatcher	gibbet	murmuring	spook
black magic	glimmer	necromancer	spooky
cadaverous	gloom	night walker	terrifying
to conjure	goblin	pact with the devil	undead
demon	gore	pallid	vampire
devil, Satan	grave robber	phantom	voodoo
dreadful	grisly	resurrectionist	werewolf
evil spirit	hangman	revolting	wolfman
fiend	to haunt	sorcery	wraith
frightful	hell fire	seance	zombie

130

Communicative Functions

The sub-aspect of Communicative Functions is similar to a notional-functional syllabus. However, we have used the term communicative function to focus on the how and why of the communicative exchange. To relate this sub-aspect to the Situations and Topics, we can say that the Situation is concerned with the "where" of the exchange, the Topic the "what" and the Function the "how" and "why."

To organize the various communicative functions in some useful way, we have presented them as a kind of syllabus/check list. We have used as a sequential basis, four levels of language sophistication. These levels represent a transition from beginning language student to fully functioning bilingual person. These four levels are:

- ❑ Level 1 **Surviving** (Beginner)   132
- ❑ Level 2 **Adjusting; Settling In** (Advanced beginner)   133
- ❑ Level 3 **Participating** (Intermediate)   134
- ❑ Level 4 **Integrating** (Advanced)   135

Within each level we have organized the functions into general types as described below:

A. **Basic Needs.** Using the language to satisfy basic physical requirements of food, shelter, and clothing.

B. **Socializing.** Using the language to make social links with native speakers. At its lowest level it satisfies basic emotional needs.

C. **Metalinguistic.** Using the language to deal with the language. This includes certain fundamental linguistic labels (noun, etc.) and tactics and strategies for managing communication (paraphrasing, interrupting, clarifying, etc.).

D. **Professional.** Using the language to make a living.

E. **Cultural.** Using the language to deal with the social and cultural milieu.

Level 1: Surviving

(Beginner)

A. Basic Needs

❑ 1. Respond physically to simple instructions such as **give, take, stand, sit, open, close, pick up, put down, put on, take off**, etc.

❑ 2. Give another person simple instructions to perform the actions above.

❑ 3. Give and understand basic warnings such as **Look out! Stop! Freeze!**

❑ 4. State basic wants and needs.

❑ 5. Request and comprehend simple information.

❑ 6. Ask for and respond to simple street directions and give simpe directions to a taxi driver.

❑ 7. Ask for assistance.

❑ 8. Get someone's attention and also use appropriate gestures.

❑ 9. Buy a small item.

❑ 10. Use a menu and order something to eat and drink.

B. Socializing

❑ 1. Greet others.

❑ 2. Take leave of another person or a group of people.

❑ 3. Arrange to meet someone.

❑ 4. Introduce yourself.

❑ 5. Identify yourself. (**I'm a**　　　)

❑ 6. Use ritual apologies.

❑ 7. Reject unwanted attention firmly and simply.

❑ 8. Agree.

❑ 9. Express thanks.

❑ 10. State and comprehend simple biographical and family information.

C. Metalinguistic

❑ 1. Use and identify basic numbers.

❑ 2. Ask and tell time.

❑ 3. Use simple time expressions such as **today, yesterday, tomorrow morning, noon.**

❑ 4. Use and comprehend days of the week, months, and ways of expressing dates.

❑ 5. Control a conversation with simple phrases such as **speak slowly, please,** or **please repeat that.**

❑ 6. Identify and label the environment. (**What's that? It's a _**)

❑ 7. Decipher simple signs and notices.

❑ 8. Use appropriate basic gestures.

Level 2: Adjusting; Settling In

(Advanced Beginner)

A. Basic Needs

❏ 1. State plans for the future.

❏ 2. Ask to borrow something.

❏ 3. Respond to a loan request.

❏ 4. Complain mildly.

❏ 5. Ask about the purpose of something.

❏ 6. Purchase household objects, equipment and clothing.

❏ 7. Make travel arrangements.

❏ 8. Describe a physical health problem.

❏ 9. Carry out a limited financial transaction such as cashing a check.

❏ 10. Fill out life forms such as a credit card application, a work permit, a school registration.

B. Socializing

❏ 1. Introduce another person.

❏ 2. Make small talk.

❏ 3. Share simple likes and dislikes.

❏ 4. Issue an invitation.

❏ 5. Decline an invitation.

❏ 6. Visit.

❏ 7. Entertain a visitor.

❏ 8. Play simple games/sports.

❏ 9. Recount past events.

❏ 10. Express basic emotions.

❏ 11. Apologize for a specific error.

❏ 12. Request and give permission to do something.

❏ 13. Compliment another person.

❏ 14. Accept a compliment.

❏ 15. Explain personal plans.

❏ 16. Express a personal opinion.

❏ 17. Express doubt.

❏ 18. Express irritation.

❏ 19. Express disappointment.

C. Metalinguistic

❏ 1. Clarify misunderstandings.

❏ 2. Use simple interjections.

❏ 3. Make a basic phone call.

❏ 4. Perform arithmetic operations aloud.

❏ 5. Spell words aloud.

❏ 6. Comprehend ads and announcements on radio and TV.

❏ 7. Read advertisements.

❏ 8. Read short notices, time tables, menus, etc.

❏ 9. Take simple dictation.

❏ 10. Write short informational notes.

D. Professional

❏ 1. Describe one's job.

❏ 2. Describe one's profession in general terms.

❏ 3. Explain professional objectives.

❏ 4. Express a basic professional opinion..

E. Cultural

❏ 1. Follow or sing-along with popular songs and/or folk songs.

❏ 2. Identify folk tale characters and national heroes.

❏ 3. Make general cultural comparisons in these areas:

❏ etiquette

❏ mealtimes

❏ kinship terms

❏ housing

❏ cooking

❏ gift-giving

❏ holidays and festivals

Level 3: Participating
(Intermediate)

A. Basic Needs

- ❑ 1. Ask for favors.
- ❑ 2. Grant favors.
- ❑ 3. Sell a personal possession.
- ❑ 4. Make arrangements with household help.
- ❑ 5. Arrange for repairs and service (household; automotive).
- ❑ 6. Make substantial purchases such as a TV or refrigerator.
- ❑ 7. Apply for specific status (insurance, citizenship, etc.)
- ❑ 8. Retrieve a borrowed item.
- ❑ 9. Dispute a bill.

B. Socializing

- ❑ 1. Plan a social event.
- ❑ 2. Attend a recreational event.
- ❑ 3. Discuss current events.
- ❑ 4. Comment on sports events.
- ❑ 5. Avoid commitments.
- ❑ 6. Sympathize.
- ❑ 7. Share personal hopes and dreams.
- ❑ 8. Tell an anecdote.
- ❑ 9. Understand jokes.
- ❑ 10. Give personal advice.
- ❑ 11. Disagree tactfully.
- ❑ 12. Ask for forgiveness.
- ❑ 13. Make an excuse.

C. Metalinguistic

- ❑ 1. Understand radio and TV news.
- ❑ 2. Break social contact with appropriate mannerisms,
- ❑ 3. Summarize.
- ❑ 4. Ask for definitions.
- ❑ 5. Make a complicated telephone call.
- ❑ 6. Translate for a new-comer.
- ❑ 7. Swear.
- ❑ 8. Use verbal gestures such as **uh-uh, hm, well, huh?**
- ❑ 9. Read newspapers.
- ❑ 10. Read professional material.
- ❑ 11. Read magazine articles.
- ❑ 12. Write social notes and letters.
- ❑ 13. Write professional reports.

D. Professional

- ❑ 1. Allow or not allow another's requests.
- ❑ 2. Give professional advice.
- ❑ 3. Give detailed instructions and explanations.
- ❑ 4. Evaluate.
- ❑ 5. Give short talks/speeches on professional matters.

E. Cultural

- ❑ 1. Explain institutions of native country.
- ❑ 2. Compare major cultural differences.
- ❑ 3. Discuss major aspects of host culture, including:

❑ courtship	❑ government	❑ education
❑ marriage	❑ religion	❑ superstitions
❑ sex	❑ death	❑ folklore
❑ family	❑ mourning	❑ hospitality
❑ racial and ethnic groups	❑ funerals	❑ humor

Level 4: Integrating
(Advanced)
A. Basic Needs

❑ 1. Act in emergencies.

B. Socializing

❑ 1. Share secrets.
❑ 2. Flirt.
❑ 3. Speak of personal accomplishments.
❑ 4. Tease.
❑ 5. Break off a relationship.
❑ 6. Counsel.
❑ 7. Praise.

❑ 8. Flatter.
❑ 9. Insult.
❑ 10. Plead.
❑ 11. Soften the truth.
❑ 12. Chastise another person.
❑ 13. Threaten.
❑ 14. Tell jokes.

C. Metalinguistic

❑ 1. Interpret and translate.
❑ 2. Paraphrase.
❑ 3. Play word games such as crossword puzzles.

❑ 4. Use source materials such as the Oxford English Dictionary.
❑ 5. Read books.
❑ 6. Write letters to the editor.

D. Professional

❑ 1. Debate ideas.
❑ 2. Negotiate.

❑ 3. Give professional direction.
❑ 4. Exercise leadership.

E. Cultural

❑ 1. Take and defend a stand on a current national issue.

❑ 2. Discuss, study, and critique the following aspects of the culture:
❑ arts
❑ law
❑ attitudes toward animals and nature
❑ community organization
❑ residence rules
❑ property rights
❑ status differentiation
❑ social mobility
❑ ethics

The
Cultural
Aspect

Language and culture are intertwined. In the previous section on the communicative aspect, North American culture makes its presence felt, especially in the lists of communicative situations and topics. To a lesser extent, communicative functions are also modified by culture. Ways of expressing thanks or extending invitations can be quite different in the English typical of Toronto, Los Angeles, Boston, or Bombay.

Because we have already listed communicative situations, topics, and functions in Part II, we will not repeat those lists here. Instead we will present cultural information that does not fit under these categories.

In other, paralinguistic ways, notably in body language and gestures, culture also impinges on communication, but we will deal with that in Part V.

And then there are all the cultural practices (customs) that can only be hinted at in a book such as this. Rather than attempt to describe North American cultural practices, we will instead present a list of Cultural Common Denominators. This list can be used as a checklist by both teacher and student to see if these areas have been adequately explored in class.

In this part of The ESL Miscellany, we will attempt to deal with the huge body of information that is commonly known by most contemporary Americans and Canadians. For example, the foreigner, unaware that the New York Yankees is a baseball team, could easily be mystified by overhearing one American ask another, "How did the Yankees do last night?" or, even more mystified when they are invited to go watch the Blue Jays play.

Obviously, it takes years to learn everything there is to know about North American culture; it is even possible that some native speakers do not know who Babe Ruth was. The capsule summaries of selected areas of North American culture contained in this section are at best a starting point for discussion, research, explanation, and study. Once again our lists should be considered only guidelines.

Cultural Information

Cultural Checklist

Cultural Common Denominators*

Every culture has customs, traditions, practices, and beliefs associated with the following cultural items. Each item in the list represents an essay, if not an entire book, but we will do no more here than suggest that the list can be used as a guideline for an orientation to North American culture. Incidentally, the list can also serve as a checklist for a series of fascinating discussions of a cross-cultural nature.

- ❏ numerals
- ❏ calendar
- ❏ personal names
- ❏ greetings
- ❏ gestures
- ❏ etiquette
- ❏ mealtimes
- ❏ kinship nomenclature
- ❏ age-grading
- ❏ athletic sports
- ❏ games
- ❏ leisure activities
- ❏ music
- ❏ dancing
- ❏ feasting
- ❏ bodily adornment
- ❏ folklore
- ❏ luck superstitions
- ❏ cooking
- ❏ food and food taboos
- ❏ family
- ❏ marriage
- ❏ kin-groups
- ❏ housing
- ❏ hospitality
- ❏ visiting
- ❏ gift-giving
- ❏ friendship customs
- ❏ courting
- ❏ joking
- ❏ sexual restrictions
- ❏ incest
- ❏ taboos
- ❏ modesty in natural functions
- ❏ funeral rites
- ❏ mourning
- ❏ medicine
- ❏ education
- ❏ law
- ❏ land-use policies
- ❏ attitude toward animals
- ❏ community organization
- ❏ residence rules
- ❏ property rights
- ❏ status differentiation
- ❏ racial and ethnic groups
- ❏ mobility
- ❏ trade
- ❏ government
- ❏ patriotism
- ❏ religious practices

*Adapted from George P. Murdock, "The Common Denominators of Culture," in *The Science of Man in the World Crisis,* ed Ralph Linton, N.Y: Columbia University Press, 1945.

1: Immigration Statistics

U.S. Immigration by Countries (1820-1996)

COUNTRY	1820-1996	COUNTRY	1996
Germany	7,105,300	Mexico	163,572
Italy	5,353,210	West Indies	116,801
Mexico	5,246,390	Philippines*	66,100
United Kingdom	5,197,150	South America	61,769
Ireland	4,780,890	Africa	52,889
Canada	4,348,550	India	44,859
Former USSR	3,749,780	Central America	44,289
West Indies	3,372,720	Korea*	33,000
Austria	2,664,730	China	25,106
South America	1,588,410	Canada	15,825
Sweden	1,398,550	Hong Kong*	15,200
China	1,232,740	United Kingdom	13,657
Central America	1,153,220	Vietnam*	13,300
Philippines*	955,000	Poland	8,481
France	795,260	Germany	6,748
Norway	756,450	Japan	6,011
Poland	743,380	Romania	5,198
Greece	704,680	Albania	4,007
India	703,340	Lebanon*	3,800
Korea*	611,000	Jordan*	3,800
Portugal	518,750	Portugal	3,766
Japan	498,330	Turkiye	3,657
Vietnam*	444,000	Israel	3,126
Turkiye	425,600	Australia/N.Z.	2,750
Netherlands	382,110	Former USSR	2,588
Denmark	374,290	Italy	2,501
Switzerland	362,790	Bulgaria	2,066
Spain	289,610	Yugoslavia	2,011
Romania	246,660	Ireland	1,731
Belgium	212,890	Spain	1,591
Hungary	167,870	Greece	1,452
Australia/N.Z.	160,870	Netherlands	1,423
Yugoslavia	158,540	Former Czech.	1,389
Czechoslovakia	156,850	Hungary	1,183
Israel	152,470	Sweden	1,098
Bulgaria	78,029	Lithuania	1,080

* 1989 statistics

Immigration *(continued)*

Foreign-Born Population in the U.S. (1990)

25 most common places of birth

1990 Rank	Place of Birth	Number	Percent
1	Mexico	4,298,014	21.7
2	Philippines	912,674	4.6
3	Canada	744,830	3.8
4	Cuba	736,971	3.7
5	Germany	711,929	3.6
6	United Kingdom	640,145	3.2
7	Italy	580,592	2.9
8	Korea	568,397	2.9
9	Vietnam	543,262	2.7
10	China	529,837	2.7
11	El Salvador	465,433	2.4
12	India	450,406	2.3
13	Poland	388,328	2.0
14	Dominican Rep.	347,858	1.8
15	Jamaica	334,140	1.7
16	Former USSR	333,725	1.7
17	Japan	290,128	1.5
18	Colombia	286,124	1.4
19	Taiwan	244,102	1.2
20	Guatemala	225,739	1.1
21	Haiti	225,393	1.1
22	Iran	210,941	1.1
23	Portugal	210,122	1.1
24	Greece	177,398	0.9
25	Laos	171,577	0.9

2. Native Peoples of North America

U.S. and Canadian Indian Nations

Eastern Woodlands
Abenaki
Algonquian
Conoy
Delaware
Erie
Fox
Huron
Illinois
Iroquois
  Cayuga
  Mohawk
  Onondaga
  Oneida
  Seneca
  Tuscarora
Kickapoo
Laurentian
Mahican
Malecite
Massachuset
Menominee
Miami
Micmac
Mohegan
Montauk
Nanticoke
Narraganset
Nauset
Neutral
Niantic
Nipmuc
Ojibwa
Pamlico
Passamaquoddy
Pennacook
Penobscot
Pequot
Pocomtuc
Potawatomi
Powhatan
Sauk
Susquehanna
Tionontati
Wampanoag

Wappinger
Wenrohronon
Winnebago
Wyandot

Southeast
Acolapissa
Acuera
Adai
Ais
Akokisa
Alabama
Apalachee
Atakapa
Avoyel
Bayogoula
Caddo
Calusa
Cape Fear
Chatot
Cheraw
Cherokee
Chiaha
Chickasaw
Chitimacha
Choctaw
Congaree
Coosa
Coweta
Creek
Cusabo
Dakota
  Biloxi
  Catawba
  Ofo
  Tutelo
Eno
Eufaula
Fresh Water
Guacata
Guale
Hasinai
Hitchiti
Houma
Jeaga
Kasihta

Koasati
Manahoac
Mobile
Mococo
Monacan
Nahyssan
Naniaba
Natchez
Ocale
Occaneechi
Onatheaqua
Pascagoula
Pedee
Pensacola
Pohoy
Potano
Santee
Saponi
Saturiwa
Sewee
Sugeree
Surruque
Tacatacuru
Taensa
Tamathli
Tekesta
Timucua
Tocobaga
Tohome
Tunica
Tuskegee
Uamasee
Utina
Waccamaw
Wateree
Waxhau
Winyaw
Woccon
Yuchi
Yui
Yustaga

Plains
Arapaho
Arikara
Assiniboin

Atsina
Blackfoot
  Blood
  Northern
  Piegan
Cheyenne
Comanche
Crow
Dakota
  Santee
  Teton
  Yankton
Hidatsa
Iowa
Kansa
Kiowa Apache
Mandan
Missouri
Omaha
Osage
Ota
Oto
Pawnee
Plains Cree
Plains Ojibwa
Ponca
Quapaw
Scarcee
Wichita
Dakota

Northwest
Cayuse
Coeur D'Alene
Columbia
Cowlitz
Flathead
Kalispel
Klamath
Klickitat
Kutenai
Lake
Lillooet
Modoc
Molala
Nespelem

Nez Perce
Okanagon
Sanpoil
Shuswap
Sinkaietk
Spohan
Tenino
Thompson
Umatilla
Walla Walla
Wenatchee
Yakima

Great Basin
Chemehuevi
Fish Lake
Gosiute
Kaibab
Kawaiisu
Las Vegas
Moapa
Mono
  Eastern Mono
  Western Mono
Numic
  Central Numic
  Southern
Numic
  Western Numic
Pahvant
Paiute
  Northern
Paiute
  Southern
Paiute
  Owens Valley
Paiute
Red Lake
Shivwits
Shoshoni
  Bannock
  Eastern
Shoshoni
  Lemhi
  Northern
Shoshoni

Native Peoples of North America (continued)

Panamint	Sandia	Karok	Kamia	Aleut
Sheep Eater	Santa Clara	Kwalhioqua	Kawaiisu	American Indian
Western	Taos	Makah	Kitanemuk	Ingalik
Shoshoni	Tesuque	Quileute	Luiseno	Kutchin
Tumpanogots	Papago	Siuslaw	Maidu	Tanaina
Uinkarets	Pima	Tillmook	Miwok	Tinneh
Ute	Western Pueblo	Tututni-Tolowa	Mojave	Tlingit
"Weber Ute"	Acoma	Umpqua	Mono	Tsimshian
Northern Ute	Hano	Wiyot	Nisenan	
Southern Ute	Hopi	Yurok	Patwin	**Puerto Rico**
Eastern Mono	Laguna		Poma	Taino
Western Mono	Zuni	**California**	Saboba	
	Yuma	Achomawi	Salinan	**Hawaii**
Southwest	Cocopa	Akwa'ala	Serrano	Hawaiian
Apache	Havasupai	Atsugewi	Shasta	
Central Pueblo	Hualapai	Cahuilla	Tubatulabal	**Canada***
Cochiti	Maricopa	Chimariko	Wappo	Abenaki
Jemez	Mojave	Chumash	Washo	Algonkin
San Felipe	Yavapai	Coast Miwok	West Diegueno	Huron
Santa Ana		Cocopa	Wintu	Inuit
Santo Domingo	**Northwest**	Costanoan	Wintun	Iroquois
Zia	**Coast**	Cupeno	Yana	Micmac
Eastern Puelo	Alsea	East Diegueno	Yokut	Montagnais
Isleta	Chimakum	Esselen	Yuki	Nipissing
Nambe	Chinook	Fernandeno	Yuma	Ojibwa
Picuris	Coos	Gabrieleno		Ottawa
San Ildefonso	Hupa	Halchidhoma	**Alaska**	Pennacook
San Juan	Kalapuya	Juaneno	Inuit	Potawatomi

* There are 630 Indian groups in Canada; these are referred to as First Nations and Indian Bands. Other Aboriginal peoples are called Inuit (also called Eskimos) and Métis (people of mixed heritage). This table is based on the most recent, 1996, census:

	Indians/First Nations	Métis	Inuit	Total Aboriginal
Newfoundland	5,430	4,685	4,265	14,205
Prince Edward Island	825	120	15	950
Nova Scotia	11,340	860	210	12,380
New Brunswick	9,189	975	120	10,250
Quebec	47,600	16,075	8,300	71,415
Ontario	118,830	22,790	1,300	141,525
Manitoba	82,990	46,195	360	128,685
Saskatchewan	75,205	36,535	190	111,245
Alberta	72,645	50,745	795	122,840
British Columbia	113,315	26,750	815	139,655
Yukon	5,530	565	110	6,175
Northwest Territories*	11,400	3,895	24,600	39,690
Canada (total)	**554,290**	**210,190**	**41,080**	**799,010**

As of 1999, many of these people live in the new territory of Nunavut. See the next page.

144

Native Peoples of North America (continued)

Largest U.S Indian Reservations (1987)

Reservation	Nation	Population	Location
Navajo	Navajo	173,018	Arizona, New Mexico, Utah
Cherokee	Cherokee	58,232	Oklahoma
Creek	Creek	54,606	Oklahoma
Choctaw	Choctaw	21,858	Oklahoma
Pine Ridge	Dakota	19,246	South Dakota
Southern Pueblos		17,079	New Mexico
Chicksaw	Chicksaw	11,780	Oklahoma
Rosebud	Dakota	11,685 *	South Dakota
Gila River	Pima	10,688	Arizona
Papago-Sells	Papago	10,138	Arizona
Turtle Mountain	Ojibwa	9,889	North Dakota
Hopi	Hopi	9,040	Arizona
Standing Rock	Dakota	8,612	North Dakota, South Dakota
Fort Apache	Apache	8,421	Arizona
Zuni	Zuni	8,135	New Mexico
Pawnee	Pawnee	7,657	Oklahoma
Northern Pueblos		7,651	New Mexico
Shawnee	Shawnee	7,263	Oklahoma, Texas
Blackfoot	Blackfoot	7,193	Montana
Yakima	Yakima	6,846	Washington
Wind River	Shoshone, Arapaho	5,124	Wyoming

* 1984 data

Canada

In 1996 there were 77 Indian reserves and communities in the Canadian census. On April 1st, 1999, a large territory in the north of Canada was established by the Canadian government taking the central and eastern portions of the Northwest Territories. The new self-governing territory is called Nunavut, which means "Our Land" in Inuit. 85 percent of the population are Inuit. With an area of 2 million square kilometers, Nunavut represents one fifth of the Canadian land mass.

Sources: The 1990 Information Plesse Almanac, Boston © 1989
           The Encyclopaedia Brittanica, Chicago ©1990
           North American Indians, Alice B. Kehow
           Indian and Northern Affairs Canada website, www.ina.gc.ca 1999
           1996 Census/Statistics Canada website, www.statcan.ca 1999

3: Population by Ethnic Identity

Note: The U.S. Census asks Americans to identify themselves by race, nationality, and ethnic origin. The following information from the 1990 census shows how they identify themselves.

Racial and National Origin for the U.S., 1990

Origin	Population	Percentage			
White	199,686,070	80.3	Vietnamese	614,547	0.2
Black	29,986,060	12.1	Hawaiian	211,014	0.1
American Indian	1,878,285	0.8	Eskimo	62,964	0.0
Inuit	57,152	0.0	Samoan	49,345	0.0
Aleut	23,797	0.0	Guamanian	821,692	0.3
Chinese	1,645,742	0.7	Other Asian-Pacific	9,804,847	3.9
Filipino	1,406,770	0.6	Hispanic (total)	22,354,059	9.0
Japanese	847,562	0.3	Mexican	13,495,938	5.4
Asian Indian	815,447	0.3	Puerto Rican	2,727,754	1.1
Korean	798,849	0.3	Cuban	1,043,932	0.4
			Other Hispanic	5,086,435	2.0

Black and Hispanic State Populations

	BLACK		HISPANIC	
Rank	State	Population	State	Population
1	New York	2,401,842	California	4,543,770
2	California	1,819,282	Texas	2,985,643
3	Texas	1,710,250	New York	1,609,245
4	Illinois	1,675,229	Florida	857,898
5	Georgia	1,465,457	Illinois	635,525
6	Florida	1,342,478	New Jersey	491,867
7	North Carolina	1,316,050	New Mexico	476,089
8	Louisiana	1,237,263	Arizona	440,915
9	Michigan	1,198,710	Colorado	337,300
10	Ohio	1,076,734	Michigan	162,388

Black Proportions of State Populations

Note: During the Civil War (1860-1864), 11 slave states seceded from the nation: Mississippi, South Carolina, Louisiana, Georgia, Alabama, North Carolina, Virginia, Arkansas, Tennessee, Florida, and Texas; four slave states remained in the Union: Maryland, Delaware, Missouri, and Kentucky.

Rank	State	Percentage	Rank	State	Percentage
1	Mississippi	35.2	11	Tennessee	15.8
2	South Carolina	30.4	12	Illinois	14.7
3	Louisiana	29.4	13	Florida	13.8
4	Georgia	26.8	14	New York	13.7
5	Alabama	25.6	15	Michigan	12.9
6	Maryland	22.7	16	New Jersey	12.6
7	North Carolina	22.4	17	Texas	12.0
8	Virginia	18.9	18	Missouri	10.5
9	Arkansas	16.3	19	Ohio	10.0
10	Delaware	16.1		**United States**	11.7

146

4: Major U.S. Cities

1990 Rank	City	State	Population 1990	Rank 1980
1	New York	New York	7,322,564	1
2	Los Angeles	California	3,485,398	3
3	Chicago	Illinois	2,783,726	2
4	Houston	Texas	1,630,553	5
5	Philadelphia	Pennsylvania	1,585,577	4
6	San Diego	California	1,110,549	8
7	Detroit	Michigan	1,027,974	6
8	Dallas	Texas	1,006,877	7
9	Phoenix	Arizona	983,403	9
10	San Antonio	Texas	935,933	11
11	San Jose	California	782,248	17
12	Indianapolis	Indiana	741,952	12
13	Baltimore	Maryland	736,014	10
14	San Francisco	California	723,959	13
15	Jacksonville	Florida	672,971	19
16	Columbus	Ohio	632,910	20
17	Milwaukee	Wisconsin	628,088	16
18	Memphis	Tennessee	610,337	14
19	Washington	District of Columbia	606,900	15
20	Boston	Massachusetts	574,283	21
21	Seattle	Washington	516,259	23
22	El Paso	Texas	515,342	28
23	Nashville-Davidson	Tennessee	510,784	25
24	Cleveland	Ohio	505,616	18
25	New Orleans	Louisiana	496,938	22
26	Denver	Colorado	467,610	24
27	Austin	Texas	465,622	42
28	Fort Worth	Texas	447,619	33
29	Oklahoma City	Oklahoma	444,719	31
30	Portland	Oregon	437,319	35
31	Kansas City	Missouri	435,146	27
32	Long Beach	California	429,433	37
33	Tucson	Arizona	405,390	45
34	St. Louis	Missouri	396,685	26
35	Charlotte	North Carolina	395,934	47
36	Atlanta	Georgia	394,017	29
37	Virginia Beach	Virginia	393,069	56
38	Albuquerque	New Mexico	384,736	44
39	Oakland	California	372,242	43
40	Pittsburgh	Pennsylvania	369,879	30
41	Sacramento	California	369,365	52
42	Minneapolis	Minnesota	368,383	34
43	Tulsa	Oklahoma	367,302	38
44	Honolulu	Hawaii	365,272	36
45	Cincinnati	Ohio	364,040	32

5: States of the United States

Union*	State	Seats**	Capital	Union*	State	Seats**	Capital
1819	Alabama	9	Montgomery	1889	Montana	3	Helena
1959	Alaska	3	Juneau	1867	Nebraska	5	Lincoln
1912	Arizona	8	Phoenix	1864	Nevada	4	Carson City
1836	Arkansas	6	Little Rock	1788	New Hampshire	4	Concord
1850	California	54	Sacramento	1787	New Jersey	15	Trenton
1876	Colorado	8	Denver	1912	New Mexico	5	Santa Fe
1788	Connecticut	8	Hartford	1788	New York	33	Albany
1787	Delaware	3	Dover	1789	North Carolina	14	Raleigh
1845	Florida	25	Tallahassee	1889	North Dakota	3	Bismarck
1788	Georgia	13	Atlanta	1803	Ohio	21	Columbus
1959	Hawaii	4	Honolulu	1907	Oklahoma	8	Oklahoma City
1890	Idaho	4	Boise	1859	Oregon	7	Salem
1818	Illinois	22	Springfield	1787	Pennsylvania	23	Harrisburg
1816	Indiana	12	Indianapolis	1790	Rhode Island	4	Providence
1846	Iowa	7	Des Moines	1788	South Carolina	8	Columbia
1861	Kansas	6	Topeka	1889	South Dakota	3	Pierre
1792	Kentucky	8	Frankfort	1796	Tennessee	11	Nashville
1812	Louisiana	9	Baton Rouge	1845	Texas	32	Austin
1820	Maine	4	Augusta	1896	Utah	5	Salt Lake City
1788	Maryland	10	Annapolis	1791	Vermont	3	Montpelier
1788	Massachusetts	12	Boston	1788	Virginia	13	Richmond
1837	Michigan	18	Lansing	1889	Washington	11	Olympia
1858	Minnesota	10	St. Paul	1863	West Virginia	5	Charleston
1817	Mississippi	7	Jackson	1848	Wisconsin	11	Madison
1821	Missouri	11	Jefferson City	1890	Wyoming	3	Cheyenne
				1846	District of Columbia	1	

* The date the state entered the union. The original states (1787) are listed below.

** Seats in the House of Congress. Each state (except the District of Columbia) has 2 senators and at least one representative. The number of representatives is based on the population of the state. The total number of senators and representatives is also the number of votes the state may cast for the President of the U.S. (electoral votes). The District of Columbia has only one representative, but 3 electoral votes.

The Thirteen Original States

Connecticut	New Hampshire	Pennsylvania
Delaware	New Jersey	Rhode Island
Georgia	New York	South Carolina
Maryland	North Carolina	Virginia
Massachusetts		

These states were the original 13 British colonies that established the United States of America starting with the Declaration of Independence in 1776. The dates given for entering the union are the dates they ratified the constitution between 1787 and 1790. They were the only states until the independent Republic of Vermont joined the union as the fourteenth state in 1791.

State Ranking by Population (1990 Census)

Rank	State	Population	Rank	State	Population
1	California	29,279,000	27	Connecticut	3,226,929
2	New York	17,627,000	28	Oklahoma	3,124,000
3	Texas	16,825,000	29	Oregon	2,828,214
4	Florida	12,775,000	30	Iowa	2,766,658
5	Pennsylvania	11,764,000	31	Mississippi	2,534,814
6	Illinois	11,325,000	32	Kansas	2,467,000
7	Ohio	10,778,000	33	Arkansas	2,337,395
8	Michigan	9,179,000	34	West Virginia	1,782,958
9	New Jersey	7,617,418	35	Utah	1,711,117
10	North Carolina	6,553,000	36	Nebraska	1,572,503
11	Georgia	6,387,000	37	New Mexico	1,490,381
12	Virginia	6,128,000	38	Maine	1,218,053
13	Massachusetts	5,928,000	39	Nevada	1,193,000
14	Indiana	5,499,000	40	New Hampshire	1,103,063
15	Missouri	5,079,385	41	Hawaii	1,095,000
16	Wisconsin	4,869,640	42	Idaho	1,003,558
17	Washington	4,827,000	43	Rhode Island	988,609
18	Tennessee	4,822,134	44	Montana	794,329
19	Maryland	4,733,000	45	South Dakota	693,294
20	Minnesota	4,358,864	46	Delaware	658,031
21	Louisiana	4,180,831	47	North Dakota	634,223
22	Alabama	3,984,000	48	District of Columbia*	575,000
23	Kentucky	3,665,220	49	Vermont	560,029
24	Arizona	3,619,000	50	Alaska	546,000
25	South Carolina	3,407,000	51	Wyoming	449,905
26	Colorado	3,272,000		*Not a state.*	

Associated Free States

Name	Capital	Population (1998 est.)	Organization
Guam	Agana	148,060	Self-governing territory
Puerto Rico	San Juan	3,857,000	Commonwealth
Virgin Islands	Charlotte Amalie	118,211	Self-governing territory
American Samoa	Pago Pago	62,093	Self-governing territory
Northern Mariana Islands	Chalan Kanoa	66,561	Commonwealth
Micronesia	Kolonia	107,900	Independent state
Belau	Koror	13,870	Republic
Marshall Islands	Darap-Uliga-Darrit	43,420	Republic

Non Self-Governing Possessions

Name	Population
Baker, Howland and Jarvis Islands	Uninhabited
Johnston Atoll	Military personnel
Kingman Reef	Military personnel
Palmyra	Government personnel
Navassa	Uninhabited
Midway Islands	Military personnel
Wake Island	Military personnel

6: Provinces and Major Cities of Canada
Provinces and Territories by Population (1996 Census)

Rank	Province	Population	Date*	Capital
1	Ontario	10,642,790	1867	Toronto
2	Quebec	7,045,080	1867	Quebec City
3	British Columbia	3,689,755	1871	Victoria
4	Alberta	2,669,195	1905	Edmonton
5	Manitoba	1,100,295	1870	Winnipeg
6	Saskatchewan	976,615	1905	Regina
7	Nova Scotia	899,970	1873	Halifax
8	New Brunswick	729,630	1873	Fredericton
9	Newfoundland including Labrador	547,160	1949	St. John's
10	Prince Edward Island	132,855	1873	Charlottetown
	Territory			
11	Northwest Territories	64,120*	1867	Yellowknife
12	Yukon Territory	30,655	1867	Whitehorse
13	Nunavut	24,000*	1999	Iqaluit
	Canada (total)	28,528,125	1867	Ottawa, Ontario

*On April 1, 1999, the Northwest Territories was split and the Nunavut Territory was created. The 1996 census shows 64,120 people in the Northwest Territories. The 1999 estimate of the population of Nunavut is 24,000, 85% of whom are Inuit (Esquimo). "Nunavut" means "Our Land" in the Inuit language.

Major Cities of Canada (1996 Census)

Rank	City, Province	Population
1	Toronto, Ontario	4,263,757
2	Montreal, Quebec	3,326,510
3	Vancouver, BC	1,831,665
4	Ottawa, Ontario	1,010,498
5	Edmonton. Alberta	862,597
6	Calgary, Alberta	821,628
7	Quebec City, Quebec	671,889
8	Winnipeg, Manitoba	667,209
9	Hamilton, Ontario	624,360
10	London, Ontario	398,616

Sources: 1996 Census/Statistics Canada website, www.statcan.ca 1999

7: Government Structure of the U.S.

There are three basic levels of government: local, state, and federal (national). At each level, there are three, independent branches: the legislative, the executive, and the judicial. Because each branch is independent, it can check and balance (control) the authority of the other branches. This is called the balance of powers.

The United States is a democracy; it is controlled by its citizens. As Abraham Lincoln said, it is a "government of the people, by the people, and for the people." The United States is also a republic, to be specific, a democratic republic. This means that its laws are made and administered by representatives elected by the people. (In this sense, the President, senators, and even local mayors are representatives.)

The only governments in the U.S. run directly by the people (pure democracies) are those of small towns, like those in New England, which make all basic decisions in Town Meetings, and even in those towns elected volunteers (selectpersons) run the town between Town Meetings.

Federal Government

The structure and function of the federal government are established and limited by the Constitution of the United States and its twenty-six amendments. The responsibilities of the federal government are for the common defense and the general welfare of the citizens, for the regulation of interstate commerce, and for relations with other countries and between the states. All powers not specifically given to the federal government by the Constitution or prohibited by the Bill of Rights (the first ten amendments) are left to the states.

How laws are made and used: The executive branch can suggest laws to the congress (the legislative branch) or the congress can originate laws. Laws authorizing the government to tax or spend money are written by the House of Representatives. All laws must be passed by both houses of congress and signed by the President. If the President will not sign (vetoes) a law, the congress can vote to override the veto.

The executive branch uses the laws made by congress; it spends the government's money and runs most of the functions of government following the instructions (laws) passed by congress, and it makes the people obey the law (enforces the law).

When people or the government are accused of breaking the law, the courts (the judiciary branch) judge whether the law has been broken and what the government should do if it has been. The courts interpret the laws made by congress, but they also base their decisions on previous decisions made by the courts. Under this system (called "common law"), the courts make decisions which function as new laws.

Legislative Branch

The Congress of the U.S. has two houses (a bicameral structure). The congress makes laws, advises the President, and must consent (agree with) his appointments and certain of his decisions such as treaties with other countries and declarations of war.

U.S. Senate: There are 100 senators, two from each state, elected directly by popular vote to serve six-year terms. Each senator has their own office and staff.

Officers: President of the Senate (the Vice President of the U.S.), President Pro Tempore, Majority Leader and Whip, Minority Leader and Whip.
Annual salary of a senator: $141,300.

U.S. House of Representatives: There are 435 Representatives, apportioned to the states based on the size of each state's population, elected directly by popular vote to serve two-year terms. Each representative has their own office and staff. Officers: Speaker of the House, Majority Leader and Whip, Minority Leader and Whip.
Annual salary of a representative: $141,300

Major Offices of the Congress:
- General Accounting Office
- Government Printing Office
- Office of Technology Assessment
- Congressional Budget Office
- Library of Congress

151

Executive Branch

President: The President is the Chief Executive Officer of the federal government and Commander-in-Chief of the Armed Forces. He or she serves a four-year term. No president can be elected for more than two, four-year terms.

Annual salary of the President: $400,000 plus expenses.

The President is the head of the administration. The administration runs the government. The White House staff and the President's Cabinet work directly for the President. They are all political appointees; most of these appointments are then sent to the congress for its advice and consent (approval). The staff advises the President and does his planning and office work. The cabinet advises the President and runs the many departments and agencies of the federal government.

Election of the President: People who want to become President usually try to become the nominees of one of the two major political parties. They run in the primary elections held in some of the states. In these primaries, delegates to each party's national convention are elected by direct popular vote. In some states, the parties choose their delegates in political caucuses. At the national conventions, the delegates elect the man or woman who will be the nominee of their party.

During the presidential campaign, the two major party candidates and sometimes candidates representing minor, third parties or independent candidates try to win the support of the majority of voters in each state. No third party has won the presidency since the new Republican Party won its first election under Abraham Lincoln in 1860.

In the general election in November, the voters in each state elect electors to represent their state in the electoral college; these electors vote for the candidate who won the election in their state. Each state has as many electors (the electoral vote) as it has senators and representatives, which gives smaller states some extra influence. The candidate who wins the greatest number of electoral votes becomes president; this is not necessarily the candidate who gets the greatest number of popular votes nationwide. The winner of the popular vote has failed to become president three times, in 1824, 1876, and 1888

Order of presidential succession: When a President dies or leaves office for any reason during his or her term, he or she is succeeded by the Vice President, Speaker of the House, President Pro Tempore of the Senate, Secretary of State.

The President (or Vice President) can be removed from office only by being impeached by the House of Representatives and convicted by the Senate presided over by the Chief Justice of the Supreme Court. The congress also has the power to impeach, convict, and remove from office federal judges and other civil officers.

Vice President: The Vice President is the successor to the President if he or she leaves office, a member of the President's Cabinet, and the President of the Senate. Recently, he has also been an adviser on most of the President's decisions.

Annual salary of the Vice President: $181,400 plus expenses.

Election of the Vice President: After he or she is elected by the national convention of his or her party, each presidential candidate chooses a running mate, a nominee for Vice President. After he or she is elected by the convention, the candidate joins the presidential ticket for the election campaign. The President and Vice President win the election together.

Other parts of the executive branch:

The Civil Service: Most employees of the federal government are not political appointees but civil servants who stay in the government from one administration to the next.

The Diplomatic Corps: The ambassador and delegation to the United Nations, other ambassadors, their staffs, and the rest of the diplomatic service are directed by the Secretary and Department of State.

Legal Services: All the departments and agencies of the federal government have lawyers. The Department of Justice under the Attorney General reviews and coordinates all laws proposed to the congress, enforces the law, and represents the executive branch in the courts. The FBI (Federal Bureau of Investigation) is part of this department.

The Military: The Army, the Navy and Marines, and the Air Force are under the direct command of the President through the Secretary of Defense and then the Chairman of the Joint Chiefs of Staff, who is the nation's top military officer.

Judicial Branch

General: The legal system in the U.S. is Common Law rather than Civil Law. Laws are written and enacted by the legislatures of the states and by congress, but the decisions of the courts in interpreting these laws are based on precedents (earlier court decisions). Court decisions function as new laws; the courts have a powerful influence on all levels of government.

Some judges at the state and local levels are elected for specific terms in some states. Federal judges are appointed by the President and confirmed with the advice and consent of the Senate. They all serve for life or until they choose to resign; this protects them from political influence.

Criminal Law: All people accused of breaking criminal law before the state or federal courts have the right to be tried by a jury of either six or twelve citizens who will decide if they are guilty or innocent. They are indicted (formally accused) by the government, sometimes by a grand jury of citizens. In court they are prosecuted by a government prosecutor and defended by their own lawyer or a public defender. If they are found guilty, they can appeal the decision of the jury or the judge to a higher court, a court of appeals. If the verdict is innocent, the government cannot appeal. The constitution says nobody can be tried twice for the same crime.

If a defendant does not appeal a guilty verdict, punishment is decided on by the judge following the penal code (penalty law). Sometimes the judge is advised by the jury; sometimes his or her choice of judgments is limited by a uniform sentencing law enacted by the legislature. The punishment is then administered by the justice department of the executive branch (the police and prison system). Punishments may be appealed to the Supreme Court if they may be cruel or unusual because such punishments are forbidden by the Constitution's Bill of Rights.

Civil Law: All forms of business and relations between people, companies, and states are regulated (ruled) by either criminal or civil law. Conflicts between people, etc., which do not involve criminal activity, are resolved by the courts using civil law. Juries are used in some cases; others are decided by a judge or a panel of judges.

Federal and State Jurisdictions: The federal courts have authority (jurisdiction) in all criminal and civil cases involving the federal government or law, federal officers, and other countries, their officers or their citizens. The federal courts also have authority in cases between states, between any state and a citizen of another state, or between citizens of different states. This includes most cases involving big businesses. All other cases are tried in the state courts.

The U.S. District Courts: These courts are the lowest level of the federal court system. Most cases involving federal law, both civil and criminal, begin at this level.

There are 91 district courts, at least one and sometimes several in each state and in the territories of Guam, Puerto Rico, and the Virgin Islands.

The U.S. Courts of Appeals: There are eleven Circuit Courts, each covering a multistate region, plus two special courts, one for the District of Columbia and one for temporary emergencies. Each court holds court in several places which make up a circuit. These Circuit Courts hear appeals brought to them from the lower district courts and cases involving federal regulatory agencies.

The U.S. Supreme Court: There are nine justices of the Supreme Court (one Chief Justice and eight Associate Justices). They are appointed by the President and confirmed with the advice and consent of the Senate. The justices serve for life unless they choose to retire or they are impeached by the House and convicted by the Senate.

Annual salary of the Chief Justice: $175,400;

Annual salary of the Associates Justices: $167,900.

The Supreme Court is the highest court of appeals; its main function is to decide whether decisions of the lower courts and laws passed by the states or federal government are constitutional (in accord or agreement with the Constitution and the Bill of Rights.) The Supreme Court also decides cases when there is a conflict between the laws of one state and another or the federal government. It chooses the cases it will hear from among cases appealed to it from the lower courts and cases involving challenges to state and federal laws.

Because the Supreme Court interprets the Constitution and either cancels or defines the meaning of laws based on its interpretations of the Constitution, it has a great influence on the way the laws of the country are used. From the beginning of U.S. history, the Supreme Court has often used its power to change the political and social development of the country.

State Governments

There are 50 states in the U.S. and 15 associated states and possessions in the Caribbean and Pacific. Each has its own government. Although their structures vary in many ways, each of these governments has three branches like the federal government. The following descriptions are generally true for most states.

LEGISLATIVE BRANCH: The legislative branch of each state has a bicameral (two-house) structure like the federal government. There is an upper house called the senate and a lower house called the house or assembly of representatives. The state legislatures make both civil and criminal laws for their states.

EXECUTIVE BRANCH: Each state has a governor and a lieutenant governor, who are elected by the people of the state. The structure and functions of the executive branch differ from state to state. Most states have a secretary of state, a treasurer, a comptroller and an attorney general.

JUDICLAL BRANCH: The highest court is called the appellate court, the court of appeals, or the supreme court. Below it are the superior and inferior courts, which in some states include all local and municipal courts.

Local Governments

There are many variations in the structures of local governments. The smallest government structures are villages. Towns are generally larger, and cities are larger still. The whole state is divided into counties. In some states, each county is divided into several townships, each containing several towns and villages. In other states, each county is divided into towns, which may have several villages, town centers, or hamlets in them. The open (unincorporated) countryside between villages is governed by the township (town) or the county.

LEGISLATIVE BRANCH: Villages, towns, and cities (municipalities) always have some form of legislative board, which is directly elected by the local citizens. In cities and large towns it is called the town or city council or the board of alderpersons. In smaller towns and villages, the town council is sometimes called the board of selectpersons. The local legislatures make regulations and spend local tax money. To help them plan for changes, they often appoint local zoning and planning boards.

In most municipalities, the school system is run by a local school board, which is also directly elected by the people. Sometimes there is a township school board.

EXECUTIVE BRANCH: The smallest towns are run by the selectpersons with the help of an elected town clerk or manager. In larger towns and cities there is always an independent town or city manager or mayor.

JUDICIAL BRANCH: Villages and small towns have elected justices of the peace or local town magistrates. Larger towns and cities have municipal courts. In some states, these are part of the state court system; in others, they are independent.

Other Organizations

There are other organizations which govern life in the United States, usually through political and financial influence.

POLITICAL PARTIES: There are two major political parties, the Democratic Party and the Republican Party. There are also many minor, special interest, and regional and local parties including the Libertarian Party, Socialist Party, Socialist Labor Party, Communist Party, and Socialist Workers Party. Individuals may also run for political office as independents (without party support).

Other Groups With Political Influence:
- Business and trade associations
- Chambers of commerce
- Professional organizations
- Labor unions
- Public service boards
- Civil rights organizations
- Political action committees
- Veteran's and Fraternal organizations
- Alumni associations
- Consumer and public interest groups
- Churches
- Other special interest groups

8: U.S. Departments and Agencies

Departments and The Cabinet

Note: Each department is headed by a member of the president's Cabinet, who is given the title of secretary, with the exception of the Department of Justice, which is headed by the attorney general. The vice president is also a member of the Cabinet.

Department of Agriculture
Department of Commerce
Department of Defense
Department of Education
Department of Energy
Department of Health and Human Services
Department of Housing and Urban Development
Department of Justice
Department of Labor
Department of State
Department of the Interior
Department of the Treasury
Department of Transportation
Department of Veterans' Affairs

White House Staff

Chief of Staff
Assistant to the President/Deputy Chief of Staff
Assistants to the president:
    Cabinet Secretary
    Communications
    Counsel to the President
    Deputy Counsel to the President
    Counselor to the President
    Special Counsel
    Domestic Policy Council
    Intergovernmental Affairs
    Legislative Affairs
    Management and Administration
    National AIDS Policy
    National Economic Policy
    National Security
    Presidential Personnel
    Press Secretary
    Political Affairs
    Public Liaison
    Staff Secretary
    Director of Scheduling
    Director of Speechwriting
    Chief of Staff to the First Lady
    Special Projects

Executive Agencies

Council of Economic Advisers
Council on Environmental Quality
Office of Administration
Office of Management and Budget
Office of National Drug Control Policy
Office of Science and Technology Policy
U.S. Trade Representative

Major Independent Agencies

Central Intelligence Agency (CIA)
Commission on Civil Rights
Commodity Futures Trading COmmission
Consumer Product Safety Commission
Environmental Protection Agency (EPA)
Equal Employment Opportunity Commission (EEOC)
Export-Import Bank of the U.S.
Farm Credit Administration
Federal Communications Commission (FCC)
Federal Deposit Insurance Commission (FDIC)
Federal Election Commission
Federal Emergency Management Agency
Federal Energy Regulatory Agency
Federal Maritime Commission
Federal Mine Safety and Health Review Commission
Federal Reserve System
Federal Trade Commission (FTC)
General Services Administration (GSA)
Inter-American Foundation
National Aeronautics and Space Administration (NASA)
National Archives and Records Administration
National Endowment for the Arts
National Endowment for the Humanities
National Labor Relations Board (NLRB)
National Railroad Passenger Corporation (AMTRAK)
National Science Foundation
National Transportation Safety Board
Nuclear Regulatory Commission
Occupational Safety and Health Review Commission
Office of Government Ethics
Office of Personnel Management
Office of Special Counsel
Peace Corps
Postal Rates Commission
Securities and Exchange Commission (SEC)
Selective Service System (SSS)
Small Business Administration (SBA)
Social Security Administration
Tennessee Valley Authority (TVA)
Trade and Development Agency
U.S. International Trade Commission
U.S. Postal Service (USPS)

9: Government Structure of Canada

There are three basic levels of government: local, state, and federal (national). Although the legislative, the executive, and the judicial functions are done at all levels, under a parliamentary system like Canada's the executive function is dependent on the legislature.

Canada is a democracy, controlled by its citizens. On the national level, it is a federation of provinces and territories. There are ten provinces: Alberta, British Columbia, Manitoba, New Brunswick, Newfoundland (including Labrador), Nova Scotia, Ontario, Prince Edward Island, Quebec, and Saskatchewan. There are three territories: the Northwest Territories, Nuvavut, and the Yukon.

On a less formal but politically very important basis, Canada is a federation of two peoples, one English speaking and the other French. The history of the union of these two peoples has been one of political strain. The nation as a whole is officially bilingual. Although the distinct French character of Quebec culture and society have always been recognized in Canada, the increasing population, prosperity, and political power of English speaking Canada have stimulated a seperatist movement in Quebec that has been a major political factor throughout the 1970's, '80's, and '90's.

On another level, Canada is a monarchy. This is important historically and today many Canadians are loyal to Elizabeth II as Queen of Canada, as well as Great Britain. She is officially Head of State. The Queen's representative in Canada is the Governor General.

Canada gained functional independence from Great Britain with the British North America Act of 1867. The Constitution Act of 1982 formally ended the colonial control of Canada by the British Parliament. The government of Canada was transferred under the Constitution to the Canadian people.

Federal Government

The Head of State is the Queen, represented by the Governor General. This is a ceremonial and advisory position. The real leader of the country is the Prime Minister, who is the leader of the majority party in the House of Commons. The Prime Minister and his cabinet are members of the Commons. They serve as the executive branch, advising the Governor General and running the civil service. The capital city of Canada is Ottawa, Ontario.

There are two houses of parliament, the Commons with 301 members and the Senate with 104. Members of the Commons are elected by the people in elections every five years or when the Prime Minister and his government are voted down in the Commons and they decide to call for an election. The Senators are appointed for terms ending with their 75th birthdays. Laws must be passed by both houses of the legislature and signed by the Governor General in the Queen's name.

Provincial Government

Each of the ten provincial governments is offically headed by a Lieutenant Governor, appointed by the federal government. This is a largely formal, symbolic position, like that of the Governor General on the federal level. The real executive head of each province is the Premier, the leader of the majority party in the provincial legislature.

These are single-house legislative bodies elected every four years . In eight of the provinces, the legislature is called the Legislative Assembly. In Newfoundland, which became a province in 1949, it is traditionally called the House of Assemblies, and in Quebec it is significantly called the National Assembly.

156

10: U.S. Presidents

1. George Washington
(1732-1799)
Party: Federalist
Term: 1789-1797
Birthplace: Virginia

2. John Adams
(1735-1826)
Party: Federalist
Term: 1797-1801
Birthplace: Massachusetts

3. Thomas Jefferson
(1743-1826)
Party: Democratic-Republican
Term: 1801-1809
Birthplace: Virginia

4. James Madison
(1751-1836)
Party: Democratic-Republican
Term: 1809-1817
Birthplace: Virginia

5. James Monroe
(1758-1831)
Party: Democratic-Republican
Term: 1817-1825
Birthplace: Virginia

6. John Quincy Adams
(1767-1848)
Party: Democratic-Republican
Term: 1825-1829
Birthplace: Massachusetts

7. Andrew Jackson
(1767-1845)
Party: Democratic
Term: 1829-1837
Birthplace: South Carolina

8. Martin Van Buren
(1782-1862)
Party: Democratic
Term: 1837-1841
Birthplace: New York

157

9. William Harrison
(1773-1841)
Party: Whig
Term: 1841 *
Birthplace: Virginia

10. John Tyler
(1790-1862)
Party: Whig
Term: 1841-1845
Birthplace: Virginia

11. James Polk
(1795-1849)
Party: Democratic
Term: 1845-1849
Birthplace: North Carolina

12. Zachary Taylor
(1784-1850)
Party: Whig
Term: 1849-1850 *
Birthplace: Virginia

13. Millard Fillmore
(1800-1874)
Party: Whig
Term: 1850-1853
Birthplace: New York

14. Franklin Pierce
(1804-1869)
Party: Democratic
Term: 1853-1857
Birthplace: New Hampshire

15. James Buchanan
(1791-1868)
Party: Democratic
Term: 1857-1861
Birthplace: Pennsylvania

16. Abraham Lincoln
(1809-1865)
Party: Republican
Term: 1861-1865 **
Birthplace: Kentucky

17. Andrew Johnson
(1808-1875)
Party: Union
Term: 1865-1869
Birthplace: North Carolina

18. Ulysses S. Grant
(1822-1885)
Party: Republican
Term: 1869-1877
Birthplace: Ohio

19. Rutherford B. Hayes
(1822-1893)
Party: Republican
Term: 1877-1881
Birthplace: Ohio

20. James Garfield
(1831-1881)
Party: Republican
Term: 1881 **
Birthplace: Ohio

21. Chester Arthur
(1829-1886)
Party: Republican
Term: 1881-1885
Birthplace: Vermont

22. Grover Cleveland
(1837-1908)
Party: Democratic
Term: 1885-1889
Birthplace: New Jersey

23. Benjamin Harrison
(1833-1901)
Party: Republican
Term: 1889-1893
Birthplace: Ohio

24. Grover Cleveland
(second nonconsecutive term)
Term: 1893-1897

25. William McKinley
(1843-1901)
Party: Republican
Term: 1897-1901 **
Birthplace: Ohio

26. Theodore Roosevelt
(1858-1919)
Party: Republican
Term: 1901-1909
Birthplace: New York

27. William Taft
(1857-1930)
Party: Republican
Term: 1909-1913
Birthplace: Ohio

28. Woodrow Wilson
(1856-1924)
Party: Democratic
Term: 1913-1921
Birthplace: Virginia

29. Warren Harding
(1865-1923)
Party: Republican
Term: 1921-1923 *
Birthplace: Ohio

30. Calvin Coolidge
(1872-1933)
Party: Republican
Term: 1923-1929
Birthplace: Vermont

31. Herbert Hoover
(1874-1964)
Party: Republican
Term: 1929-1933
Birthplace: Iowa

32. Franklin D. Roosevelt
(1882-1945)
Party: Democratic
Term: 1933-1945 *
Birthplace: New York

33. Harry S. Truman
(1884-1972)
Party: Democratic
Term: 1945-1953
Birthplace: Missouri

34. Dwight D. Eisenhower
(1890- 1969)
Party: Republican
Term: 1953-1961
Birthplace: Texas

35. John F. Kennedy
(1917-1963)
Party: Democratic
Term: 1961-1963 **
Birthplace: Massachusetts

36. Lyndon B. Johnson
(1908-1973)
Party: Democratic
Term: 1963-1969
Birthplace: Texas

37. Richard Nixon
(1913- 1994)
Party: Republican
Term: 1969-1974 §
Birthplace: California

38. Gerald Ford
(1913-)
Party: Republican
Term: 1974-1977
Birthplace: Nebraska

39. Jimmy Carter
(1924-)
Party: Democratic
Term: 1977-1981
Birthplace: Georgia

40. Ronald Reagan
(1911-)
Party: Republican
Term: 1981-1989
Birthplace: Illinois

41. George Bush
(1924-)
Party: Republican
Term: 1989 - 1993
Birthplace: Massachusetts

42. Bill Clinton
(1946-)
Party: Democrat
Term: 1993 - 2001
Birthplace: Massachusetts

* Died in office
** Assassinated in office
§ Resigned from office

41.George W. Bush
(1946-)
Party: Republican
Term: 2001-
Birthplace: Connecticut

11: Canadian Governors General and Prime Ministers

Term	Governor General	Term	Prime Minister, Party
1867-1868	Viscount Monck	1867-1873	Sir John A. Macdonald, Conservative
1869-1872	Baron Lisgar	1873-1878	Alexander Mackenzie, Liberal
1872-1878	Earl of Dufferin	1878-1891	Sir John A. Macdonald, Conservative
1878-1883	Marquess of Lome	1891-1892	Sir John J. C. Abbott, Conservative
1883-1888	Marquess of Lansdowne	1892-1894	Sir John S. D. Thompson, Conservative
188-1893	Baron Stanley of Preston	1894-1896	Sir Mackenzie Bowell, Conservative
1893-1898	Earl of Aberdeen	1896	Sir Charles Tupper, Conservative
1898-1904	Earl of Minto	1896-1911	Sir Wilfrid Laurier, Liberal
1904-1911	Earl Grey	1911-1917	Sir Robert Borden, Conservative
1911-1916	Duke of Connaught	1917-1920	Sir Robert Borden, Unionist
1916-1921	Duke of Devonshire	1920-1921	Arthur Meighen, Unionist
1921-1926	Baron Byng of Vimy	1921-1926	W. L. Mackenzie King, Liberal
1926-1931	Viscount Willingdon	1926	Arthur Meighen, Conservative
1931-1935	Earl of Bessborough	1926-1930	W. L. Mackenzie King, Liberal
1935-1940	Baron Tweedsmuir	1930-1935	Richard B. Bennett, Conservative
1940-1948	Earl of Athlone	1935-1948	W. L. Mackenzie King, Liberal
1948-1952	Viscount Alexander	1948-1957	Louis S. St. Laurent, Liberal
1952-1959	Viscount Massey	1957-1963	John G. Diefenbaker, Conservative
1959-1967	Georges P. Vanier	1963-1968	Lester B. Pearson, Liberal
1967-1973	Roland Michener	1968-1979	Pierre Elliott Trudeau, Liberal
1974-1979	Jules Léger	1979-1980	Charles Joseph Clark, Conservative
1979-1984	Edward R. Schreyer	1980-1984	Pierre Elliott Trudeau, Liberal
1984-1990	Jeanne Sauvé	1984	John Turner, Liberal
1990-1995	Raymond John Hnatyshyn	1984-1993	Brian Mulroney, Conservative
1995-	Roméo LeBlanc	1993	Kim Campbell, Conservative
		1993-	Jean Chrétien, Liberal

12: U.S. Industries

Largest U.S. Corporations (1997)

Rank	Company	Sales
1	General Motors	$178,174,000,000
2	Ford Motor Company	153,627,000,000
3	Exxon (petroleum)	122,379,000,000
4	Walmart (discount department stores)	119,299,000,000
5	General Electric	90,840,000,000
6	IBM (business machines,computers)	78,508,000,000
7	Chrysler (motors)	61,147,000,000
8	Mobil (petroleum)	59,978,000,000
9	Philip Morris (tobacco)	56,114,000,000
10	AT & T (telecommunications)	53,261,000,000
11	Boeing (aircraft)	45,800,000,000
12	Texaco (petroleum)	45,187,000,000
13	State Farm Insurance	43,957,000,000
14	Hewlett-Packard (computers)	42,985,000,000
15	Du Pont (chemicals)	41,304,000,000
16	Sears Roebuck (department/mail order stores)	41,296,000,000
17	Travelers Group (insurance)	37,609,000,000
18	Prudential (insurance)	37,073,000,000
19	Chevron (petroleum)	36,376,000,000
20	Procter & Gamble (toiletries)	35,764,000,000
21	Citicorp (banking)	34,697,000,000
22	Amoco (petroleum)	32,836,000,000
23	Kmart (discount department stores)	32,183,000,000
24	Merrill Lynch (investments)	31,731,000,000
25	J.C. Penney (department stores)	30,546,000,000

Leading U.S. Franchises (1997)

McDonald's	Dunkin' Donuts	Proforce, USA (cleaning)
Burger King	Carlson Wagonlit (travel)	General Nutrition Stores
Yogen Fruz/Bresler's/ICBIY	Jazzercise	Domino's Pizza
7-11 Convenience Stores	Bimple International (food)	KFC (chicken)
Jani-King (cleaning)	Mail Boxes, Etc.	Church's Chicken
Subway	Miracle Ear	Orion (fast) Foods
Baskin-Robbins	Futurekids (computers)	Great Clips (hair salons)
Coverall Cleaning	Papa John's Pizza	Re/Max (real estate)
Arby's	Holiday Inn	Super 8 Motels
Taco Bell	Choice Hotels	

13: Some Famous Americans

Before 1812

Adams, Samuel	(1722-1803)	Patriot, Boston Tea Party firebrand
Allen, Ethan	(1738-1789)	Leader of the Green Mountain Boys
Arnold, Benedict	(1741 -1801)	Treasonous Revolutionary War general
Attucks, Crispus	(c.1723-1770)	Led group that began the Boston Massacre in 1770
Boone, Daniel	(1734-1820)	Frontiersman
Clark, William	(1770-1838)	Explored the northwest with Lewis in 1804
Crockett, Davy	(1786-1836)	Frontiersman, died at the Alamo
Franklin, Benjamin	(1706-1790)	Writer, statesman, scientist
Hale, Nathan	(1755-1776)	Revolutionary War officer
Hamilton, Alexander	(1755-1894)	Statesman, author, first secretary of the treasury
Hancock, John	(1737-1793)	Statesman, Declaration of Independence signer
Henry, Patrick	(1736-1799)	Revolutionary war figure, orator
Jones, John Paul	(1747-1792)	Naval hero
LaSalle, Sieur de (R.C.)	(1643-1687)	Explored and claimed Mississippi Basin for France
Lewis, Meriwether	(1774-1809)	Explored the northwest with Clark in 1804
Pilgrims		Founded Plymouth Plantation Colony in 1720
Pocahontas	(c. 1595-1617)	Indian princess, saved explorer John Smith's life
Revere, Paul	(1735-1818)	Silversmith, hero of famous ride in 1775
Ross, Betsy	(1752-1836)	Designed and sewed first American flag
Sacagawea	(1784-1884)	Guided Lewis and Clark
Smith, Capt. John	(c. 1580-1631)	Led first colony (1607-9) in Jamestown, Virginia
Thomas Paine	(1737-1809)	Political philosopher
Turnbull, John	(1756-1843)	Historical themes painter
Whitney, Eli	(1765-1825)	Invented cotton gin and manufacture

1812-1865

Audubon, John James	(1785-1851)	Artist, ornithologist
Brown, John	(1800-1859)	Abolitionist
Carson, Kit	(1809-1868)	Scout
Clay, Henry	(1777-1852)	Political leader
Custer, George	(1839-1876)	Union general in Civil War, killed by Indians
Davis, Jefferson	(1808-1889)	President of the Confederacy
Douglass, Frederick	(1817-1895)	Author, diplomat, abolitionist
Emerson, Ralph Waldo	(1803-1882)	Philosopher, author, lecturer
Geronimo	(1829-1909)	Apache chieftain
Jackson, Thomas (Stonewall)	(1824-1863)	Confederate general in Civil War
Key, Francis Scott	(1779-1843)	Author of national anthem
Lee, Robert E.	(1807-1870)	Confederate general in Civil War
Sherman, William T.	(1820-1891)	Union general in Civil War
Sitting Bull	(1835-1890)	Dakota chief
Thoreau, Henry David	(1817-1862)	Philosopher, author, naturalist
Truth, Sojourner	(1797-1883)	Suffragette, abolitionist
Tubman, Harriet	(1820-1913)	Abolitionist, liberator
Webster, Daniel	(1782-1852)	Statesman
Webster, Noah	(1759-1843)	Lexicographer
Young, Brigham	(1801-1877)	Mormon leader, colonized Utah

1866-1916

Anthony, Susan B.	(1820-1906)	Suffragette
Barton, Clara	(1821 -1906)	Organizer of American Red Cross
Bell, Alexander Graham	(1847-1922)	Inventor of telephone, teacher of deaf
Buffalo Bill (William Cody)	(1846-1917)	Scout, showman
Carver, George Washington	(1861-1943)	Educator, botanist
Cassatt, Mary	(1845-1926)	Impressionist painter
Crazy Horse	(1849-1877)	Dakota war chief victorious at Little Bighorn
DuBois, W. E. B.	(1868-1963)	Historian, sociologist, founded NAACP
Edison, Thomas	(1847-1931)	Inventor of lightbulb, practical electric power
Ford, Henry	(1863-1947)	Industrialist, built first assembly-line cars
Homer, Winslow	(1836-1910)	Painter of marine themes
Liliuokalani, Lydia Kamekeha	(1838-1917)	Last monarch of Hawaii
Long, Huey	(1893-1935)	Politician
Peary, Adm. Robert E.	(1856-1920)	Explorer, first to reach North Pole 1909
Rockefeller, John D.	(1839-1937)	Established Standard Oil, philanthropist
Sargent, John Singer	(1856-1925)	Portrait artist
Washington, Booker T.	(1856-1915)	Educator
Wright, Orville	(1871 -1948)	Built first powered airplane with brother Wilbur

1917-1970

Bethune, Mary McLeod	(1875-1955)	Educator
Copland, Aaron	(1900-1990)	Composer
Cronkite, Walter	(1916-)	Television journalist
Disney, Walt	(1901-1966)	Film animator and producer
Earhart, Amelia	(1898-1937)	Aviatrix
Freidan, Betty	(1921 -)	Feminist, author
Goddard, Robert	(1882-1945)	Physicist, father of modern rocketry
Hearst, William Randolph	(1863-1951)	Publisher
Hopper, Edward	(1882-1967)	Painter of realistic urban scenes
Keller, Helen	(1880-1968)	Educator and writer
King Jr., The Rev. Dr. Martin Luther	(1929-1968)	Civil rights leader
MacArthur, Douglas	(1880-1964)	General in WW II, Korean War
Malcolm X	(1925-1965)	Civil rights leader
Marshall, Thurgood	(1980-1993)	Supreme Court justice, appointed 1967
McCarthy, Joseph	(1908-1957)	Anti-communist, politician
Moses, Grandma	(1860-1961)	Folk painter
O'Keeffe, Georgia	(1887-1986)	Painter of southwestern motifs
Oppenheimer, J. Robert	(1904-1967)	Physicist, father of atomic bomb
Patton, George S.	(1885-1945)	General in WW II
Pollock, Jackson	(1912-1956)	Abstract expressionist painter
Rockwell, Norman	(1894-1978)	Illustrator
Roosevelt, Eleanor	(1884-1962)	Humanitarian, UN delegate
Spock, Benjamin	(1903-1998)	Pediatrician
Steinem, Gloria	(1934-)	Feminist, author
Stevenson, Adlai	(1900-1965)	Statesman
Warhol, Andy	(1928-1989)	Pop artist
Wright, Frank Lloyd	(1867-1959)	Architect

1970-1985

Brokaw, Tom	(1940-)	Television news anchor
Brothers, Joyce	(1928-)	Psychologist
Brown, Helen Gurley	(1922-)	Publisher
Child, Julia	(1912-)	Chef
Chung, Connie	(1946-)	Television journalist, anchor
Donaldson, Sam	(1934-)	Television journalist
Eisner, Michael	(1942-)	Chairman of Walt Disney
Falwell, Jerry	(1933-)	Televangelist
Graham, Billy	(1918-)	Evangelist, author
Graham, Katharine	(1917-)	Publisher of *Washington Post*
Hefner, Hugh	(1926-)	Publisher of *Playboy*
Iacocca, Lee	(1924-)	Chairman of Chrysler
Jackson, The Rev. Jesse	(1941-)	Civil Rights leader, politician
Jennings, Peter	(1938-)	Television news anchor
Karan, Donna	(1948-)	Fashion designer
Klein, Calvin	(1942-)	Fashion designer
Landers, Ann	(1918-)	Advice columnist
Lauren, Ralph	(1939-)	Fashion designer
Nader, Ralph	(1934-)	Consumer advocate
O'Connor, Sandra Day	(1930-)	Supreme Court justice
Onassis, Jacqueline	(1929-1998)	Widow of John F. Kennedy
Pei, I.M.	(1917-)	Architect
Quinn, Jane Bryant	(1939-)	Economist
Rather, Dan	(1931-)	Television anchor
Ride, Sally K.	(1952-)	Astronaut
Sagan, Carl	(1934-1996)	Astronomer, author
Steinbrenner, George	(1930-)	Owner of the New York Yankees
Van Buren, Abagail	(1918-)	Advice columnist
Westheimer, Ruth	(1928-)	Sex therapist

1985-2000

Madeline Albright	(1937-)	Secretary of State
Neil Armstrong	(1930-)	Astronaut
Pat Buchanan	(1938-)	Journalist, presidential candidate
William F. Buckley	(1925-)	Columnist, author
Noam Chomsky	(1928-)	Linguist, political activist
Hillary Rodham Clinton	(1947-)	First Lady, politician
Bob Dole	(1923-)	Senator, presidential candidate
John Kenneth Galbraith	(1908-)	Economist
Bill Gates	(1955-)	Microsoft Chairman
John Glenn	(1921-)	Senator, astronaut
Al Gore	(1948-)	Vice-President
Edward Kennedy	(1960-)	Senator
Jack Kevorkian	(1928-)	Assisted suicide activist
Henry Kissinger	(1923-)	Statesman
Estee Lauder	(1908-)	Cosmetics Line Founder
Monica Lewinsky	(1973-)	White House intern
Rush Limbaugh	(1951-)	Radio talk show host
H. Norman Schwarzkopf	(1934-)	Desert Storm general
Ted Turner	(1938-)	TV executive
Jody Williams	(1950-)	Nobel Prize winner

14: Entertainers

Name	Occupation	Dates
Allen, Woody	Actor, director, screenwriter	(1935-)
Andrews, Julie	Actress	(1935-)
Armstrong, Louis	Jazz musician	(1900-1971)
Astaire, Fred	Actor, dancer	(1904-1983)
Baez, Joan	Singer	(1941-)
Balanchine, George	Choreographer	(1904-1983)
Ball, Lucille	Actress, comedienne	(1911-1989)
Barnum, P. T.	Circus master	(1810-1891)
Baryshnikov, Mikhail	Dancer, actor	(1948-)
Bernstein, Leonard	Conductor, composer	(1918-1990)
Bogart, Humphrey	Actor	(1899-1957)
Brando, Marlon	Actor	(1924-)
Cage, Nicolas	Actor	(1964-)
Capra, Frank	Director	(1897-1991)
Carey, Mariah	Singer	(1970-)
Carson, Johnny	Comedian, TV entertainer	(1925-)
Cash, Johnny	Country musician	(1932-)
Charles, Ray	Blues & rock musician	(1930-)
Cher	Actress	(1946-)
Clark, Dick	TV entertainer	(1929-)
Close, Glenn	Actress	(1947-)
Cody, Buffalo Bill	Creator of wild west show	(1846-1917)
Como, Perry	Singer	(1912-)
Connery, Sean	Actor	(1930-)
Coppola, Francis Ford	Director	(1939-)
Cosby, Bill	Actor, comedian	(1937-)
Costner, Kevin	Actor, director	(1955-)
Crosby, Bing	Actor, singer	(1904-1977)
Cruise, Tom	Actor	(1962-)
Davis, Bette	Actress	(1908-1990)
Davis, Sammy Jr.	Actor, singer	(1925-1990)
De Niro, Robert	Actor	(1943-)
Denver, John	Singer	(1943-1997)
Dietrich, Marlene	Actress	(1901-)
Dillon, Matt	Actor	(1964-)
Disney, Walt	Director, cartoonist	(1901-1966)
Domino, Fats	Musician	(1928-)
Donahue, Phil	Talk show host	(1935-)
Douglas, Michael	Actor	(1944-)
Dunaway, Faye	Actress	(1941-)
Duvall, Robert	Actor	(1931-)
Dylan, Bob	Rock musician	(1941-)
Eastwood, Clint	Actor, director	(1930-)
Ellington, Duke	Composer, pianist, band leader	(1899-1974)
Fiedler, Arthur	Conductor	(1894-1979)
Fields, W. C.	Actor, comedian	(1880-1946)
Fitzgerald, Ella	Jazz musician	(1918-)
Flynn, Errol	Actor	(1909-1959)

Fonda, Henry	Actor	(1905-1982)
Fonda, Jane	Actress	(1937-)
Fontaine, Joan	Actress	(1917-)
Ford, Harrison	Actor	(1942-)
Fosse, Bob	Director	(1927-1987)
Foster, Jodie	Actress	(1962-)
Franklin, Aretha	Soul and Gospel singer	(1942-)
Gable, Clark	Actor	(1901-1960)
Gabor, Zsa Zsa	Actress	(19?-)
Garbo, Greta	Actress	(1905-1990)
Garland, Judy	Actress	(1922-1969)
Gershwin, George	Composer	(1898-1937)
Gish, Lillian	Actress	(1896-1993)
Goldberg, Whoopi	Actress, commedienne	(1949-)
Griffin, Merv	Producer	(1925-)
Griffith, Andy	Actor	(1926-)
Guthrie, Woody	Folk singer	(1912-1967)
Hayworth, Rita	Actress	(1918-1987)
Hendrix, Jimi	Rock musician	(1942-1970)
Henie, Sonja	Actress, skater	(1910-1969)
Hepburn, Audrey	Actress	(1929-)
Hepburn, Katharine	Actress	(1909-)
Heston, Charlton	Actor	(1923-)
Hines, Gregory	Actor, tap dancer	(1946-)
Hitchcock, Alfred	Director	(1899-1980)
Ho, Don	Singer	(1930-)
Hoffman, Dustin	Actor	(1937-)
Holiday, Billie	Blues singer	(1915-1959)
Hope, Bob	Comedian	(1903-)
Horne, Lena	Singer	(1917-)
Houdini, Harry	Magician	(1874-1926)
Huston, John	Director	(1906-1987)
Iglesias, Julio	Singer	(1943-)
Ives, Burl	Folk singer	(1909-1995)
Jackson, Michael	Rock musician	(1958-)
Jagger, Mick	Rock musician	(1943-)
John, Elton	Rock musician	(1947-)
Jones, James Earl	Actor	(1931-)
Joplin, Scott	Composer, pianist	(1868-1917)
Keaton, Diane	Actress	(1946-)
Kelly, Grace	Actress	(1929-1982)
King, B.B.	Blues musician	(1925-)
Lancaster, Burt	Actor	(1913-)
Landon, Michael	Actor	(1936-)
Lansbury, Angela	Actress	(1925-)
Lee, Spike	Director	(1957-)
Lennon, John	Rock musician, composer	(1940-1980)
Leno, Jay	Talk show host	(1950-)
Letterman, David	Talk show host	(1947-)
Lewis, Jerry	Comedian, Actor	(1935-)
Liberace	Pianist	(1919-1987)
Lloyd-Webber, Andrew	Composer	(1948-)
MacLaine, Shirley	Actress	(1934-)
Madonna	Rock singer, actress	(1958-)
Martin, Steve	Actor, comedian	(1945-)
Marx, Groucho	Actor,comedian	(1890-1977)

McEntire, Reba	Country musician	(1955-)
Miller, Glenn	Band leader	(1904-1944)
Monroe, Marilyn	Actress	(1926-1962)
Morrison, Jim	Rock singer	(1943-1971)
Murphy, Eddie	Actor, comedian	(1961-)
Nelson, Willie	Country singer	(1933-)
Newhart, Bob	Actor, comedian	(1929-)
Newman, Paul	Actor	(1925-)
Nicholson, Jack	Actor	(1937-)
Nimoy, Leonard	Director, actor	(1931-)
Oakley, Annie	Sharp shooter	(1860-1926)
Orbison, Roy	Rock musician	(1936-1988)
Ozawa, Seiji	Conductor	(1935-)
Parton, Dolly	Actress, country singer	(1946-)
Peck, Gregory	Actor	(1916-)
Poitier, Sidney	Actor	(1927-)
Porter, Cole	Composer	(1893-1964)
Presley, Elvis	Actor, rock singer	(1935-1977)
Quinn, Anthony	Actor	(1915-)
Redford, Robert	Actor	(1937-)
Rogers, Ginger	Actress, dancer, singer	(1911-1995)
Rooney, Mickey	Actor	(1920-)
Sarandon, Susan	Actress	(1946-)
Schwarzenegger, Arnold	Actor	(1947-)
Scorsese, Martin	Director	(1942-)
Scott, George C.	Actor	(1927-)
Selznick, David O.	Producer	(1902-1965)
Shepard, Sam	Actor, playwright	(1943-)
Simon, Paul	Singer, musician	(1942-)
Sinatra, Frank	Singer	(1915-1998)
Sousa, John Philip	Composer	(1854-1932)
Spielberg, Steven	Director	(1947-)
Springsteen, Bruce	Rock musician	(1949-)
Stallone, Sylvester	Actor	(1946-)
Stanwyck, Barbara	Actress	(1907-1990)
Stewart, James	Actor	(1908-1997)
Stone, Oliver	Director	(1946-)
Stravinsky, Igor	Composer	(1882-1971)
Streep, Meryl	Actress	(1949-)
Sullivan, Ed	Variety show host	(1901-1974)
Taylor, Elizabeth	Actress	(1932-)
Temple, Shirley	Actress	(1928-)
Tracy, Spencer	Actor	(1900-1967)
Turner, Tina	Rock musician, actress	(1939-)
Waller, Fats	Composer	(1904-1943)
Wayne, John	Actor	(1907-1979)
Welk, Lawrence	Band leader	(1903-1992)
Welles, Orson	Director	(1915-1985)
West, Mae	Actress	(1893-1980)
Williams, Hank	Country musician	(1923-1953)
Winfrey, Oprah	Talk show host, actress	(1954-)

15: Heroes

Folk Heroes and Cultural Icons

Horatio Alger
Muhammad Ali
Johnny Appleseed
Billy the Kid
Bonnie and Clyde
Buffalo Bill
Daniel Boone
John Brown
Paul Bunyan
Al Capone
Kit Carson
Cesar Chavez
Davy Crockett
James Dean
Amelia Earhart
Wyatt Earp
Thomas Edison
Benjamin Franklin
Barbara Fritchie
John Henry
Wild Bill Hickock
Jesse James

Casey Jones
Martin Luther King, Jr.
Charles Lindbergh
Malcolm X
Marilyn Monroe
Mickey Mouse
John Muir
Annie Oakley
Jessie Owens
Rosa Parks
Pecos Bill
Molly Pitcher
Pocahontas
Elvis Presley
Paul Revere
Jackie Robinson
Betsy Ross
Babe Ruth
Tom Swift
Uncle Sam
Rip Van Winkle
Sergeant York

Presidential Icons

George Washington
Thomas Jefferson
Andrew Jackson

Abraham Lincoln
Teddy Roosevelt
Franklin Roosevelt

Comic Book Heroes

Alfred E. Newman
Batman and Robin
Betty Boop
Bill the Cat
Buck Rogers
Bugs Bunny
Calvin and Hobbes
Charlie Brown
Daffy Duck
Dagwood and Blondie
Dick Tracy
Donald Duck
Elmer Fudd
Felix the Cat
Fred Flintstone
Garfield

George Jetson
Little Orphan Annie
Mickey Mouse
Mike Doonesbury
Mutt 'n' Jeff
Nancy
Opus
Popeye
Scooby Doo
Snoopy
Spiderman
Superman
Sylvester and Tweety
Wile E. Coyote and the Roadrunner
Wonder Woman
Woody Woodpecker

16: Points of Interest

State	Site
Alabama	First capital of the Confederacy in Montgomery
Alaska	Denali National Park, wildlife sanctuary surrounding Mt. McKinley
Arizona	Taliesin West in Scottsdale, home of Frank Lloyd Wright
Arkansas	Eureka Springs, resort since 1880s
California	Disneyland in Anaheim
Colorado	Mesa Verde National Park, cliff-dwelling Indians' cities
Connecticut	Mark Twain House in Hartford
Delaware	John Dickinson home in Dover, residence of "Penman of the Revolution"
Florida	Cape Kennedy, NASA Space Center
	Saint Augustine, oldest city in U.S., est. by Spanish in 1565
Georgia	Chickamauga Battlefield Park, site of decisive 1863 victory for South in Civil War
Hawaii	Iolani Palace in Honolulu, last residence of Hawaiian royalty
Idaho	Hell's Canyon, deepest gorge in North America
Illinois	Lincoln shrines in Springfield, New Salem and Sangamon
Indiana	Fort Vincennes, one of the first white settlements west of the Appalachians
Iowa	Herbert Hoover birthplace and library in West Branch
Kansas	Dodge City, frontier town on Santa Fe Trail
Kentucky	Churchill Downs in Louisville, home of Kentucky Derby since 1875
Louisiana	Mardi Gras in New Orleans
Maine	Seacoast, Acadia National Park
Maryland	U.S. Naval Academy in Annapolis
Massachusetts	Plymouth Plantation, pilgrims' first colony
	Old North Church in Boston, beginning of Paul Revere's ride
	Witch trials in Salem in 1692
Michigan	Sault Ste. Marie, French settlement est. 1668
Minnesota	Minnehaha Falls in Minneapolis, inspiration for Longfellow's "Hiawatha"
Mississippi	Vicksburg National Military Park and Cemetery
Missouri	Pony Express Museum in St. Joseph
Montana	Custer Battlefield National Cemetery at Little Bighorn River
Nebraska	Buffalo Bill Ranch State Historical Park in Nebraska City
Nevada	Legalized gambling casinos in Las Vegas, Reno and Tahoe
New Hampshire	Strawbery Banke in Portsmouth, historical buildings dating to 17th century
New Jersey	Miss America Pageant and casinos in Atlantic City
New Mexico	Carlsbad Caverns, a national park with caverns on three levels and the largest natural cave in the world
New York	Ellis Island, immigration station for East Coast
North Carolina	Kitty Hawk, Wright brothers' first flight
	Roanoke Island, first English colony in America
North Dakota	Theodore Roosevelt National Park in Badlands, contains the president's Elkhorn Ranch
Ohio	Mound City National Monuments, group of 24 prehistoric Indian burial mounds

171

State	Site
Oklahoma	National Cowboy Hall of Fame, Oklahoma City
Oregon	Columbia River Gorge
Pennsylvania	Valley Forge, encampment grounds for Gen. Washington and troops in 1777
	Gettysburg, site of Civil War battle, turning point in war for Union
Rhode Island	John Brown House in Providence, residence of 18th century merchant
South Carolina	Fort Sumter National Monument, Union troops were overrun by Confederate soldiers to start the Civil War in 1861
South Dakota	Black Hills
Tennessee	Graceland in Memphis, home of Elvis Presley
	The Grand Ole Opry in Nashville, country music show est. 1925
Texas	The Alamo in San Antonio, fort was overrun by Santa Anna in1836
Utah	Temple Square in Salt Lake City, Mormon Church headquarters
Vermont	Bennington Battle Museum
Virginia	Monticello in Charlottesville, Jefferson's home
	Mount Vernon, Washington's home
	Appomattox, site of surrender of Gen. Lee and Confederacy in 1865
	Lexington, birthplace and tomb of Gen. Lee
Washington	Mount St. Helens, volcanic eruption in 1989
West Virginia	Harper's Ferry, John Brown led slave uprising in 1859
Wisconsin	Heritage Hill in Green Bay, museum of historical buildings and artifacts
Wyoming	Yellowstone National Park
District of Columbia	Washington Monument
	Lincoln Monument
	White House
	Jefferson Memorial
	Vietnam War Memorial
	National Archives
	Capitol

17: National Parks

Name	Location	Est.	Features
Acadia	Maine	1916	Mt. Desert Island and adjacent mainland
Arches	Utah	1929	Stone arches and pedestals caused by erosion
Badlands	South Dakota	1929	Arid land inhabited by bison, antelope, deer
Big Bend	Texas	1935	Mountains and desert bordering Rio Grande
Biscayne	Florida	1968	Coral reef south of Miami
Bryce Canyon	Utah	1923	Brilliantly colored eroded rocks
Canyonlands	Utah	1964	Red-rock canyons, spires and arches
Capitol Reef	Utah	1937	Sedimentary rock formations in high narrow gorges
Carlsbad Caverns	New Mexico	1923	World's largest known caves
Channel Islands	California	1938	Marine mammals, endangered species, archaeology
Crater Lake	Oregon	1902	Lake in the heart of an inactive volcano
Denali	Alaska	1917	North America's highest mountain, Mt. McKinley
Everglades	Florida	1934	Subtropical swamp
Gates of the Arctic	Alaska	1978	Diverse wilderness, part of the Brooks Range
Glacier	Montana	1910	Rocky Mountains
Glacier Bay	Alaska	1925	Whales, glaciers
Grand Canyon	Arizona	1908	Mile-deep gorge, 4-18 miles wide, 217 miles long
Grand Teton	Wyoming	1929	High mountain range
Great Basin	Nevada	1922	Biological and geological attractions
Great Smoky Mts.	NC, TN	1926	Highest mountain range east of Black Hills
Guadalupe Mts.	Texas	1966	Highest peak in Texas (8751 ft.)
Haleakala	Hawaii	1916	Dormant Haleakala volcano (10,023 ft.)
Hawaii Volcanoes	Hawaii	1916	Volcanoes, luxuriant vegetation at lower levels
Hot Springs	Arkansas	1832	47 hot springs
Isle Royale	Michigan	1931	Largest wilderness island in Lake Superior
Katmai	Alaska	1918	Dormant volcano, bears
Kenai Fjords	Alaska	1978	Mountain goats, marine mammals, birdlife
Kings Canyon	California	1890	Huge canyons, high mountains, giant sequoias
Kobuk Valley	Alaska	1978	Native culture and anthropology center
Lake Clark	Alaska	1978	Across Cook Inlet from Anchorage
Lassen Volcanic	California	1907	Impressive volcanic phenomena
Mammoth Cave	Kentucky	1926	Limestone labyrinth with underground river
Mesa Verde	Colorado	1906	Best-preserved prehistoric cliff dwellings in U.S.
Mount Rainier	Washington	1899	Single peak glacial system, dense forest
North Cascades	Washington	1968	Alpine landscape, glaciers, mountain lakes
Olympic	Washington	1909	Finest Pacific Northwest rainforest
Petrified Forest	Arizona	1906	Extensive natural exhibit of petrified wood
Redwood	California	1968	Coastal redwood forests, world's tallest known tree
Rocky Mountain	Colorado	1915	107 named Rocky Mountain peaks over 10,000 ft.
Samoa	American Samoa	1988	Two rainforest preserves and a coral reef
Shenandoah	Virginia	1926	Scenic Skyline Drive
Theodore Roosevelt	North Dakota	1947	Roosevelt Ranch, valley of the Little Missouri River
Virgin Islands	U.S. Virgin Islands	1956	Prehistoric Caribbean Indian relics, beaches
Voyageurs	Minnesota	1971	Wildlife, canoeing, fishing, hiking
Wind Cave	South Dakota	1903	Limestone caverns in the Black Hills, buffalo herd
Wrangell-St. Elias	Alaska	1978	Second highest peak in U.S. (Mt. Elias)
Yellowstone	WY, MT, ID	1872	World's greatest geyser area, falls and canyons
Yosemite	California	1890	Giant sequoias, enormous gorges and waterfalls
Zion	Utah	1909	Multicolored gorge in southwestern Utah desert

18: Natural Features

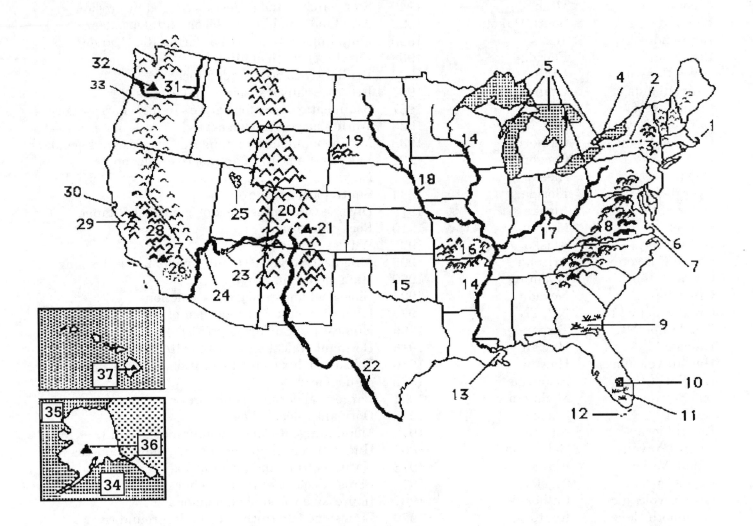

1. Cape Cod	14. Mississippi River	26. Death Valley
2. Erie Canal	15. Arkansas River	27. Mt. Whitney
3. Catskill Mountains	16. Ozark Mountains	28. Sierra Nevada Mountains
4. Niagara Falls	17. Ohio River	29. Big Sur Coastline
5. Great Lakes	18. Missouri River	30. San Francisco Bay
6. Chesapeake Bay	19. Black Hills	31. Columbia River
7. Cape Hatteras	20. Rocky Mountains	32. Mt. St. Helens
8. Appalachian Mountains	21. Pike's Peak	33. Cascade Range
9. Okefenokee Swamp	22. Rio Grande	34. Aleutian Islands
10. Lake Okeechobee	23. Grand Canyon	35. Bering Strait
11. Everglades Swamp	24. Colorado River	36. Mt. McKinley
12. Key West (islands)	25. Great Salt Lake	37. Kilauea Volcano
13. Mississippi Delta		

19: Important Days and Holidays: U.S. & Canada

US Holidays	Date	*Federal legal holidays in the U.S.*
* New Year's Day	January 1	
*Martin Luther King Day	Third Monday in January	
Chinese New Year	First new moon after the sun enters Aquarius	
Groundhog Day	February 2	
Boy Scouts' Day	February 8	
Lincoln's Birthday	February 12	
Saint Valentine's Day	February 14	
Susan B. Anthony Day	February 15	
*Presidents' Day	Third Monday in February	
Washington's Birthday	February 22	
Leap Year Day	February 29	
Johnny Appleseed Day	March 11	
Girl Scouts' Day	March 12	
St. Patrick's Day	March 17	
April Fool's Day	April 1	
Daylight Saving Time begins	First Sunday in April	
World Health Day	April 7	
Jefferson's Birthday	April 13	
Income taxes due	April 15	
Patriots' Day	April 19	
National Secretaries' Day	April 23	
Arbor Day	Last Tuesday in April	
May Day	May 1	
Law Day	May 1	
Lei Day (Hawaii)	May 1	
Cinco de Mayo	May 5	
Mother's Day	Second Sunday in May	
*Memorial Day	Last Monday in May	
Children's Day	June 8	
Flag Day	June 14	
Emancipation Day	June 19	
Fathers' Day	Third Sunday in June	
*Independence Day	July 4	
*Labor Day	First Monday in September	
Grandparents' Day	September 7	
Citizenship Day	September 17	
World Peace Day	September 21	
Native American Day	September 26	
Leif Erikson Day	October 9	
*Columbus Day	Second Monday in October	
Daylight Saving Time Ends	Last Sunday in October	
Halloween	October 31	
Election Day	First Tuesday after the first Monday in November	
*Veterans' Day	November 11	
Sadie Hawkins Day	First Sunday after November 11	
*Thanksgiving	Fourth Thursday in November	
Human Rights Day	December 10	
Bill of Rights Day	December 15	
*Christmas	December 25	

175

Canadian Federal Holidays

Victoria Day	Penultimate Monday in May	Thanksgiving Day	2nd Monday in October
Canada Day	July 1	Remembrance Day	November 11
Labour Day	1st Monday in September	Boxing Day	December 26

Major Jewish and Christian Holidays

Holiday	Religion	Date
Epiphany	Christian	January 6
Three King's Day	Christian	January 6
Eastern Orthodox Christmas	Christian	January 7
Shrove Tuesday (Mardi Gras)	Christian	Day before Ash Wednesday
Ash Wednesday	Christian	40 days (excluding Sundays) before Easter
World Day of Prayer	Inter-faith	March 7
Saint Patrick's Day	Christian	March 17
Palm Sunday	Christian	Sunday before Easter
Purim (Feast of Lots)	Jewish	14th or 15th of Hebrew month of Adar
Good Friday	Christian	Friday before Easter Sunday
Easter Sunday	Christian	The first Sunday after the full moon occurring on or after March 21
Passover (Pesach)	Jewish	15-22 of Hebrew month of Nisan
Ascension Day	Christian	Ten days before Pentecost
Pentecost	Christian	50 days after Easter
Trinity Sunday	Christian	Sunday after Pentecost
Shavuot (Feast of Weeks)	Jewish	6th or 7th of Hebrew month of Sivan
Rosh Hashanah (New Year)	Jewish	First day of Hebrew month of Tishri
Yom Kippur (Day of Atonement)	Jewish	10th day of Tishri
Sukkot (Tabernacles)	Jewish	15-21 Tishri
All Saint's Day	Christian	November 1
Advent	Christian	Four-week period before Christmas
Baha'U'Llah Birthday	Baha'i	November 12
Saint Lucia's Day	Christian	December 13
Christmas	Christian	December 25
Hanukkah	Jewish	25th of Hebrew month of Kislev

Major Islamic Holidays

Note: Because the Muslim calendar, containing only 354 days, is shorter than the Gregorian calendar Islamic holidays do not always fall on the same days of the Gregorian calendar and so are listed seperately.

Holiday	Date
Islamic New Year	First day of Islamic month of Muharram
Mawlid an-Nabi (Muhammad's Birthday)	12th of Islamic month of Rabi
Fast of Ramadan	9th month of Islamic calendar
Id al-Fitr (Festival of Fast Breaking)	29th or 30th of Ramadan to 3rd of following month of Shawwal
Beiram (The first day of spring)	10th of Islamic month of Zu'lhijjah
Id al-Adhh (The Great Festival)	10th to 13th of the Islamic month of Zu'lhijjah

20: Major Religions in the U.S. & Canada

MAJOR RELIGIOUS GROUPS IN THE U.S.

Membership of 100,000 or more (1998)

Group	Number of Churches	Membership
Protestant		
Adventist	4,770	840,777
Baptist	95,109	33,209,484
Brethren (German Baptists)	1,552	195,680
Christian and Missionary Alliance	1,850	311,612
Disciples of Christ	3,840	910,297
Churches of Christ	14,000	2,250,000
Church of Christ Scientist	2,200	unavailable
Churches of God	3,110	281,673
Church of the Nazarene	5,135	608,008
Episcopal	7,415	2,536,550
Evangelical Churches	2,121	348,255
Friends (Quakers)	2,472	189,466
Jehovah's Witnesses	10,671	975,829
Latter-day Saints (Mormons)	12,160	4,977,779
Lutheran	19,103	8,302,584
Mennonite	3,168	350,547
Methodist	52,761	14,183,130
Pentecostal	46,170	12,602,982
Presbyterian	14,416	4,160,154
Reformed and United Church of Christ	1,700	522,079
Salvation Army*	1,264	453,150
Unitarian Universalist	1,010	215,000
Protestant Totals (1998)	**305,997**	**88,425,036****
Roman Catholic	22,728	61,207,914
Moslems	n/a	3,332,000***
Jewish	2,440	3,500,000***
Eastern Orthodox	1,678	5,013,821
Baha'i Faith	7,200	133,000***
Buddhist	62	780.000***

*   Religious charitable organization with missions
**   Total includes estimates for some denominations/churches, and it does not include a
    figure for the Christian Scientists, a large organization.
*** Estimated membership

MAJOR RELIGIOUS GROUPS IN CANADA

Religion	Members
Anglican	780,897
Antiochian Orthodox	350,000
Apostolic Church of Pentecost	13,500
Armenian Holy Apostolic Church	75,000
Baha'i Faith	28,500
Baptist	293,279
Christian and Missionary Alliance	87,197
Christian Reformed Church	79,235
Evangelical Free Curch	22,528
Evangelical Lutheran	198,751
Greek Orthodox	350,000
Hindu	90,000
Islam	120,000
Jehovah's Witnesses	112,960
Latter Day Saints (Mormon)	130,000
Lutheran	250,000
Mennonite	38,453
Orthodox	1,000,000
Pentecostal	249,774
Presbyterian	211,075
Roman Catholic	12,498,605
Salvation Army	95,763
Seventh Day Adventist	46,113
United Church of Canada	1,835,215

21: A Brief History of the U.S.

c. 1000   Leif Erikson explores North America.

1492- 1502   Columbus explores the Caribbean for Spain in four voyages and publicizes the New World.

1497   John Cabot explores the Northeast American coast to Delaware.

1513   Juan Ponce de Leon explores Florida, searches for the Fountain of Youth.

1519   Cortes conquers Mexico.

1539   Hernando de Soto explores Florida, travels past the Mississippi River.

1540   Coronado and other Spanish explorers explore Northern Mexico, the Southwest U.S. and California.

1607   English found Jamestown.

1609   Henry Hudson explores New York Harbor and the Hudson River; Samuel de Champlain explores Lake Champlain; Santa Fe, New Mexico, founded.

1619   First black laborers brought to Jamestown as indentured servants. Slavery legalized in 1650.

1620   Plymouth Plantation, Massachusetts, founded by the Pilgrims, who came on the *Mayflower*.

1626   Peter Minuet buys Manhattan Island for the Dutch; pays the Indians $24 in trinkets.

1634   Frenchman Jean Nicolet explores the Great Lakes to Lake Michigan.

1636   First college, Harvard, founded. Roger Williams founds Rhode Island with democratic rule and religious toleration.

1654   First Jewish settlers come to New Amsterdam (later New York).

1664   British seize Dutch colony of New Netherland and rename it New York.

1673   Father Jacques Marquette and Louis Jolliet explore the upper Mississippi, claiming it for France.

1682   Sieur de La Salle explores the Mississippi south to the Gulf of Mexico.

1692   Witchcraft trials in Salem, Massachusetts.

1704   First regular newspaper, *Boston News Letter,* founded.

1741   Capt. Vitus Bering discovers Alaska for Russia.

1744-1763   French lose Canada and Ohio Valley to British after 20 years of war. Indians fight on both sides

1754-1776   British attempts to tax and control the colonies cause resentment and rebellion.

1773   Boston Tea Party.

1775   Battles of Lexington and Concord—"The shot heard 'round the world." Capture of Fort Ticonderoga, New York, and the Battle of Bunker Hill in Massachusetts are colonial victories. Gen. George Washington takes charge of the colonial army in Boston.

1776   Colonies declare independence from Britain on July 4.

1777   First constitution (Articles of the Confederation) adopted.

1781   British lose Revolutionary War

1784   Peace treaty signed with British.

1787   New constitution written and adopted.

1791   Bill of Rights enacted.

1793   Eli Whitney's invention of the cotton gin makes slavery profitable for the Southern states.

1797   Navy started with three ships.

1803   U.S. under President Thomas Jefferson buys Louisiana from Napoleon.

1804-1806   Lewis and Clark, with Sacagawea, an Indian woman guide, explore the Louisiana Purchase.

1808   Slave importation outlawed. Illegal imports continue until 1860.

1812   War with Britain.

1814   In Washington, D.C., the new Capitol and White House are burned by British. Peace treaty of Ghent.

1815   British are defeated in Battle of New Orleans.

1818   Troops under Gen. Andrew Jackson invade Florida to attack the Seminole Indians and weaken the Spanish government.

1819   Spain, whose American empire from Chile and Argentina in the south to Mexico and Florida in the north is collapsing, gives Florida to the U.S.

1823   Monroe Doctrine opposes any new colonies or any European intervention in the Americas.

1825   The Erie Canal, stretching from the Great Lakes to the Hudson River, is completed. The settlement of the MiddleWest and the growth of its towns and industries is stimulated. New York, New York, the largest city in the U.S. since 1790, expands rapidly.

1828   "Jacksonian Revolution." The new Democratic Party under Andrew Jackson wins the presidency and takes power in Washington. This first major political change, staged without violence, proves the stability of the government.

1836   Mexican-U.S. struggle for Texas. Mexican Gen. Santa Anna takes the Alamo in San Antonio and is then captured by Sam Houston at San Jacinto.
First wagon train of settlers travels from Missouri to California.

1848   Gold discovered in California. Development of the West is accelerated.

1853   Commodore Matthew C. Perry opens trade with Japan for U.S. ships.

1860   Abraham Lincoln elected.

1861   Seven Southern states withdraw from the U.S., set up the Confederate States of America and start the Civil War.

1863   Lincoln legally frees the slaves. Battle of Gettysburg. Lincoln's Gettysburg address.

1865   Civil War ends with Northern victory. Lincoln is re-elected and then assassinated. Thirteenth Amendment abolishes slavery.

1866   Reconstruction of the South. Ku Klux Klan formed secretly.

1867   U.S. buys Alaska from Russia.

1869   Transcontinental railroad completed. Knights of Labor founded.

1871   Fire burns the center of Chicago.

1872   Amnesty Act restores civil rights to the South.

1876   U.S. Centennial celebrated. Gen. Custer's last stand: 265 soldiers killed by Dakota Indians. Reconstruction ended in the South.

1886   Haymarket riot and other labor unrest. American Federation of Labor (AFL) formed.

1890   "Battle" of Wounded Knee; 200 Indian men, women, and children, and 29 U.S. soldiers killed in last major conflict of the Indian wars. Sherman Antitrust Act begins to curb big business monopolies.

1898   U.S. begins to take an aggressive interest in international affairs. Spanish-American War fought to aid independence of Cuba. U.S. annexes Hawaii.

1899   U.S. attempts to save Chinese independence and make China an international market by declaring the Open Door Policy.

1903   U. S. fosters Panama's independence from Colombia to get treaty to build Panama Canal. Wright brothers fly first airplane at Kitty Hawk.

1906   San Francisco earthquake. Pure Food and Drug and Meat Inspection acts.

1911   Supreme Court breaks up Rockefeller's Standard Oil Co. monopoly.

1914   Henry Ford raises pay of his workers from $2.40 for a nine-hour day to $5 for an eight-hour day so they can afford to buy a car. The sales of Ford cars booms.

1915   The Great War starts in Europe. U.S. remains neutral. Clayton Antitrust Act spurs anti-monopoly suits by federal government. U.S. frees Haiti to make it a "protectorate." U.S. actively supports various factions in Mexican Revolution of 1913-1916. U.S. hegemonyexpands in Carribbean.

1917   U.S. declares war on Germany. Prohibition amendment submitted; enacted 1919-1933.

1918   World War I ends November 11.

1919   First transatlantic flight.

1920   U.S. refuses to join the League of Nations.

1921   Congress curbs immigration and sets national quotas. Ku Klux Klan revives terror against blacks and Jewish Americans.

1924   Indians are made U.S.citizens.

1925   Scopes Monkey Trial dramatizes the changing understanding of evolution, science versus religion, and education in the U.S.

1926   Robert Goddard fires first fuel rocket.

1927   Marines are sent into China to protect U.S. interests duringcivil war. Charles Lindbergh crosses Atlantic solo.

1929   St. Valentine's Day Massacre dramatizes the power and violence of gangsters. Stock market crash begins the Great Depression.

1932   Roosevelt initiates new federalist approach to solving the crisis in the economy. To give Americans a "New Deal" and try to end the Depression Roosevelt rapidly increases the size and spending of the federal government over the next eight years.

1935   Committee for Industrial Organization(CIO) forms, promoting stronger unions in auto, steel and other heavy industry. Congress passes the Social Security Act.

1939   World War II begins in Europe. U.S. remains neutral but rearms and supports Britain more and more actively through 1941.

1941   Japan attacks Pearl Harbor December 7. U.S. declares war on Axis Powers (Japan, Germany and Italy).

1945   Germany surrenders May 7. First atomic bomb dropped on Hiroshima August 6. Second atomic bomb destroys Nagasaki August 9. Japan surrenders August 15. United Nations founded.

1946   Philippines given independence by U.S. on July 4.

1947   Truman Doctrine combats communism. The Marshall Plan aids reconstruction in Europe. Congress passes the Taft-Hartley Labor Relations Act over President Truman's veto to curb strikes.

1948   U.S.S.R. blockades West Berlin. British and U.S. break blockade with a massive airlift. Organization of American States founded.

1949   NATO founded for mutual protection of West Europe, Canada and U.S. People's Republic of China established under Mao Tse-tung; U.S. refuses recognition and maintains relations with the Nationalist government in exile in Taiwan (Formosa).

1950   Korean War begins; UN (including U.S.) sides with South Korea against Communist China-backed North Korea. U.S. agrees to give economic and military support to South Vietnam.

1951   Senate investigations, led by Estes Kefauver, expose the power of the Mafia and organized crime. Popular Gen. Douglas MacArthur is fired from his command in Korea.

1953   Peace is declared in Korea. U.S. supports anti-communists with massive aid in Indochina War.

1954   Anti-communist investigations by Senator Joseph McCarthy end in his condemnation by Senate.

1955   AFL-CIO formed. Rosa Parks refuses to give up her bus seat, beginning a citywide boycott in Birmingham, Alabama, led by Martin Luther King, Jr. Federal court overturns bus segregation law. Civil Rights movement gains strength.

1956   Supreme Court requires schools to desegregate.

1957   Congress passes the first civil rights bill on voting rights since Reconstruction.

1958   U.S.S.R.'s successful launch of the first man-made satellite, *Sputnik,* spurs U.S. scientific efforts and the space race. U.S. *Explorer I* launched.

1959   Alaska and Hawaii become states. St. Lawrence Seaway opens.

1960   Congress passes a stronger voting rights bill.

1961   Cuban exiles, with help from the CIA, invade Cuba at the Bay of Pigs; they fail to inspire a revolt and withdraw against Fidel Castro.

1962   Military advisors sent to Vietnam are permitted to "fire if fired upon." John Glenn is the first American in space.

1963   President John F. Kennedy is assassinated.

1964   Major civil rights legislation is proposed. President Johnson and Congress begin a great increase in government spending on social welfare programs to create Johnson's "Great Society."

1965   President Johnson orders continuous bombing in South Vietnam and sends 184,300 troops. Riots in Watts section of Los Angeles, California.

1966   U.S. fights in North Vietnam and Cambodia.

1967   Riots in Newark, New Jersey, and Detroit, Michigan. 475,000 troops in Vietnam.

1968   Vietnam War peace talks begin in Paris. Martin Luther King, Jr., and Robert Kennedy are assassinated.

1969   President Nixon expands the peace talks and begins phased withdrawal of U.S. troops from Vietnam. Neil Armstrong walks on the moon.

1970   U.S. and South Vietnamese fight in Cambodia.

1972   President Nixon reopens relations with China.

1973   Vietnamese peace pacts signed.

1974   President Nixon resigns when threatened with impeachment for covering up evidence on the 1972 break-in at the Democratic National Committee offices in Watergate in Washington.

1975   South Vietnam, without U.S. military support, falls to North Vietnam.

1978   The U.S. agrees to hand the Panama Canal over to Panama in 1999.

1979   90 hostages are taken in Iran as the Shah's U.S.-backed government falls in a popular uprising. The crisis continues for 444 days.

1981   President Reagan's tax cuts are passed by Congress. The economy grows for nine years, but so does the national debt.

1982   The Equal Rights Amendment, guaranteeing women and others equal rights, fails to be ratified by enough states to change the Constitution. The Space Shuttle *Columbia* successfully returns from space.

1983   281 U.S. and French military personnel serving in a UN peacekeeping force in Lebanon are killed by terrorist bombs. President Reagan and six Carribbean nations send troops into Grenada to restore democratic government.

1984   Marines are withdrawn from Lebanon; civil war continues.

1985   President Reagan and Soviet leader Mikhail Gorbachev hold their first summit. Congress passes GrammRudman bill to try to reduce government spending.

1986   Space Shuttle *Challenger* explodes while the world watches on TV. U.S. war planes attack Libya in response to terrorism. AIDS is acknowledged as an international health emergency.

1989   President Bush sends troops into Panama and ousts Gen. Manuel Noriega. U.S., U.S.S.R. and their allies declare the end of the Cold War.

1990   U.S. sends troops to Saudi Arabia to protect Middle East allies after Iraqi leader Saddam Hussein seizes Kuwait.

1991   U.S. and other UN forces bomb Iraq and reclaim Kuwait.

1992   Bill Clinton elected president. U.S. with U.N. enters Somalia.

1993   World Trade Center bombed. Great flood in the Midwest. Brady Bill (gun law) signed.

1994   NAFTA takes effect. Earthquake in L.A. Republican party gains control of congress.

1995   U.S. with the U.N. enters Haiti. Truck bomb destroys federal building in Oklahoma City. Diplomatic relations with Vietnam re-established. War ends in Bosnia. U.S. sends peacekeepers.

1996   TWA flight 800 crashes. Bomb explodes at the Olympics in Atlanta. Clinton re-elected.

1997   Madeline Albright becomes 1st woman Secretary of State. Tobacco companies agree to settlements in anti-smoking suits.

1998   Clinton sex scandal erupts. El Nino weather patterns prevail. Unrest in Kosovo. House votes to impeach Clinton. Senate does not remove Clinton from office. Terrorists bomb embassies in Kenya and Tanzania.

1999   U.S. leads the world in preparations to avoid computer system disruption, "Y2K bug;" there is little disruption at 1/1/2000. Children attack several schools around the country. Millennium terrorist attacks, expected at the New Year, don't occur. U.S. economic expansion and prosperity and explosive growth in the use of the internet, third-world population, and AIDS continue.

2000   Vice-President Al Gore (Democrat) and Texas Governor George W. Bush, son of President George Bush, (Republican) ran in the 2000 presidential election. Improvements in health care and education as well as violence and smoking among children were issues in the presidential campaign. The election was a virtual tie. Al Gore won the popular vote, but George W. Bush won the majority of the Electoral College and became president. The final decision depended on who would get Florida's electors, and the decision was delayed for weeks while Florida recounted votes.

2001   Before leaving office, President Clinton ordered several regulatory changes that he had not been able to get through Congress, and, like most presidents, he gave out several presidential pardons. President Bush reversed some of the regulatory changes, and Clinton's pardons caused the last scandal of his administration. Bush appointed popular General Colin Powell as Secretary of State, but some of his more conservative cabinet appointments caused controversy. A major campaign financing reform bill, trying to reduce the influence of "big money" on politics, and the President's budget providing a $1.6 trillion tax cut over ten years dominated the work of Congress early in the year. Incidents of violence by children in the public schools continued. The U.S. economy slowed down and the stock market, particularly technology stocks, continued a drop begun in 2000. This raised questions about future surpluses politicians around the country were counting on.

22: Folk Songs

Places

The Banks of the Ohio
Dixie
Down in the Valley
The Eyes of Texas
Home on the Range
My Old Kentucky Home
Red River Valley
The Sidewalks of New York
The Streets of Laredo

Traveling

Five Hundred Miles
Freight Train
The Golden Vanity
Sloop John B.
The Wabash Cannonball

Work

Blow the Man Down
Drill, Ye Tarriers, Drill
The Erie Canal
Git Along Little Dogies
Goodbye, Old Paint
I've Been Working on the Railroad

Children's Songs

Bingo
Hush Little Baby
This Old Man
Pop Goes the Weasel
Rock-a-Bye Baby
Row, Row, Row Your Boat
Skip to My Lou
Old MacDonald
Three Blind Mice

People

Barbara Allen
Casey Jones
Clementine
Dan Tucker
Go Tell Aunt Rhodie
Jeanie with the Light Brown Hair
John Henry
Oh, Susanna
She'll Be Coming 'Round the Mountain
Sweet Betsy from Pike
Tom Dooley

Love

Black Is the Color of My True Love's Hair
Goodnight Irene
House of the Rising Sun
In the Good Old Summertime
My Bonnie Lies over the Ocean
On Top of Old Smokey

Animals

Blue Tail Fly
The Fox
Froggie Went A-Courtin'
The Old Gray Mare

Play

A Bicycle Built for Two
Camptown Races
For He's a Jolly Good Fellow
Happy Birthday
Mountain Dew
Turkey in the Straw

Spirituals

Amazing Grace
Joshua Fought the Battle of Jericho
Kum Bay Yah
Nobody Knows the Trouble I've Seen
Old Folks at Home
Rock of Ages
Rock-a My Soul
Swing Low, Sweet Chariot
When the Saints Go Marching In

Patriotism

The Battle Hymn of the Republic
When Johnny Comes Marching Home Again
Yankee Doodle

Modern

Blowin' in the Wind
Brother, Can You Spare a Dime?
City of New Orleans
If I Had a Hammer
Old Man River
We Shall Overcome

23: Nursery Rhymes

Common Nursery Rhymes

Humpty Dumpty
Humpty Dumpty sat on a wall,
Humpty Dumpty had a great fall.
All the king's horses and all the king's men
Couldn't put Humpty together again.

There Was an Old Woman
There was an old woman
Who lived in a shoe,
She had so many children
She didn't know what to do.
She gave them some broth,
Without any bread,
Whipped them all soundly,
 And sent them to bed.

The Cat and the Fiddle
Hey diddle diddle,
The cat and the fiddle,
The cow jumped over the moon.
The little dog laughed to see such sport,
And the dish ran away with the spoon.

Old Mother Hubbard
Old Mother Hubbard went to the cupboard
To get her poor dog a bone.
But when she got there, the cupboard was bare,
And so the poor dog had none.

Jack and Jill
Jack and Jill went up the hill
To fetch a pail of water.
Jack fell down and broke his crown
And Jill came tumbling after.

Baa, Baa, Black Sheep
Baa, baa, black sheep, have you any wool?
Yes, sir, yes, sir, three bags full.
One for my master and one for my dame
And one for the little boy who lives down the lane
Baa, baa, black sheep, have you any wool?
Yes, sir, yes, sir, three bags full.

Hickory Dickory Dock
Hickory dickory dock,
The mouse ran up the clock
The clock struck one,
The mouse ran down,
Hickory dickory dock.

Mary Had a Little Lamb
Mary had a little lamb,
Little lamb, little lamb,
Mary had a little lamb
Its fleece was white as snow.
And everywhere that Mary went,
Mary went, Mary went,
Everywhere that Mary went
The lamb was sure to go.

Old King Cole
Old King Cole was a merry old soul,
And a merry old soul was he.
He called for his pipe
And he called for his bowl
And he called for his fiddlers three.
Every fiddler had a very fine fiddle
And a very fine fiddle had he.
Oh, there's none so rare as can compare
With King Cole and his fiddlers three.

Rain, Rain, Go Away
Rain, rain, go away,
Come again some other day.

Rock-a-bye Baby
Rock-a-bye, baby, on the treetop
When the wind blows the cradle will rock.
When the bough breaks, the cradle will fall,
And down will come baby, cradle and all.

Thirty Days
Thirty days hath September,
April, June and November.
All the rest have thirty-one,
Save February which alone
Has twenty-eight and one day more
When Leap Year comes one year in four.

Solomon Grundy
Solomon Grundy,
Born on Monday,
Christened on Tuesday,
Married on Wednesday,
Sick on Thursday,
Worse on Friday,
Died on Saturday,
Buried on Sunday.
That was the end
Of Solomon Grundy.

One, Two, Buckle My Shoe
One, two, buckle my shoe,
Three, four, open the door,
Five, six, pick up sticks,
Seven, eight, lay them straight.
Nine, ten, a big fat hen,
Eleven, twelve, dig and delve,
Thirteen, fourteen, maids a-courting,
Fifteen, sixteen, maids in the kitchen,
Seventeen, eighteen, maids a-waiting,
Nineteen, twenty, food's a-plenty,
My plate is empty.

ABCs
A,b,c,d,e,f,g,
H,i,j,k,l,m,n,o,p,
Q,r,s,t,u,v,
W. x, y and z.
Now I know my ABCs,
Next time won't you sing with me?

Others

Bow, Wow, Wow, Whose Dog Art Thou?
Bye, Baby Bunting
Cock-a-doodle Doo
Cock Robin
Diddle, Diddle, Dumpling, My Son John
Doctor Foster Went to Gloucester
Georgie Porgie
Goosey Goosey Gander
Hark, Hark, the Dogs Do Bark
Here We Go Round the Mulberry Bush
Hot Cross Buns
Jack Be Nimble
Jack Sprat
Little Bo Peep
Little Boy Blue
Little Jack Horner
Little Miss Muffet
Mistress Mary, Quite Contrary

Now I Lay Me Down to Sleep
Old Mother Goose
Pat-a-cake, Pat-a-cake, Baker's Man
Pease Porridge Hot
Peter, Peter, Pumpkin Eater
Pussy Cat, Pussy Cat
The Queen of Hearts
Ride a Cock Horse
Ring around the Roses
Simple Simon
Sing a Song of Sixpence
There Was a Crooked Man
This is the House that Jack Built
Three Little Kittens
Tom, Tom, the Piper's Son
To Market, to Market, to Buy a Fat Pig
Wee Willie Winkie
What Are Little Boys Made of?

Tongue Twisters

Peter Piper picked a peck of pickled peppers,
A peck of pickled peppers, Peter Piper picked.
If Peter Piper picked a peck of pickled peppers,
Where's the peck of pickled peppers
   Peter Piper picked?

She sells sea shells by the seashore.
The shells she sells are seashore shells.

Round and round the rough and ragged rock the
ragged rascal ran.

Rubber baby buggy bumpers

The sixth sheik's sixth sheep's sick.

Betty bought some butter, "But," she said, "this butter's bitter, and a bit of better butter would make a better batter." So she bought a bit of butter better than the bitter butter, and it made her batter better—so it was that Betty bought a bit of better butter!

A tutor who tooted a flute
Tried to teach two tooters to toot.
Said the two to the tutor,
"Is it harder to toot or
To tutor two tooters to toot?"

24: Light Verse

Light Verse

The Owl and the Pussy-cat

The Owl and the Pussy-cat went to sea
    In a beautiful pea-green boat.
They took some honey, and plenty of money,
    Wrapped up in a five-pound note.
The Owl looked up to the stars above,
    And sang to a small guitar,
"O lovely Pussy! O Pussy, my love,
  What a beautiful Pussy you are,
    You are,
    You are!
What a beautiful Pussy you are!

Pussy said to Owl, "You elegant fowl!
    How charmingly sweet you sing!
O let us be married! too long we have tarried:
    But what shall we do for a ring?"
They sailed away, for a year and a day,
    To the land where the Bong-tree grows
And there in a wood a Piggy-wig stood
    With a ring at the end of his nose,
    His nose,
    His nose,
    With a ring at the end of his nose.

"Dear Pig, are you willing to sell for one shilling
    Your ring?" Said the Piggy, "I will."
So they took it away, and were married next day
    By the Turkey who lives on the hill.
They dined on mince, and slices of quince,
    Which they ate with a runcible spoon;
And hand in hand, on the edge of the sand,
    They danced by the light of the moon,
    The moon,
    The moon,
    They danced by the light of the moon.
    —*Edward Lear, 1851*

Wynken, Blynken, and Nod

Wynken, Blynken, and Nod one night
    Sailed off in a wooden shoe,—
Sailed on a river of crystal light
    into a sea of dew.
"Where are you going, and what do you wish?"
    The old moon asked the three.

"We have come to fish for the herring-fish
    That live in this beautiful sea;
Nets of silver and gold have we,"
    Said Wynken,
      Blynken,
        And Nod.

The old moon laughed and sang a song,
    As they rocked in the wooden shoe;
And the wind that sped them all night long
    Ruffled the waves of dew;
The little stars were the herring-fish
    That lived in the beautiful sea.
"Now cast your nets wherever you wish,—
    Never afraid are we!"
So cried the stars to the fishermen three,
    Wynken,
      Blynken,
        And Nod.

All night long their nets they threw
    To the stars in the twinkling foam,—
Then down from the skies came the wooden shoe,
    Bringing the fishermen home:
'Twas all so pretty a sail, it seemed
    As if it could not be;
And some folk thought 'twas a dream they'd dreamed
    Of sailing that beautiful sea;
But I shall name you the fishermen three:
    Wynken,
      Blynken,
        And Nod.

Wynken and Blynken are two little eyes,
    And Nod is a little head,
And the wooden shoe that sailed the skies
    Is a wee one's trundle-bed;
So shut your eyes while Mother sings
    Of wonderful sights that be,
And you shall see the beautiful things
    As you rock in the misty sea
Where the old shoe rocked the fishermen three:—
    Wynken,
      Blynken,
        And Nod.
    —*Eugene Field*

As I Was Going to Saint Ives

As I was going to Saint Ives
I met a man with seven wives.
Every wife had seven sacks,
Every sack had seven cats,
Every cat had seven kits.
Kits, cats, sacks and wives,
How many were going to Saint Ives?

Paul Revere's Ride

Listen my children, and you shall hear
Of the midnight ride of Paul Revere,
On the eighteenth of April in Seventy-five;
Hardly a man is now alive
Who remembers that famous day and year . . .
—*Henry Wadsworth Longfellow*

Nonsense Verse

Jabberwocky

'Twas brillig, and the slithy toves
    Did gyre and gimble in the wabe;
All mimsy were the borogroves,
    And the mome raths outgrabe.

"Beware the Jabberwock, my son!
    The jaws that bite, the claws that catch!
Beware the Jubjub bird, and shun
    The frumious Bandersnatch!"

He took his vorpal sword in hand;
    Long time the manxome foe he sought—
So rested he by the Tumtum tree,
    And stood awhile in thought.

And, as in uffish thought he stood,
    The Jabberwock, with eyes of flame,
Came whiffling through the tulgey wood,
    And burbled as it came!

One, two! One, two! And through and through
    The vorpal blade went snicker-snack!
He left it dead, and with its head,
    He went galumphing back.

"And hast thou slain the Jabberwock?
    Come to my arms, my beamish boy!
O frabjous day! Callooh! Callay!"
    He chortled in his joy.

'Twas brillig, and the slithy toves
    Did gyre and gimble in the wabe;
All mimsy were the borogroves,
    And the mome raths outgrabe.
    —*Lewis Carroll, 1871*

As I was going up the stair

As I was going up the stair,
    I met a man who wasn't there.
He wasn't there again today –
    I wish that he would go away!

    —*Anonymous*

The Jumblies

They went to sea in a sieve, they did;
    In a sieve they went to sea;
In spite of all their friends could say,
On a winter's morn, on a stormy day,
    In a sieve they went to sea.

And when the sieve turned round and round,
    And everyone cried, "You'll be drowned!"
They called aloud, "Our seive ain't big,
But we don't care a button, we don't care a fig—
    In a seive we'll go to sea!"

Far and few, far and few,
    Are the lands where the Jumblies live.
Their heads are green, and their hands are blue;
    And they went to sea in a sieve.
    —*Edward Lear, 1871*

The Crocodile

How doth the little crocodile
    Improve his shining tail,
And pour the waters of the Nile
    On every golden scale!

How cheerfully he seems to grin,
    How neatly spreads his claws,
And welcomes little fishes in,
    With gently smiling jaws.
    —*Lewis Carroll, 1871*

The Common Cormorant

The common cormorant or shag
    Lays eggs inside a paper bag.
The reason you will see no doubt
    It is to keep the lightning out.
But what these unobservant birds
    Have never noticed is that herds
Of wandering bears may come with buns
    And steal the bags to hold the crumbs.
    —*Anonymous*

25: American Literature and Cinema

1776-1830

Cooper, James Fenimore	(1789-1851)	The Last of the Mohicans
Franklin, Benjamin	(1706-1790)	Poor Richard's Almanack
Irving, Washington	(1783-1859)	"Rip Van Winkle," "Legend of Sleepy Hollow"
Paine, Thomas	(1737-1809)	Common Sense, The Crisis

The American Rennaissance (1830-1870)

Alcott, Louisa May	(1832-1888)	Little Women
Emerson, Ralph Waldo	(1803-1882)	Essays, Nature
Fuller, Margaret	(1810-1850)	Woman in the Nineteenth Century
Hawthorne, Nathaniel	(1804-1864)	The Scarlet Letter
Melville, Herman	(1819-1891)	Moby Dick, Billy Budd
Poe, Edgar Allen	(1809-1849)	The Fall of the House of Usher
Stowe, Harriet Beecher	(1811-1896)	Uncle Tom's Cabin
Thoreau, Henry David	(1817-1862)	Walden

Modern Literature (1870-1940)

Anderson, Sherwood	(1876-1941)	Winesburg, Ohio
Cather, Willa	(1876-1947)	Death Comes for the Archbishop
Chopin, Kate	(1851-1904)	The Awakening
Crane, Stephen	(1871-1900)	The Red Badge of Courage
Dreiser, Theodore	(1871-1945)	Sister Carrie
Faulkner, William	(1897-1962)	The Sound and the Fury
Fitzgerald, F. Scott	(1896-1940)	The Great Gatsby
Hemingway, Ernest	(1899-1961)	The Sun Also Rises
Henry, O.	(1862-1910)	The Gift of the Magi
James, Henry	(1843-1916)	Portrait of a Lady, The Bostonians
Lewis, Sinclair	(1885-1951)	Babbit, Main Street, Arrowsmith
London, Jack	(1876-1916)	The Call of the Wild, Sea Wolf
Mitchell, Margaret	(1900-1949)	Gone with the Wind
Porter, Katherine Ann	(1890-1980)	Flowering Judas; Pale Horse, Pale Rider
Sinclair, Upton	(1878-1968)	The Jungle
Stein, Gertrude	(1874-1946)	Three Lives
Steinbeck, John	(1902-1968)	The Grapes of Wrath
Tarkington, Booth	(1869-1946)	Seventeen, Penrod
Twain, Mark	(1835-1910)	Huckleberry Finn, Tom Sawyer
Wharton, Edith	(1862-1937)	Ethan Frome, The Age of Innocence
Williams, William Carlos	(1883-1963)	Tempers
Wodehouse, P.G.	(1881-1975)	Anything Goes
Wolfe, Thomas	(1900-1938)	You Can't Go Home Again
Wright, Richard	(1908-1960)	Native Son, Black Boy

Contemporary Literature (1940-)

Angelou, Maya	(1928-)	I Kow Why the Caged Bird Sings
Baldwin, James	(1924- 1987)	The Fire Next Time
Bellow, Saul	(1915-)	Herzog

Bradbury, Ray	(1920-)	Farenheit 451
Capote, Truman	(1924-1984)	In Cold Blood
Cheever, John	(1912-1982)	The Wapshot Chronicle
Doctorow, E. L.	(1931-)	Ragtime
Ellison, Ralph	(1914-1994)	The Invisible Man
Heller, Joseph	(1923-1999)	Catch-22
Hersey, John	(1914-1993)	A Bell for Adano
Lee, Harper	(1926-)	To Kill a Mockingbird
Mailer, Norman	(1923-)	The Naked and the Dead
Malamud, Bernard	(1914-1986)	The Fixer, The Natural
McCullers, Carson	(1917-1967)	The Heart is a Lonely Hunter
McMurtry, Larry	(1936-)	Lonesome Dove, Leaving Cheyenne
Michener, James	(1907-1998)	Tales of the South Pacific
Morrison, Toni	(1931-)	Tar Baby, Beloved
Oates, Joyce Carol	(1938-)	Do with Me What You Will
Pynchon, Thomas	(1937-)	Gravity's Rainbow
Rand, Ayn	(1905-1982)	Atlas Shrugged
Roth, Philip	(1933-)	Portnoy's Complaint, Zuckerman Unbound
Salinger, J. D.	(1919-)	Catcher in the Rye
Tan, Amy	(1952-)	The Joy Luck Club
Updike, John	(1932-)	Rabbit, Run
Vonnegut, Kurt	(1922-)	Slaughterhouse Five, Jailbird
Walker, Alice	(1944-)	The Color Purple
Warren, Robert Penn	(1905-1989)	All the King's Men
Welty, Eudora	(1909-)	The Optimist's Daughter

Poets

Benet, Stephen Vincent	(1898-1943)	John Brown's Body
Bradstreet, Anne	(c.1612-1672)	The Tenth Muse Lately Sprung up in America
Brooks, Gwendolyn	(1917-)	The Bean Eaters, "Malcolm X"
cummings, e. e.	(1894-1962)	Tulips and Chimneys
Dickinson, Emily	(1830-1886)	"There's a Certain Slant of Light"
Eliot, T. S.	(1888-1965)	"The Waste Land," "Four Quartets"
Frost, Robert	(1874-1963)	"Birches," "Mending Wall"
Ginsberg, Allen	(1926-1998)	"Howl"
Jeffers, Robinson	(1887-1966)	"Shine Perishing Republic," "Hurt Hawks"
Longfellow, Henry W.	(1807-1882)	"Evangeline," "Hiawatha"
Nash, Ogden	(1902-1971)	I'm a Stranger Here Myself
Parker, Dorothy	(1893-1967)	Laments for the Living
Plath, Sylvia	(1932-1963)	The Colossus
Poe, Edgar Allen	(1809-1849)	"The Raven"
Pound, Ezra	(1885-1972)	The Cantos
Riley, James Whitcomb	(1849-1916)	"When the Frost is on the Pumpkin"
Robinson, Edward	(1869-1935)	"Richard Cory"
Sandberg, Carl	(1878-1967)	Chicago Poems
Teasdale, Sara	(1884-1933)	"Helen of Troy"
Millay, Edna St. Vincent	(1892-1950)	A Few Figs from Thistles
Warren, Robert Penn	(1905-1989)	"Brother to Dragons"
Whitman, Walt	(1819-1892)	"Song of Myself"

Playwrights

Albee, Edward	(1928-)	Who's Afraid of Virginia Woolf?
Baraka, Imamu Amiri	(1934-)	Dutchman, The Slave
Hart, Moss	(1904-1961)	Once in a Lifetime
Hellman, Lillian	(1904-1984)	The Little Foxes
Hughes, Langston	(1902-1967)	Shakespeare in Harlem
Mamet, David	(1947-)	American Buffalo
Miller, Arthur	(1915-)	Death of a Salesman
Odets, Clifford	(1906-1963)	Waiting for Lefty, The Golden Boy
O'Neill, Eugene	(1888-1953)	Long Day's Journey into Night
Saroyan, William	(1980-1981)	The Human Comedy
Shepard, Sam	(1943-)	True West, Buried Child
Sherwood, Robert	(1896-1955)	The Petrified Forest
Simon, Neil	(1927-)	Barefoot in the Park
Wilder, Thornton	(1897-1975)	Our Town
Williams, Tennessee	(1911-1983)	A Streetcar Named Desire

Academy Awards (Oscars) - Best Films

1960	The Apartment		1983	Terms of Endearment
1961	West Side Story		1984	Amadeus
1962	Lawrence of Arabia		1985	Out of Africa
1963	Tom Jones		1986	Platoon
1964	My Fair Lady		1987	The Last Emperor
1965	The Sound of Music		1988	Rainman
1966	A Man for All Seasons		1989	Driving Miss Daisy
1967	In the Heat of the Night		1990	Dances with Wolves
1968	Oliver!		1991	The Silence of the Lambs
1969	Midnight Cowboy		1992	Unforgiven
1970	Patton		1993	Schindler's List
1971	The French Connection		1994	Forrest Gump
1972	The Godfather		1995	Braveheart
1973	The Sting		1996	The English Patient
1974	The Godfather, Part II		1997	Titanic
1975	One Flew Over the Cuckoo's Nest		1998	Shakespeare in Love
1976	Rocky		1999	Life is Beautiful
1977	Annie Hall		2000	American Beauty
1978	The Deer Hunter		2001	Gladiator
1979	Kramer vs. Kramer			
1980	Ordinary People			
1981	Chariots of Fire			
1982	Ghandi			

26: A Few Famous Quotations

Early to bed and early to rise, makes a man healthy, wealthy and wise.

Nothing is certain but death and taxes.

There never was a good war or a bad peace.

Benjamin Franklin, *Poor Richard's Almanack*, 1732-1757

Taxation without representation is tyranny.   **James Otis, 1761**

By uniting we stand, by dividing we fall.   **John Dickinson, 1775**

Give me liberty or give me death.   **Patrick Henry, 1775**

Don't one of you fire until you see the whites of their eyes.   **William Prescott, 1775**

We must all hang together, else we shall all hang seperately.   **Benjamin Franklin, 1776**

I only regret that I have but one life to give for my country.   **Nathan Hale, 1776**

I have just begun to fight.   **John Paul Jones, 1779**

These are the times that try men's souls.   **Thomas Paine, 1785**

To be prepared for war is one of the most effectual means of preserving peace.   **George Washington, 1790**

There is always room at the top.   **Daniel Webster**

Be sure you are right, then go ahead.   **Davy Crockett, 1812**

Don't give up the ship.   **Capt. James Lawrence, 1813**

Go West, young man.   **John L. B. Soule, 1851**

The mass of men lead lives of quiet desperation.   **Henry David Thoreau, 1854**

It is well that war is so terrible—we would grow too fond of it.   **Robert E. Lee, 1862**

You can fool all of the people some of the time and some of the people all of the time, but you can't fool all of the people all of the time.   **Abraham Lincoln, 1863**

The true republic—men, their rights and nothing more; women, their rights and nothing less.   **Susan B. Anthony, 1868**

There's a sucker born every minute.   **P.T. Barnum**

Politics makes strange bedfellows.   **Charles Dudley Warner, 1871**

There's many a boy here today who looks on war as all glory, but, boys, it is all hell.   **Gen. William T. Sherman, 1888**

Everybody talks about the weather, but nobody does anything about it.   **Charles Warner, 1890**

Some Famous Quotations (Continued)

The report of my death was an exaggeration.	Mark Twain, 1897
Speak softly and carry a big stick; you will go far.	Theodore Roosevelt, 1901
Win one for the Gipper.	Knute Rockne, 1921
You are all a lost generation.	Gertrude Stein, 1926
What this country really needs is a good five-cent cigar.	Thomas Riley Marshall
Never give a sucker an even break.	W. C. Fields
I tell you, folks, all politics is apple sauce.	Will Rogers, 1932
I never forget a face, but in your case I'll make an exception.	Groucho Marx
The only thing we have to fear is fear itself.	Franklin D. Roosevelt, 1933
A radical is a man with both feet firmly in the air.	Franklin D. Roosevelt, 1939
Here's looking at you, kid. Play it again, Sam.	Humphrey Bogart, *Casablanca*, 1943
You can never be too rich or too thin.	Wallis Simpson, Duchess of Windsor
The world is run by C students. The buck stops here.	Harry S. Truman, 1945
Fasten your seat belts; it's going to be a bumpy night.	Bette Davis, *All About Eve,* 1950
Ask not what your country can do for you; ask what you can do for your country.	John F. Kennedy, 1961
You win some, you lose some, and some get rained out.	C. E. Wood
One small step for a man, one giant step for mankind.	Neil Armstrong, 1969
I cried all the way to the bank.	Liberace, 1973
Nice guys finish last.	Leo Durocher, 1975
Sometimes when I look at my children, I say to myself, "Lillian, you should have stayed a virgin."	Lillian Carter, 1980
How do I know why there were Nazis? I don't even know how to work the can opener.	Woody Allen, *Hannah and Her Sisters,* 1986

Sources: The Harper Book of American Quotations, Gordon Carruth and Eugene Ehrlich, eds. Harper & Row, New York , 1988
Wit and Wisdom of Famous American Women, Evelyn Beilenson and Ann Tenenbaum, eds. Peter Pauper Press, Inc., White Plains, 1986

27: Proverbs

Note: The list of proverbs has been correlated with the list of Topics (pp. 55-135). The assignment of a proverb to a particular semantic category can be done according to several different criteria. We have assigned the proverbs mostly on the basis of their literal, rather than figurative, meaning.

Food
Half a loaf is better than none.
Variety is the spice of life.
The bread is buttered on both sides.

Cooking
Too many cooks spoil the broth.
The pot calls the kettle black.
Out of the frying pan and into the fire.

Eating
Don't bite the hand that feeds you.
You can't eat your cake and have it too.
First come, first served.

Housing/Housekeeping
There's no place like home.
People in glass houses shouldn't throw stones.
Walls have ears.

Clothing
Too big for their britches.
If the shoe fits, wear it.
A stitch in time saves nine.

Relationships
Every man for himself.
A friend in need is a friend indeed.
Familiarity breeds contempt.
Live and let live.
It takes one to know one.
Two is company, three is a crowd.
Spare the rod and spoil the child.

Human Qualities
He who hesitates is lost.
Honesty is the best policy.
Haste makes waste.
Where there's a will, there's a way.
Beauty is only skin deep.
Beggars can't be choosers.

Human Stages
A sucker is born every minute.
Don't throw out the baby with the bath water.
Boys will be boys.
Never say die.
Dead men tell no tales.

Time
Time heals all wounds.
Never put off 'til tomorrow what you can do today.
Rome was not built in a day.
Better late than never.
Here today, gone tomorrow.
Last but not least.

Weather
Save it for a rainy day.
Make hay while the sun shines.
It never rains but it pours.
Red sky at morning, sailors take warning;
    Red sky at night, sailor's delight.

Animals
You can't make a silk purse out of a sow's ear.
Don't throw pearls before swine.
His bark is worse than his bite.
Let sleeping dogs lie.
You can't teach an old dog new tricks.
Curiosity killed the cat.
Let the cat out of the bag.
There are many ways to skin a cat.
When the cat's away the mice will play.
You can lead a horse to water but you can't
    make it drink.
Don't look a gift horse in the mouth.

Birds
The early bird catches the worm.
Kill two birds with one stone.
 A bird in the hand is worth two in the bush.
Birds of a feather flock together.
Don't count your chickens before they hatch.

Language
Easier said than done.
No sooner said than done.
Ask me no questions and I'll tell you no lies.
Actions speak louder than words.

Thinking
Seeing is believing.
Out of sight, out of mind.
Necessity is the mother of invention.
Let your conscience be your guide.
Two heads are better than one.

Numbers/ Measures

Six of one and half-dozen of another.
Give them an inch and they'll take a mile.
One picture is worth a thousand words.

Substances and Materials

A rolling stone gathers no moss.
All that glitters is not gold.
Good riddance to bad rubbish.
Every little bit helps.

Containers

Don't put all your eggs in one basket.
One rotten apple spoils the barrel.

Emotions

Love makes the world go 'round.
Absence makes the heart grow fonder.
It's no use crying over spilled milk.
Better safe than sorry.
Misery loves company.
Once bitten, twice shy.
He who laughs last, laughs best.

The Body

In one ear and out the other.
Don't cut off your nose to spite your face.
Blood is thicker than water.
Look before you leap.

Transportation

Don't put the cart before the horse.
Like carrying coals to Newcastle.
Time and tide wait for no man.

Money

Money doesn't grow on trees.
Money talks.
Money is the root of all evil.
A fool and his money are soon parted.
A penny saved is a penny earned.
The best things in life are free.
Easy come, easy go.

Recreation

All work and no play makes Jack a dull boy.
The more the merrier.
Thank God it's Friday.
All work and no play makes Jack a dull boy.

Sports and Games

Slow and steady wins the race.
Sink or swim.
It's not whether you win or lose,
    but how you play the game.
If you can't beat 'em, join 'em.
Practice makes perfect.

Medicine and health

An apple a day keeps the doctor away.
An ounce of prevention is worth a pound of cure.
One man's food is another man's poison.
What's good for the goose is good for the gander.

Business

Nothing ventured, nothing gained.
Everyone has their price.
Business before pleasure.
The customer is always right.

Shops and Tools

Jack of all trades, master of none.
Hit the nail on the head.
Give me the right tool, I will move the world.

Law

Truth will out.
Two wrongs don't make a right.
The end justifies the means.

Media

Bad news travels fast.
No news is good news.
The pen is mightier than the sword.
Don't judge a book by its cover.

Education

Practice what you preach.
Do as I say, not as I do.

War

Don't give up the ship.
All is fair in love and war.
War is hell.

Energy

Where there's smoke, there's fire.
Burn the candle at both ends.
Fight fire with fire.

Source: The Dictionary of American Proverbs, David Kin, ed. Philosophical Library.

28: Superstitions

The **ace of spades** is a sign of death.

Getting out of **bed** on the wrong side means you will have a bad day.

Letting a **black cat** cross your path brings bad luck.

The **bride** should not see the **husband** on the morning before the wedding.

Cattle lying down indicate rain.

A four-leaf **clover** brings good luck.

A **cricket** in the house is good luck.

Hanging a **horseshoe** over the door, points up, brings good luck.

Passing under a **ladder** brings bad luck.

Killing a **ladybug** beetle brings bad luck.

Lightning never strikes twice in the same place.

Lighting three cigarettes from one **match** brings bad luck or pregnancy to the third person.

Breaking a **mirror** brings seven years of bad luck.

Finding a **penny** brings good luck ("see a penny, pick it up, all day long you'll have good luck").

Carrying a **rabbit's foot** brings good luck.

Spilling **salt** brings bad luck, but a pinch of the spilled salt thrown over your right shoulder will keep away evil spirits.

Killing a **spider** brings rain.

If you make a wish on a falling **star,** your wish will come true.

The number **thirteen** brings bad luck.

Opening an **umbrella** in the house brings bad luck.

29: Curses and Oaths

Note: A word of caution is in order. This list is included for the purpose of comprehension. It is ill-advised to attempt to use these curses and oaths until one is thoroughly acculturated. The words in this list are not all equally offensive, but they are all potentially dangerous if not used properly.

Mild Words and Phrases

Cripes	Fudge	Heck	Phooey
Dang	Gee	Holy cow	Shoot
Dang it	Golly	Holy smoke	Shucks
Darn	Gosh	I'll be darned	Son of a gun
Darn it	Heavens	Jeez	Sugar

Mild Insults

Boob, Boobie	Doofus	Good for nothing	Pig
Buffoon	Dork	Harebrained	Scaredy cat
Bum	Dumb	Hopeless	Silly
Chicken	Dumbbell	Idiot	Stupid
Clown	Dummy	Jerk	Turkey
Cow	Flake	Nerd	Useless
Crazy	Fool	Nincompoop	Weenie
Creep	'Fraidy cat	Nut	Witch
Dog			Worthless

Strong Words and Phrases

Christ	Frigging	God	Jesus Christ
Crap	Fuck	God damn it	Jesus H. Christ
Damn	Fucking A	Hell	Shit
Damn it			Son of a bitch (SOB)

Strong Insults

Note to students: These words are particularly dangerous. Some native speakers of English in the U. S. and Canada use these words in a joking way – in fact some young people use them so often that the words have become almost meaningless. However, we <u>strongly</u> recommend that you avoid them. You may think you are joking, but you can hurt the person you insult or make them very angry. If you hear these words, do not assume that the person is attacking someone; they may be joking. It is good to understand these words and to know how they are used, but **do not use them yourself.**

Note to teachers: These words are not put here to encourage you to teach them. Some teachers have been angered that we have included this page. However, many more teachers have encouraged us to keep it. When they are asked by students to teach them about swearing in English, this presentation helps. If you are offended, please understand that other professionals find this page useful. This book is your reference, not a student text, but if you are uncomfortable having this page in your book, we encourage you to cut it out of the book, replacing it with a photocopy of page 195.

Ass	Dumb shit	Go fuck yourself	Shithead
Asshole	Eat me	Go to hell	Shove it up your ass
Bastard	Eat shit	Mother fucker	Slut
Bitch	Fuck face	Piss off	Son of a bitch
Cocksucker	Fucking asshole	Prick	Suck my dick
Dick	Fuck you	Queer	Up yours
Dumb fuck	Fucker	Screw you	Whore

30: Names

Most Common First Names (Given to babies in 1990s)*

Rank	Girls	Rank	Girls	Rank	Boys	Rank	Boys
1	Ashley	6	Emily	1	Michael	6	Tyler
2	Sarah	7	Megan	2	Christopher	7	Brandon
3	Jessica	8	Samantha	3	Matthew	8	Zachary
4	Kaitlyn	9	Brianna	4	Joshua	9	Jacob
5	Brittany	10	Kayla	5	Nicholas	10	Andrew

Other Common Women's Names

Alice	Catherine	Ellen	Jennifer	Lauren	Nicole
Alison	Christina	Gail	Jessica	Linda	Paula
Amanda	Claire	Hannah	Jill	Margaret	Patricia
Amber	Crystal	Heather	Joan	Mary	Rachel
Amy	Danielle	Helen	Judith	Marilyn	Rebecca
Ann	Deborah	Jackie	Karen	Martha	Ruth
Anita	Diane	Jane	Kathleen	Melissa	Susan
Barbara	Donna	Janet	Kimberly	Michelle	Stephanie
Carol	Elizabeth	Jean	Laura	Nancy	Tiffany
					Virginia

Other Common Men's Names

Adam	Daniel	George	Kevin	Raymond	Scott
Albert	David	Gerald	Kyle	Richard	Stanley
Alexander	Dennis	Henry	Lawrence	Robert	Steven
Allan	Donald	James	Louis	Roger	Stewart
Anthony	Douglas	Jason	Mark	Ronald	Theodore
Arthur	Edward	John	Patrick	Roy	Thomas
Benjamin	Eric	Jonathan	Paul	Ryan	Timothy
Brian	Frank	Joseph	Peter	Samuel	Walter
Charles	Fredrick	Justin	Ralph	Saul	William

The Sixty Most Common Surnames (Ranked)**

Smith(son)	Harri(son)	Lewis	Morri(son)	Mitchell	Rivera
Johnson	Thoma(son)	Robinson	King	Philip(son)	Hernandez
William(son)	Taylor	Walker	Wright	Campbell	Edwards
Brown	Moore	Gonzalez	Hill	Carter	Murphy
Jones	Jackson	Hall	Nelson	Evans	Rogers
Martin(ez)	White	Lee	Green	Lopez	Cook
Miller	Thompson	Peter(son)	Richard(son)	Turner	Perez
Davi(son)	Rodriguez	Allen(son)	Scott	Stewart	Griffin
Anderson	Clark(son)	Young	Baker	Collins	Christian(son)
Wilson	Robert(son)	Garcia	Adam(son)	Parker	Morgan

Sources: *Dr. Clevelnd Kent Evans, Bellevue University, Bellevue, NE
**Social Security Administration, Data and Research.

31: Place Names

Common Place Names

Washington	Brookfield	Canton	Lebanon
Jefferson	Deerfield	Elkton	New Haven
Madison	Fairfield	Evanston	Riverdale
Monroe	Greenfield	Hampton	Troy
Jackson	Springfield	Lexington	Hanover
Lincoln	Longmeadow	Princeton	Salem
Franklin	Edgewood	Wheaton	Richmond
Lafayette	Elmwood	Guilford	London
Leesburg	Pleasantville	Stratford	Dover
Libertyville	Summerville	Portland	Plymouth
Independence	Bloomington	Columbia	Highland Park
			Newport

English Elements of Common Place Names in the U.S. and Canada

Note: In both Canada and the United States, Indian and French place names are common; Spanish place names are very common in the Western and Southern United States. Some examples are: Indian – Saskatchewan, Ottawa, Massachusetts, Mississippi, Illinois; French – Montreal, New Orleans, Vermont, Louisiana; Spanish – Santa Fe, San Francisco, Florida, Nevada. Many places in Canada and the U.S. are also named after places in England: Boston, MA; London, ON. However, one of the most common ways of creating North American place names has been the practice of building the names from standard elements prefixed and/or suffixed to family names or animal names. This is typically English, and done mostly with English names. For example, using the family name Hart, East Hartford Junction. Using an animal, Little Deerfield Falls.

North-	- town	- City
East-	- ton	- Village
South-	- ville	- Park
West-	- apolis	- Valley
New-	- burg	- Junction
Old-	- bury	- Hills
Great-	- boro(ugh)	- Heights
Big-	- minster	- Mills
Little-	- stead	- Locks
Fort-	- sex	- Lake
Port-	- ford	- Beach
Brook-	- land	- Point
Glen-	- wood	- Haven
Mount-	- forest	- Harbor
Saint-	- field	- Shores
Oak-	- vale	- Rock
Elm-	- dale	- Bluffs
Pine-	- crest	- Falls
Maple-	- port	- Creek
Cedar-	- side	- Rapids
	- view	- Springs
	- bridge	- Ferry

32: Sports Teams in the U.S. and Canada
Major League Baseball
American League

Eastern Division		Central Division		Western Division	
Baltimore	Orioles	Chicago	White Sox	Anaheim	Angels
Boston	Red Sox	Cleveland	Indians	Oakland	Athletics
Detroit	Indians	Detroit	Tigers	Seattle	Mariners
New York	Yankees	Kansas City	Royals	Texas	Rangers
Tampa Bay	Devil Rays	Minnesota	Twins		
Toronto	Blue Jays				

National League

Eastern Division		Central Division		Western Division	
Atlanta	Braves	Chicago	Cubs	Arizona	Diamondbacks
Florida	Marlins	Cincinnati	Reds	Colorado	Rockies
Montreal	Expos	Houston	Astros	Los Angeles	Dodgers
New York	Mets	Milwaukee	Brewers	San Diego	Padres
Philadelphia	Phillies	Pittsburgh	Pirates	San Francisco	Giants
		St. Louis	Cardinals		

National Hockey League

Eastern Conference		Western Conference	
Atlantic Division		**Central Division**	
New Jersey	Devils	Chicago	Black Hawks
New York	Islanders	Detroit	Red Wings
New York	Rangers	Nashville	Predators
Philadelphia	Flyers	St. Louis	Blues
Pittsburgh	Penguins		

Northeast Division		**Pacific Division**	
Boston	Bruins	Anaheim	Mighty Ducks
Buffalo	Sabres	Dallas	Stars
Montreal	Canadiens	Los Angeles	Kings
Ottawa	Senators	Phoenix	Coyotes
Toronto	Maple Leafs	San Jose	Sharks

Southeast Division		**Northwest Division**	
Atlanta	Thrashers	Calgary	Flames
Carolina	Hurricanes	Colorado	Avalanche
Florida	Panthers	Edmonton	Oilers
Tampa Bay	Lightning	Vancouver	Canucks
Washington	Capitals		

National Basketball Association

Eastern Conference
Atlantic Division

Boston	Celtics
Miami	Heat
New Jersey	Nets
New York	Knickerbockers (Knicks)
Orlando	Magic
Philadelphia	'76ers
Washington	Wizards

Central Division

Atlanta	Hawks
Charlotte	Hornets
Chicago	Bulls
Cleveland	Cavaliers
Detroit	Pistons
Indiana	Pacers
Milwaukee	Bucks
Toronto	Raptors

Western Conference
Midwest Division

Dallas	Mavericks
Denver	Nuggets
Houston	Rockets
Minnesota	Timberwolves
San Antonio	Spurs
Utah	Jazz
Vancouver	Grizzlies

Pacific Division

Golden State	Warriors
Los Angeles	Clippers
Los Angeles	Lakers
Phoenix	Suns
Portland	Trail Blazers
Sacramento	Kings
Seattle	SuperSonics

National Football League

National Conference
Eastern Division

Dallas	Cowboys
New York	Giants
Philadelphia	Eagles
Arizona	Cardinals
Washington	Redskins

Central Division

Chicago	Bears
Detroit	Lions
Green Bay	Packers
Minnesota	Vikings
Tampa Bay	Buccaneers

Western Division

Atlanta	Falcons
Carolina	Panthers
New Orleans	Saints
San Francisco	'49ers
St. Louis	Rams

American Conference
Eastern Division

Buffalo	Bills
Indianapolis	Colts
Miami	Dolphins
New England	Patriots
New York	Jets

Central Division

Baltimore	Ravens
Cincinnati	Bengals
Cleveland	Browns
Jacksonville	Jaguars
Pittsburgh	Steelers
Tennessee	Titans

Western Division

Denver	Broncos
Kansas City	Chiefs
Oakland	Raiders
San Diego	Chargers
Seattle	Seahawks

33: Sports Personalities

Baseball

Aaron, Hank	(1934-)
Bench, Johnny	(1947-)
Berra, Yogi	(1925-)
Cobb, Ty	(1886-1961)
Dean, Dizzy	(1911-1974)
DiMaggio, Joe	(1914-1999)
Durocher, Leo	(1906-)
Gehrig, Lou	(1903-1941)
Gibson, Josh	(1911 1947)
Grove, Lefty	(1900-1975)
Hornsby, Rogers	(1896-1963)
Jackson, Reggie	(1946-)
Koufax, Sandy	(1935-)
Mantle, Mickey	(1931-)
Mays, Willie	(1931-)
McGwire, Mark	(1963-)
Musial, Stan	(1920-)
Ott, Mel	(1909-1958)
Paige, Satchel	(1906-1982)
Ripken, Cal	(1960-)
Robinson, Jackie	(1919-1972)
Ruth, Babe	(1895-1948)
Ryan, Nolan	(1947-)
Schmidt, Mike	(1949-)
Sosa, Sammy	(1968-)
Spahn, Warren	(1921 -)
Stengel, Casey	(1895-1975)
Wagner, Honus	(1874-1955)
Williams, Ted	(1918-)
Yastrzemski, Carl	(1939-)
Young, Cy	(1867-1955)

Basketball

Abdul-Jabbar, Kareem	(1947-)
Baylor, Elgin	(1934-)
Bird, Larry	(1956-)
Chamberlain, Wilt	(1936-)
Cousy, Bob	(1928-)
Erving, Julius	(1950-)
Johnson, Earvin "Magic"	(1959-)
Jordan, Michael	(1963-)
Malone, Karl	(1963-)
Malone, Moses	(1955-)
Mikan, George	(1924-)
Olajuwon, Hakeem	(1963-)
Pettit, Bob	(1932-)
Robertson, Oscar	(1938-)
Rodman, Dennis	(1961-)
Russell, Bill	(1934-)
Stockton, John	(1962-)
West, Jerry	(1938-)

Football

Bradshaw, Terry	(1948-)
Brown, Jim	(1936-)
Bryant, Paul "Bear"	(1913-1983)
Ditka, Mike	(1939-)
Dorsett, Tony	(1954-)
Elway, John	(1960-)
Graham, Otto	(1921-)
Grange, Red	(1903-1991)
Lombardi, Vince	(1913-1970)
Marino, Dan	(1961-)
Montana, Joe	(1956-)
Nagurski, Bronco	(1908-1990)
Namath, Joe	(1943-)
Payton, Walter	(1954-)
Rockne, Knute	(1883-1931)
Sanders, Barry	(1968-)
Simpson, O. J.	(1947-)
Smith, Emmitt	(1969-)
Starr, Bart	(1934-)
Staubach, Roger	(1942-)
Tarkenton, Fran	(1940-)
Unitas, Johnny	(1933-)

Golf

Berg, Patty	(1918-)
Boros, Julius	(1920-)
Hagen, Walter	(1892-1969)
Hogan, Ben	(1912-1997)
Jones, Bobby	(1902-1971)
Lopez, Nancy	(1957-)
Nelson, Byron	(1912-)
Nicklaus, Jack	(1940-)
Pak, Se Ri	(1977-)
Palmer, Arnold	(1929-)
Snead, Sam	(1912-)
Trevino, Lee	(1934-)
Watson, Tom	(1949-)
Woods, Tiger	(1975-)
Wright, Mickey	(1935-)

Figure Skating

Button, Dick	(1929-)
Fleming, Peggy	(1948-)
Hamill, Dorothy	(1957-)
Hamilton, Scott	(1958-)
Henie, Sonja	(1912-1969)
Kwan, Michelle	(1979-)
Lipinski, Tara	(1983-)

Boxing

Ali, Muhammad	(1942-)
Corbett, James J.	(1866-1933)
Dempsey, Jack	(1895-1983)
Foreman, George	(1949-)
Frazier, Joe	(1944-)
Leonard, Sugar Ray	(1956-)
Louis, Joe	(1914-1981)
Marciano, Rocky	(1923-1969)
Patterson, Floyd	(1935-)
Robinson, Sugar Ray	(1920-)
Sullivan, John L.	(1858-1918)
Tunney, Gene	(1897-1978)
Tyson, Mike	(1966-)

Track and Field

Bailey, Donovan	(1967-)
Benoit, Joan	(1957-)
Griffith Joyner, Florence	(1959-1998)
Jenner, Bruce	(1949-)
Johnson, Rafer	(1935-)
Joyner Kersee, Jackie	(1962-)
Lewis, Carl	(1961-)
Moses, Edwin	(1956-)
Oerter, Al	(1936-)
Owens, Jesse	(1913-1980)
Rudolph, Wilma	(1940-1994)
Ryun, Jim	(1947-)
Tyus, Wyomia	(1945-)
Thorpe, Jim	(1888-1953)
Zaharias, Babe Didrikson	(1914-1956)

Tennis

Ashe, Arthur	(1943-1993)
Austin, Tracy	(1962-)
Borg, Bjorn	(1956-)
Bueno, Maria	(1939-)
Connelly, Maureen	(1934-1969)
Connors, Jimmy	(1952-)
Evert, Chris	(1954-)
Gonzalez, Pancho	(1928-)
Gibson, Althea	(1927-)
Graf, Steffi	(1969-)
King, Billie Jean	(1943-)
McEnroe, John	(1959-)
Navratilova, Martina	(1956-)
Sampras, Pete	(1971-)
Seles, Monica	(1973-)
Tilden, Bill	(1893-1953)
Wills, Helen	(1906-1998)

Hockey

Bourque, Ray	(1960-)
Clarke, Bobby	(1949-)
Esposito, Phil	(1942-)
Gretzky, Wayne	(1961-)
Howe, Gordie	(1928-)
Hull, Bobby	(1939-)
Lemieux, Mario	(1965-)
Orr, Bobby	(1948-)
Richard, Maurice	(1921-)
Robinson, Larry	(1951-)
Shore, Eddie	(1902-1985)

Miscellaneous

Andretti, Mario	(1940-)	Stock car driving
Arcaro, Eddie	(1916-1997)	Horse racing
Biondi, Matt	(1965-)	Swimming
Butcher, Susan	(1955-)	Dogsled racing
Evans, Janet	(1971-)	Swimming
Foyt, A. J.	(1935-)	Stock car driving
Heiden, Eric	(1954-)	Speed Skating
Louganis, Greg	(1960-)	Diving
Pele	(1940-)	Soccer
Petty, Richard	(1937-)	Stock car driving
Pincay, Laffit	(1946-)	Horse racing
Plante, Jacques	(1929-1986)	Soccer
Retton, Mary Lou	(1968-)	Gymnastics
Shoemaker, Bill	(1931-)	Horse racing
Spitz, Mark	(1950-)	Swimming
Stewart, Jackie	(1939-)	Auto racing
Unser, A1	(1939-)	Stock car racing
Unser, Bobby	(1934-)	Stock car racing
Weissmuller, Johnny	(1903-1984)	Swimming

34: U.S. School System

Name of School	Grade	Age of Students	Subjects
Nursery School		3-5	Games, songs, creative play
Kindergarten	K	4-6	Games, drawing, crafts, beginning reading, writing
Elementary School 1-5 or 1-6	1 2 3	5-7 6-8 7-9	Reading, writing, spelling, adding, drawing, music Language arts, subtraction, spelling, drawing, music Language arts, social studies, multiplication, music
Middle School 5-9 or 6-9	4 5 6	8-10 9-11 10-12	Language arts, social studies, division Language arts, social studies, fractions Language arts, social studies, decimals, science
Junior High School	7 8	11-13 12-14	Language arts, social studies, math, science, foreign language Language arts, social studies, math, science, foreign language
High School Freshman	9	13-15	**Core Courses:** English, algebra, civics, biology, foreign language **Electives:** Music, art, typing, bookkeeping, economics, technical education, home economics
Sophmore	10	14-16	**Core Courses:** English, geometry, history, chemistry, foreign language **Electives:** Music, art, bookkeeping, economics, consumer education, computer applications
Junior	11	15-17	**Core Courses:** English, advanced math, history, physics, foreign language **Electives:** Music, art, bookkeeping, economics, consumer education, computer applications
Senior	12	16-18	**Core Courses:** English, calculus, history, foreign language **Electives:** Music, art, bookkeeping, economics, consumer education, computer programming

College and University

Undergraduate College	Age	Degree	Length of time required
Junior College	17-	AA	2 years
Four-Year College	18-	BA, BS	4-5 years
University Graduate School	21-	MA, MS	2-3 years plus thesis
Graduate school		PhD, LHD, Litt. D., DCL	3 years plus thesis
Medical school		MD, DDS	2 years plus residency
Law school		JS	3 years

35: Television
Traditional Programming

Morning	Game shows
	Daytime talk shows
	Cartoons (weekends)
	News programs/weather
	Religious programs (Sunday)
	Children's/educational programs
Afternoon	Movies
	Game shows
	Daytime talk shows
	Afternoon soap operas
	Sports events (weekends)
	News programs/weather/sports
	Children's/educational programs
Evenings	Movies
	Documentaries
	Special reports
	Drama programs
	Situation comedies
	Evening soap operas
	News programs/weather/sports
Late night	Movies
	Talk shows
	News programs

Television Sets

	Percent of households:
Total TV Households:	98%
Homes with:	
Color TV sets	99%
2 or more sets	34%
3 or more sets	40%
Basic cable	67%
Premium cable	35%
VCR	84%

Favorite TV Shows

1950s

A. Godfrey's Talent Scouts
I Love Lucy
You Bet Your Life
Dragnet
The Jack Benny Show
A. Godfrey and Friends
Gunsmoke
The Red Skelton Show
December Bride
I've Got a Secret
$64,000 Question
Disneyland
The Ed Sullivan Show
Have Gun—Will Travel
The Danny Thomas Show

1960s

Bonanza
The Red Skelton Show
The Andy Griffith Show
The Beverly Hillbillies
The Ed Sullivan Show
The Lucy Show/Here's Lucy
The Jackie Gleason Show
Bewitched
Gomer Pyle
Candid Camera
The Dick Van Dyke Show
The Danny Thomas Show
Family Affair
Laugh-in
Rawhide

1970s

All in the Family
M*A*S*H
Hawaii Five-O
Happy Days
The Waltons
The Mary Tyler Moore Show
Sanford & Son
One Day at a Time
Three's Company
60 Minutes
Maude
Gunsmoke
Charlie's Angels
The Jeffersons
Laverne & Shirley

1980s

Bill Cosby Show
Cheers
Dallas
Roseanne
A Different World
America's Funniest Home Videos
Golden Girls
Wonder Years
Empty Nest
60 Minutes
Dynasty
Roseanne
Unsolved Mysteries
L.A. Law
Who's the Boss?
Grand
Murder, She Wrote
NBC Sunday Night Movie

1990s

Cheers
60 Minutes
Home Improvement
Seinfeld
E.R.
Oprah Winfrey
Veronica's Chest
Touched by an Angel
Friends
NYPD Blue
The Simpsons
Everybody Loves Raymond

36: U.S. Publications

Magazines

Rank	Magazine	Circulation
1	NRTA/AARP Bulletin	20,415,981
2	Modern Maturity	20,390,755
3	Reader's Digest	15,038,788
4	TV Guide	13,103,387
5	National Geographic Magazine	9,012,074
6	Better Homes and Gardens	7,605,187
7	Family Circle	5,107,477
8	Good Housekeeping	4,739,592
9	Ladies' Home Journal	4,590,155
10	Woman's Day	4,461,023
11	McCall's	4,216,145
12	Time	4,155,808
13	People Weekly	3,608,111
14	Prevention	3,310,278
15	Sports Illustrated	3,223,810
16	Newsweek	3,177,407
17	Playboy	3,169,697
18	Redbook	2,889,466
19	Home & Away	2,759,565
20	American Legion	2,734,218
21	Cosmopolitan	2,701,916
22	Seventeen	2,567,613
23	Southern Living	2,474,463
24	Martha Stewart Living	2,339,799
25	National Enquirer	2,324,678
26	U.S. News & World Report	2,224,003
27	YM	2,221,937
28	Glamour	2,115,642
29	Smithsonian	2,065,032
30	Star	1,948,247
31	V.F.W. Magazine	1,935,807
32	Money	1,935,402
33	'Teen	1,842,846
34	Ebony	1,819,431
35	Field & Stream	1,751,772
36	Parents Magazine	1,745,292
37	Country Living	1,697,742
38	Life	1,568,565
39	Popular Science	1,558,655
40	Golf Digest	1,529,671
41	Men's Health	1,511,345
42	Woman's World	1,505,637
43	Sunset	1,471,825
44	Popular Mechanics	1,425,692
45	First for Women	1,408,419

Top U.S. Daily Newspapers

Rank	Newspaper	Circulation
1	New York (NY) *Wall Street Journal*	1,774,880
2	Arlington (VA) *USA Today*	1,629,655
3	New York (NY) *Times*	1,074,741
4	Los Angeles (CA) *Times*	1,050,176
5	Washington (DC) *Post*	775,894
6	New York (NY) *Daily News*	721,256
7	Chicago (IL) *Tribune*	653,554
8	Long Island (NY) *Newsday*	568,914
9	Houston (TX) *Chronicle*	549,101
10	Chicago (IL) *Sun-Times*	484,379
11	San Francisco (CA) *Chronicle*	484,218
12	Dallas (TX) *Morning News*	481,032
13	Boston (MA) *Globe*	476,966
14	Phoenix (AZ) *Arizona Republic*	437,118
15	New York (NY) *Post*	436,226
16	Philadelphia (PA) *Inquirer*	428,233
17	Newark (NJ) *Star-Ledger*	406,010
18	Minneapolis (MN) *Star Tribune*	387,412
19	Detroit (MI) *Free Press*	384,624
20	Cleveland (OH) *Plain Dealer*	383,586
21	San Diego (CA) *Union*	375,598
22	Miami (FL) *Herald*	356,803
23	Orange County (CA) *Register*	356,520
24	Portland (OR) *Oregonian*	342,454
25	St. Petersburg (FL) *Times*	342,189
26	Denver (CO) *Post*	337,372
27	St. Louis (MO) *Post-Dispatch*	313,594
28	Baltimore (MD) *Sun*	312,826
29	Denver (CO) *Rocky Mountain News*	302,953
30	Atlanta (GA) *Constitution*	296,669
31	San Jose (CA) *Mercury News*	290,811
32	Milwaukee (WI) *Journal*	288,173
33	Sacramento (CA) *Bee*	281,471
34	Boston (MA) *Herald*	277,106
35	Kansas City (MO) *Times*	276,349
36	Buffalo (NY) *News*	262,085
37	New Orleans (LA) *Times-Picayune*	260,552
38	Orlando (FL) *Sentinel*	258,037
39	Fort Lauderdale (FL) *Sun-Sentinel*	257,118
40	Detroit (MI) *News*	246,638
41	Columbus (OH) *Dispatch*	246,095
42	Pittsburgh (PA) *Press*	243,024
43	Tampa (FL) *Tribune*	240,990
44	Charlotte (NC) *Observer*	239,016
45	Los Angeles (CA) *Investors Business Daily*	234,596
46	Fort Worth (TX) *Star-Telegram*	229,701
47	Louisville (KY) *Courier-Journal*	228,185
48	Seattle (WA) *Times*	227,162
49	Omaha (NE) *World-Herald*	225,761
50	Indianapolis (IN) *Star*	224,372

37. Leading U.S. Advertisers

Rank	Advertiser	Rank	Advertiser
1	General Motors	26	Honda
2	Procter & Gamble	27	Circuit City Stores
3	Philip Morris	28	General Mills
4	Chrysler	29	Kellogg Co.
5	Ford	30	Bristol-Myers Squibb
6	Pepsico	31	Ford Motor Co. (local)
7	Time Warner	32	Warner-Lambert
8	Walt Disney	33	JC Penney
9	Johnson & Johnson	34	Dayton Hudson
10	Sears Roebuck & Co.	35	American Home Products
11	Diageo PLC	36	Chrysler Corp. (local)
12	Unilever PLC	37	L'Oreal
13	News Corp.	38	U.S. Government
14	Ford Motor Co. (local)	39	Coca-Cola
15	Toyota	40	American Express
16	McDonalds	41	Seagram
17	Federated Dept. Stores	42	Mars
18	General Motors (local)	43	Toyota (local)
19	Sony	44	RJR Nabisco
20	AT & T	45	Sprint
21	General Motors (local)	46	K-Mart
22	MCI-World	47	IBM
23	Nissan Motor Co.	48	Valassis Communications
24	National Amusements	49	Anheuser-Busch
25	May Dept. Stores	50	SmithKline Beacham

Ad Spending by Categories

Rank	Category	Rank	Category
1	Automotive	17	Household Equipment
2	Retail	18	Beer & Wine
3	Business, Consumer Svcs	19	Soaps & Cleansers
4	Entertainment	20	Jewelry, Optical
5	Food	21	Cigarettes
6	Drugs & Remedies	22	Miscellaneous
7	Toiletries/Cosmetics	23	Building Materials
8	Travel & Hotels	24	Pets & Pet Foods
9	Computers, Office Equip.	25	Gasoline, Lubricants
10	Direct Response Cosmetics	26	Household Furnishings
11	Candy, Snacks, Soft Drinks	27	Horticulture, Farming
12	Insurance & Real Estate	28	Liquor
13	Publishing & Media	29	Freight, Industrial
14	Apparel, Footwear	30	Industrial Materials
15	Sporting goods, Toys	31	Business Propositions
16	Electronic Equipment	32	Airplanes

38. U.S. National Documents

Declaration of Independence
Thomas Jefferson, 1776

When in the Course of human Events, it becomes necessary for one People to dissolve the Political Bands which have connected them with another, and to assume among the Powers of the Earth, the separate and equal Station to which the Laws of Nature and of Nature's God entitle them, a decent Respect to the Opinions of Mankind requires that they should declare the causes which impel them to the Separation.

We hold these Truths to be self-evident, that all Men are created equal, that they are endowed by their Creator with certain unalienable Rights, that among these are Life, Liberty and the Pursuit of Happiness— That to secure these Rights, Governments are instituted among Men, deriving their just Powers from the Consent of the Governed, that whenever any Form of Government becomes destructive of these Ends, it is the Right of the People to alter or to abolish it, and to institute new Government, laying its Foundation on such Principles, and organizings its Powers in such Form, as to then shall seem most likely to affect their Safety and Happiness. Prudence, indeed, will dictate that Governments long established should not be changed for light and transient Causes; and accordingly all Experience hath shewn, that Mankind are more disposed to suffer while Evils are sufferable, than to right themselves by abolishing the Forms to which they are accustomed. But when a long Train of Abuses and Usurpations, pursuing invariably the same Object, evinces a Design to reduce them under absolute Despotism, it is their Right, it is their Duty, to throw off such Government, and to provide new Guards for their future Security.

The Preamble of the Constitution, 1787

We the People of the United States, in order to form a more perfect Union, establish Justice, insure domestic Tranquility, provide for the common Defense, promote the general Welfare, and secure the Blessings of Liberty to ourselves and our Posterity, do ordain and establish this Constitution for the United States of America.

The Bill of Rights
The Ten Original Constitutional Amendments, 1791

First Amendment
Congress shall make no law respecting an establishment of religion, or prohibiting the free excercise thereof; or abridging the freedom of speech, or of the press; or the right of the people peaceably to assemble, and to petition the Government for a redress of grievances.

Second Amendment
A well-regulated militia, being necessary to the security of a free State, the right of the people to keep and bear arms, shall not be infringed.

Third Amendment

No soldier shall, in time of peace be quartered in any house, without the consent of the owner, nor in time of war, but in a manner to be prescribed by law.

Fourth Amendment

The right of the people to be secure in their persons, houses, papers, and effects, against unreasonable searches and seizures, shall not be violated, and no warrants shall issue, but upon probable cause, supported by oath or affirmation, and particularly describing the place to be searched, and the persons or things to be seized.

Fifth Amendment

No person shall be held to answer for a capital, or otherwise infamous crime, unless on a presentment or indictment of a Grand Jury, except in cases arising in the land or naval forces, or in the militia, when in actual service in time of war or public danger; nor shall any person be subject for the same offense to be twice put in jeopardy of life or limb; nor shall be compelled in any criminal case to be a witness against himself, nor be deprived of life, liberty, or property, without due process of law; nor shall private property be taken for public use without just compensation.

Sixth Amendment

In all criminal prosecutions, the accused shall enjoy the right to a speedy and public trial, by an impartial jury of the State and district wherein the crime shall have been committed, which district shall have been previously ascertained by law, and to be informed of the nature and cause of the accusation; to be confronted with the witnesses against him; to have compulsory process for obtaining witnesses in his favor, and to have the assistance of counsel for his defense.

Seventh Amendment

In suits at common law, where the value in controversy shall exceed twenty dollars, the right of trial by jury shall be preserved, and no fact tried by a jury shall be otherwise reexamined in a court of the United States, than according to the rules of the common law.

Eighth Amendment

Excessive bail shall not be required, nor excessive fines imposed, nor cruel and unusual punishments inflicted.

Ninth Amendment

The enumeration in the Constitution, of certain rights, shall not be construed to deny or disparage others retained by the people.

Tenth Amendment

The powers not delegated to the United States by the Constitution, nor prohibited by it to the States, are reserved to the States respectively, or to the people.

The U.S. National Anthem
The Star-Spangled Banner
Francis Scott Key, 1814

O say, can you see, by the dawn's early light,
What so proudly we hail'd at the twilight's last gleaming?
Whose broad stripes and bright stars, thro' the perilous fight,
O'er the ramparts we watch'd, were so gallantly streaming?
And the rockets' red glare, the bombs bursting in air,
Gave proof thro' the night that our flag was still there,
O say, does that star-spangled banner yet wave
O'er the land of the free and the home of the brave?

The Gettysburg Address
Abraham Lincoln, 1863

Fourscore and seven years ago our fathers brought forth on this continent a new nation, conceived in liberty and dedicated to the proposition that all men are created equal.

Now we are engaged in a great civil war, testing whether that nation or any nation so conceived and so dedicated can long endure. We are met on a great battlefield of that war. We have come to dedicate a portion of that field, as a final resting place for those who here gave their lives that that nation might live. It is altogether fitting and proper that we should do this.

But, in a larger sense, we cannot dedicate—we cannot consecrate—we cannot hallow—this ground. The brave men, living and dead, who struggled here, have consecrated it, far above our poor power to add or detract. The world will little note, nor long remember, what we say here, but it can never forget what they did here. It is for us the living, rather, to be here dedicated to the great task remaining before us—that from these honored dead we take increased devotion to that cause for which they gave the last full measure of devotion—that we here highly resolve that these dead shall not have died in vain—that this nation, under God, shall have a new birth of freedom—and that government of the people, by the people, for the people, shall not perish from the earth.

Statue of Liberty Inscription
The New Colossus
Emma Lazarus

Not like the brazen giant of Greek fame,
With conquering limbs astride from land to land;
Here at our sea-washed, sunset gates shall stand
A mighty woman with a torch, whose flame
Is the imprisoned lightning, and her name
Mother of Exiles. From her beacon-hand
Glows world-wide welcome; her mild eyes command
The air-bridged harbor that twin cities frame.
"Keep ancient lands, your storied pomp!" cries she
With silent lips. "Give me your tired, your poor,
Your huddled masses yearning to breathe free,
The wretched refuse of your teeming shore.
Send these, the homeless, tempest-tost to me,
I lift my lamp beside the golden door!"

America the Beautiful
Katherine Lee Bates, 1893

O beautiful for spacious skies,
For amber waves of grain,
For purple mountain's majesties
Above the fruited plain.
America! America!
God shed his grace on thee,
And crown thy good with brotherhood
From sea to shining sea.

"I Have a Dream"
Martin Luther King, 1963

Five score years ago, a great American, in whose symbolic shadow we stand, signed the Emancipation Proclamation. This momentous decree came as a great beacon of hope to millions of Negro slaves who had been seared in the flames of withering injustice. It came as a joyous daybreak to end the long night of captivity.

But one hundred years later, we must face the tragic fact that the Negro is still not free.

I say to you today, my friends, that in spite of difficulties and frustrations of the moments, I still have a dream. It is a dream deeply rooted in the American dream.

I have a dream that one day this nation will rise up and live out the true meaning of its creed: "We hold these truths to be self evident; that all men are created equal."

I have a dream that one day on the red hills of Georgia the sons of former slaves and the sons of former slaveowners will be able to sit down together at the table of brotherhood.

I have a dream that one day even the state of Mississippi, a desert state sweltering with the heat of injustice and oppression, will be transformed into an oasis of freedom and justice.

I have a dream that my four little children will one day live in a nation where they will not be judged by the color of their skin but by the content of their character.

I have a dream today.

I have a dream that one day the state of Alabama, whose governor's lips are presently dripping with the words of interposition and nullification, will be transformed into a situation where little black boys and girls will be able to join hands with little white boys and white girls and walk together as sisters and brothers.

I have a dream today.

I have a dream that one day every valley shall be exalted, every hill and mountain shall be made low, the rough places will be made plains, and the crooked places will be made straight, and the glory of the Lord shall be revealed, and all flesh shall see it together.

This is our hope. This is the faith with which I return to the South. With this faith we will be able to hew out of the mountain of despair a stone of hope. With this faith we will be able to transform the jangling discords of our nation into a beautiful symphony of brotherhood. With this faith we will be able to work together, to pray together, to struggle together, to go to jail together, to stand up for freedom together, knowing that we will be free one day.

This will be the day when all God's children will be able to sing with new meaning:

> My country, 'tis of thee,
> Sweet land of liberty,
> Of thee I sing:
> Land where my fathers died,
> Land of the pilgrims' pride,
> From every mountain side
> Let freedom ring.

And if America is to be a great nation, this must become true. So let freedom ring from the prodigious hilltops of New Hampshire. Let freedom ring from the mighty mountains of New York. Let freedom ring from the heightening Alleghenies of Pennsylvania. Let freedom ring from the snowcapped Rockies of Colorado. Let freedom ring from the curvaceous peaks of California. But not only that; let freedom ring from Stone Mountain of Georgia. Let freedom ring from Lookout Mountain of Tennessee. Let freedom ring from every hill and molehill of Mississippi. From every mountainside, let freedom ring.

When we let freedom ring, when we let it ring from every village and every hamlet, from every state and every city, we will be able to speed up that day when all of God's children, black men and white men, Jews and Gentiles, Protestants and Catholics, will be able to join hands and sing in the words of the old Negro spiritual, "Free at last, free at last, thank God almighty, we are free at last!"

Pledge of Allegiance

I pledge allegiance to the flag of
the United States of America and
to the republic for which it stands,
one nation under God, indivisible,
with liberty and justice for all.

213

39. Canadian National Anthem

Official Lyrics in English

O Canada! Our home and native land!
True patriot love in all thy sons command.
With glowing hearts we see thee rise,
The True North strong and free
From far and wide,O Canada,
We stand on guard for thee.
Chorus.
God keep our land glorious and free!
O Canada, we stand on guard for thee.
O Canada, we stand on guard for thee.

Official Lyrics in French

O Canada! Terre de nos aïeux,
Ton front est ceint de fleurons glorieux.
Car ton bras sait porter l'épée,
Il sait porter la croix!
Ton histoire est une épopée
Des plus brillants exploits.
Chorus.
Et ta valeur, de foi trempée!
Protègera nos foyers et nos droits.
Protègera nos foyers et nos droits.

English Translation of the Official French Lyrics

O Canada! Land of our forefathers,
Thy brow is wreathed with a glorious garland of flowers.
As is thy arm ready to wield the sword,
So also is it ready to carry the cross!
Thy history is an epic
Of the most brilliant exploits.
Chorus.
And thy valour steeped in faith!
Will protect our homes and our rights.
Will protect our homes and our rights.

Note: This material is from the Canadian National website: www.pch.gc.ca/ceremonial-symb/english/emb_anthem.html.
There are many variations of both the French and English versions. The original French poem was by Sir Adolphe-Basile
Routhier. It was first sung in 1880, and the first widely known translation was written by R. Stanley Weir in 1908.

The Metalinguistic Aspect and Miscellaneous Materials

Contents

1: Glossary of Grammatical Terms

Absolute construction
A word or phrase which modifies the sentence as a whole, not any single element in it.
The game over, the players left the field.
The cattle having been branded, the cowboys saddled up and rode off.

Active
See Voice

Adjective
A word which modifies a noun or a pronoun.
The old man walked across the narrow street.

Adjective clause
A dependent clause serving an adjective function. See **Relative clause.**
*The woman **who performed** lives next door to me.*

Adjective phrase
A word or group of words that functions as an adjective.
dull, exceedingly dull, so very dull

Adverb
A word which modifies a verb, an adjective, or another adverb.
*The car moved **slowly** in very heavy traffic.*

Adverbial
A word or group of words which functions as an adverb.
*He works **in a large university.***
*It rained **very hard.***
*He was happy **when his friend arrived.***

Adverbial clause
A dependent clause serving an adverbial function, Common adverbial clauses include:
Comparison (as...as, as...than)
*I can't run **as fast as I used to.***
Concession (though, although, even if)
***Although I had a good time,** I was happy to leave.*
Condition - See Conditional sentences.
Purpose (so as to, in order to, so that, in order that)
*We are going to France **to learn French.***
Reason (because, as, since)
*They turned on the lights **because it was too dark.***
Result (so...that, such ...that)
*He spoke **so fast that no one understood a thing.***

Time (when, as, while, until, as soon as)
***As soon as he lit his cigar,** people began to leave the room.*

Agreement
Correspondence between grammatically related elements. Agreement in number and person between a subject and its verb.
*The **children play.** The **child plays.***
Agreement in gender, number, and person between a pronoun and its antecedent.
*The girl washed **her face.***

Antecedent
The word to which a pronoun refers.
***Aunt Mary** fainted when **she** heard the news.*

Appositive
A word, phrase, or clause used as a noun and placed next to another noun to modify it.
*George Washington, **the president,** slept here.*

Article
A and *an* are indefinite articles. *The* is the definite article.

Auxiliary
Function words which help other verbs indicate tense, mood, or voice (be, do, have). Modal auxiliaries *(can, may, might, must, should, etc.)* serve also as structural signals and have a meaning of their own *(ability, obligation, possibility).*

Case
English has the remnants of three cases: *subjective, possessive,* and *objective.* Nouns are inflected for case in the possessive *(John's).* Some pronouns and the relative pronoun *who* are inflected.
subjective: I, *he, she, we, they, who.*
possessive: my (mine), your (yours), his, her (hers), its, our (ours), their (theirs), whose.
objective: me, him, her, us, them, whom.

Clause
A group of words containing a subject and a predicate. See Independent clause and Dependent clause.

Collective noun
A noun singular in appearance which indicates a class or group of persons or things.
*a **committee** of citizens, an **army***

216

Comparative

The form of adjectives and adverbs which is used to indicate relative superiority.

tall	**taller**	**less tall**
important	**more important**	**less important**
slowly	**more slowly**	**less slowly**

Complement

A word or group of words used to complete a predicate. Predicate nominatives, predicate adjectives, direct objects, and indirect objects are complements.

Compound sentence

A sentence which combines two or more independent clauses.

He whistled, and she worked.

Complex sentence

A sentence which contains one or more dependent clauses.

He whistled while she worked.

Compound complex sentence

A sentence which contains two or more independent clauses and one or more dependent clauses.

He whistled and she worked until they both got tired.

Conditional sentences

Conditional sentences have two parts, the conditional clause and the main clause. There are three types:

1. Real condition:

   If you bother the cat, it will scratch you.

2. Unreal, contrary-to-fact condition (present):

   If I were you, I would keep the money.
   If you took a trip, where would you go?

3. Unreal, contrary-to-fact condition (past):

   If I had known you were coming, I would have baked you a cake.
   If I had been Lincoln, I wouldn't have gone to the theater that night.

Conjunction

A word used to connect sentences or sentence parts. See also **Coordinating conjunctions, Subordinating conjunctions.**

Connective

See **Conjunction.**

Conjunctive adverbs

Adverbs used to relate two independent clauses separated by a semicolon:

then, consequently, however, moreover, therefore, etc.

Coordinating Conjunctions

The simple conjunction that connect sentences and sentence parts of equal rank:

and, but, or, nor, for, yet, so.

Correlative conjunctions

Pairs of conjunctions which join sentence parts:

either. . .or, neither. . . nor, not only...but also, but...and.

Count noun

A noun that can be made plural, usually by adding -s.

Demonstrative adjectives and pronouns

Words used to point out someone or something:

this, that, these, those.

Also called demonstrative determiners.

Dependent (subordinate clause)

A group of words which contains both a subject and a predicate but which does not stand alone as a sentence. A dependent clause always serves a noun, adverb, or adjective function. See **Noun clause, Adjective clause, Adverbial clause, Relative clause.**

Determiners

A class of modifiers which includes articles *(a, an, the)*, possessives *(my, John's, his)*, demonstratives *(this, that)*, interrogatives *(which, what)*, indefinite *(some, any)*, numerals, and *each, every.*

Diphthong

Two vowel sounds joined in one syllable to form one speech sound:

out, oil, I.

Direct object

A noun, pronoun, or other substantive which receives the action of the verb.

*Jack climbed the **beanstalk** into the sky.*

Direct speech

Repeats the speaker's exact words, enclosing them in quotation marks.

He said, "I've lost my umbrella."

Elliptical clause

A clause in which one or more words necessary for the full subject-predicate structure are omitted but "understood."

*The manager admired no one else as much as **(he admired**—"understood") her.*

Expletive

The *it* or *there* which serves to fill the subject slot in *it is, there is,* and *there are* sentences.

It *is easy to understand.*
There is *a fly in my soup.*

Finite verb

A verb in the present or past form, e.g., the finite forms of the verb *be* are *is, am, are, was,* and *were*. The non-finite forms are *be, being,* and *been.*

Function words

Words which establish grammatical relationships within a sentence: articles, auxiliaries, conjunctions, prepositions, pronouns, determiners, intensifiers, and interjections.

Future

I will work, I shall work, I am going to work, I work tomorrow, etc.

Gender

The quality of nouns and pronouns that determines the choice between masculine, female, or neuter *(he, she, it.)*

Gerund

See **Verbal**.

Idiom

An expression that does not conform to general grammatical patterns but is established through usage as the way of conveying a given meaning. *hold up, hold down, be beside oneself, kick the bucket.*

Indefinite pronouns

Pronouns not pointing out a particular person, thing, or definite quantity. *Some, any, each, every, everyone, everybody, nobody, anyone, anybody, one, neither* are among the most common.

Independent clause

A group of words which contains a subject and a predicate and which can stand alone as a sentence.

Indirect object

A word which indirectly receives the action of the verb.
The witch gave **the pretty girl** *a poisoned apple.*

Indirect speech

Paraphrases of the speaker's words.
He said he had lost his umbrella.

Infinitive

See **Verbal.**

Inflection

Changes in the form of words to reflect changes in grammatical relationships:
the cabins; he walks; she's talking; quickest.

Intensifier

Words that modify adjectives or adverbs and express degree: **very** *beautiful,* **quite** *young,* **rather** *old.*

Intensive pronoun

A reflexive pronoun ending in *-self -selves,* and used for emphasis.
I'd rather do it **myself**

Interjection

A word used to exclaim or to express emotion: *ah, oh, ouch.*

Interrogative pronouns

Who, whose, whom, what, which, when used in questions.

Intonation

The rising and falling of the pitch of the voice in speech.

Intransitive verb

A verb which has no direct object
The tide **turned** *at noon.*

Linking verb

A verb which does not express action but links the subject to another word which names or describes it. *Be, become, seem, appear,* and *look* are common linking verbs.

Mass noun (Non-count noun)

A noun that refers to a quantity and cannot be preceded by a cardinal number, such as *three: sugar, milk, hunger.*

Modifier

A word, phrase, or clause which limits or describes other sentence elements or the sentence as a whole.

Mood

The classification of verb forms as
indicative (plain or factual):
I am ready;
imperative (request or command):
Be ready at six; and
subjunctive (hypothetical or contrary-to-fact):
I wish you were ready.

Nominal

Any structure that functions as a noun.

Nominative case

See Case, subjunctive.

Non-restrictive relative clause
A clause which provides further information not essential to identification of the subject or complement and is set off usually with commas.
*John Jones, **who spends a lot of money**, has many friends.*

Noun
A word which names and classifies people, animals, things, ideas.
Thomas Jefferson, lemon, religion, alligator, Paris, worm, justice, school, committee.

Noun clause
A dependent clause serving a nominal function.
Everyone agrees that the play was a success.

Noun phrase
The element in the sentence which functions as subject, object, or complement.
The pretty girl standing in the corner is my sister.
She and her friends never dance.

Number
Choice of appropriate forms to indicate singular or plural.

Object of a preposition
Completes the idea of time, position, direction, etc., begun by a preposition.
at his desk, towards the door

Objective complement
A complement after the direct object that provides another name for the object or otherwise amplifies it.
They elected him president.
The war made many women widows.
Everyone believed him crazy.

Participle
See **Verbal.**

Parts of speech
Noun, pronoun, adjective, adverb, conjunction, interjection, preposition, article.

Past
I worked, etc.

Phoneme
A basic unit *of* sound in a language. (/i/, /p/, /iy/)

Perfect
I have worked, I had worked, I will have worked.

Person
Choice of the appropriate forms to express the person speaking:
first person: I, *we*
second person: *you*
third person: *he, she, it, they*

Possessive adjectives
My, your, his, her, its, our, their.

Predicate adjective
An adjective following a linking verb and describing the subject.
The flowers look artificial.

Predicate nominative
A word or group of words which follows a linking verb and identifies the subject.
The book is a bestselling science-fiction novel.

Preposition
A connective which joins a noun or a pronoun to the rest of the sentence. A prepositional phrase may serve either an adverb or an adjective function.
adverb: *The guide led us into the forest.*
adjective: *Jack is a master of many trades.*

Present
I work, she/he works, etc.

Progressive (Continuous)
I am working, I was working, I have been working.

Pronouns
Words which stand for nouns, classified as:
personal: (I, you, *he*)
possessive: *(mine, yours, his, hers)*
reflexive/intensive: *(myself, himself, ourselves)*
demonstrative: *(this, that, those)*
relative: *(who, which, what, that, whose)*
interrogative: *(who, which, what)*
indefinite: *(one, anyone, everyone)*

Quantifiers
Words denoting how much *(some, any, most, few, one, two, three)*

Reciprocal pronouns
Each other, one another.

Relative clause
A dependent clause that is related to the main clause by a relative pronoun.
*The book **that he recommended** is* on sale.
Restrictive relative clause: A clause that contributes to the identification of the noun it modifies, not separated by a comma from the noun. See Non-restrictive relative clause.
The man who called me up was a complete stranger.

Sentence

A grammatically complete unit of thought or expression, containing at least a subject and a predicate.

Simple sentence

A sentence consisting of only one independent clause.

Stress

Pronouncing a syllable or a word in such a way that it makes it more prominent in a word or sentence respectivley.

conductor, Let's go.

Substantive

See **Nominal.**

Subject

A word or group of words about which the sentence or clause makes a statement.

The dog jumped into the car.

Subject complement

See **Predicate nominative; Predicate adjective**

Subjunctive

See **Mood.**

Subordinating conjunctions

Conjunctions which join sentence parts of unequal rank. Usually they begin dependent clauses. Some of the most common ones are:

because, since, though, although, if, when, while, before, after, as, until, so that, as long as, whereas, in order that.

Superlative

The form of adjectives and adverbs used to express absolute superiority.

the tallest	***the least tall***
the most important	*the least important*
the most slowly	*the least slowly*

Syntax

The rules of sentence formation.

Tag questions

Short *yes / no* questions added to statements.

*It's a beautiful day, **isn't it?***
*You haven't seen the film, **have you?***

Tense

The system of verb forms expressing primarily different relationships in time.

Transitive verb

A verb which normally requires an object.

*Monkeys **love** bananas.*

Two-word verbs

A combination of a verb and a preposition or an adverb which forms a new vocabulary item. Two-word verbs are classified as *intransitive, separable,* and *non-separable.*

intransitive: *John **got up** early this morning.*
separable: *John **calls up** his wife from the office.*
   *John **calls** his wife **up** from the office.*
   *John **calls** her **up** from the office.*
non-separable:
   *Everybody **picks on** fat people.*

Verb

A word or group of words expressing action, being, or state of being.

*I **swallowed** a fly.*
*What **is** man ?*
*The table **has been** set.*

Verbal

A word or phrase derived from a verb and used as a noun, an adjective, or an adverb. Verbals consist of infinitives, gerunds, or participles.

infinitive: begins with to (sometimes understood) and is used as a noun, an adverb,or an adjective.
   noun: ***To do such a thing*** *would be disastrous.*
   adverb: *Many people jog **to keep physically fit.***
   adjective: *I'm ready **to testify,** your Honor.*
gerund: ends in -ing and is used as a noun.
   Playing with matches *is a favorite passtime among children.*
participle: ends in -*ing, -ed,* and is used as an adjective.
   *I can't live without **running** water.*
   ***Accompanied** by his faithful dog, Daniel roamed the woods.*

Verb phrase

Consists of the main verb and one or more auxiliaries.

*It **is beginning** to rain.*
*It **has been raining** for a long time.*

Modern grammarians use the term **verb phrase** to indicate the verb and all that goes with it (predicate) or the verb and its modifiers.

*The old man and the boy **had quietly taken the book from the library.***

Voice

A distinction in verb forms between *active* (the subject is acting) and passive (the subject is acted upon).

active: *Elmer **fed** the chickens.*
passive: *The chickens **were fed** by Elmer.*

2: A Comparison of Three Phonetic Alphabets

Consonants

Sounds   Representations

	I.P.A.*	T-S.**	Dict.***
may	/m/	/m/	/m/
bay	/b/	/b/	/b/
pay	/p/	/p/	/p/
way	/w/	/w/	/w/
whey	/hw/	/hw/	/hw/
vee	/v/	/v/	/v/
fee	/f/	/f/	/f/
thee	/ð/	/ð/	/th/
thigh	/θ/	/θ/	/th/
new	/n/	/n/	/n/
dew	/d/	/d/	/d/
too	/t/	/t/	/t/
Lou	/l/	/l/	/l/
zoo	/z/	/z/	/s/
Sue	/s/	/s/	
you	/j/	/y/	/y/
rue	/r/	/r/	/r/
measure	/ʒ/	/ž/	/ž/
show	/ʃ/	/š/	/š/
joke	/dʒ/	/ǰ/	/ǰ/
choo	/tʃ/	/č/	/č/
bang	/ŋ/	/ŋ/	/ŋ/
bag	/g/	/g/	/g/
back	/k/	/k/	/k/
hi	/h/	/h/	/h/

*International Phonetic Alphabet
**Trager-Smith System
***Merriam-Webster dictionary

221

Vowels

Sounds	I.P.A.*	T-S.**	Dict.***
		Representations	
beat	/i/	/iy/	/ē/
bit	/ɪ/	/i/	/i/
bait	/e/	/ey/	/ā/
bet	/ɛ/	/e/	/e/
bat	/æ/	/æ/	/a/
but	/ʌ/	/ə/	/ə/
alone	/ə/	/ə/	/ə/
boot	/u/	/uw/	/ü/
put	/ʊ/	/u/	/u̇/
boat	/o/	/ow/	/ō/
bought	/ɔ/	/ɔ/	/ȯ/
father	/a/	/a/	/ä/
how	/aw/	/aw/ /æw/	/au̇/
I	/aj/	/ay/	/ī/
boy	/ɔi/	/oy/	/ȯi/
ear		/ir/	
air		/er/	
marry		/ær/	
father		/ər/	
fur		/ər/	/ər/
poor		/ur/	
or		/or/	
are		/ar/	

222

3: A Brief Guide to Punctuation

Punctuation		Used for	Example(s)
Apostrophe	'	to indicate omissions in contractions	doesn't, won't
		to indicate possession	Mary's, the Joneses'
		to indicate plurals of letters and numerals	1870's, p's and q's
Brackets	[ ]	to indicate comment or question in quoted material	"He [Lincoln] was assassinated by a mad actor."
		to indicate comment or question within material in parentheses	(Kuwait was liberated [was turned into a desolate battleground] by the U.N. forces in March,1991).
Colon	:	in writing clock time	9:15, 2:47,17:09
		to introduce a list	We need the following items: soap, toothpaste, and hand lotion.
		after the names of speakers in a dialogue	Joe: Will you come, Honey? Sue: Are you nuts? No way!
		before a formal quotation	The tall speaker began: "Four score and seven years ago,....
		after salutations in formal or business letters	Dear Sir: Dear Ms. Landsdowne:
Comma	,	after *yes* or *no* in a response	Yes, we have no bananas.
		before the conjunction in a compound sentence except when the clauses are short	The oldest boy is going to school, and the youngest is going to work. He walked and she rode.
		to separate the elements in an address	New Orleans, Louisana, U. S. A. They live at 418 Cedar Street, Winnetka, Illinois
		to separate the elements in a date	He was born on Tuesday, January 25, 1944, in Chicago.
		to separate equivalent elements in a series	Watch the stocks of Target, Ames, and Walmart.
		to separate a speaker's words from the introductory statement	John asked, "May I leave?"
		to group large numbers into thousands	9,121; 1,268,421,135
		to set off the name of a person spoken to in direct speech	Mary, take this ring.
		to separate an introductory clause from the sentence	When the party was over, I walked home.

Punctuation	Used for	Example(s)
Comma, cont.	after a mild exclamation	Well, I don't care.
	before and after an appositive	George, a famous poet, spoke next.
	to separate a tag question from the rest of the sentence	It's cold, isn't it?
	before and after a non-restrictive adjective clause	Punctuation, which is essential for writing, seems complicated at first.
Dash —	to indicate an interruption or an afterthought	We'll be there—at last—in an hour! I'll do it—at least, I'll try.
	to indicate special emphasis in place of a comma	Give people what they want—money, fame, and power.
Exclamation Point !	to indicate strong feeling or emotion or for emphasis	Help! Watch out! She said she'd jump and she did!
Hyphen -	in certain fixed expressions	person-to-person, matter-of-fact, station-to-station
	in writing out compound numbers	twenty-one, ninety-nine, twenty-first, ninety-ninth
	in expressions of clock time	It's seven-thirty. It's one-fifteen.
	in joining a prefix to a proper name	pre-Columbian, post-Roosevelt, un-Christian
	in joining a prefix to a noun whose first letter is the same as the last letter of the prefix	anti-intellectual, pre-existing, post-temperance
Parenthesis ( )	to enclose remarks, comments, explanations that interrupt the main thought	She invited the two men (they are cousins) to the party. If it rains (it usually doesn't this time of year), we'll postpone the picnic.
Period .	at the end of a statement	I want to be alone.
	after initials and abbreviations	Mr. P. T. Barnum. It's 7 p.m.
	to indicate cents/decimals	$5.39; 257.0932; .00906
Question Mark ?	at the end of a direct question	Where does it all end?
	after a tag question	You like to talk, don't you?

224

Punctuation	Used for	Example(s)
Quotation " "	to enclose direct quotations	"Come here," Jim said.
Marks	around titles of chapters	"The Return to Witchwood"
	articles in magazines or newspapers	"Wood Stove Madness," *Country Journal*
	songs, poems, radio and TV programs	"Michelle, Ma Belle" "Hurt Hawks" "Music from the Hearts of Space" "I Love Lucy"
	with other punctuation, as follows:	"Come, " he said. "I'm going." I said, "I will;" I followed. "Can you see?" he asked. Did I answer, "No?"
Semicolon ;	in a compound sentence without a connective	The singular form is "mouse;" the plural form is "mice."
	in a sentence with two main clauses joined by a conjunctive adverb.	The teacher was sick; therefore, the class was called off. Roseanne ran a good race; however, she failed to qualify for the finals.
Underlining and *Italics*	Use underlining in handwritten or typed material and Italics in printed material:	
	for titles of periodicals and books	Newsweek, A Farewell to Arms
	foreign phrases and words used in an English context	And then, alors, there she was. "Cuidado," I warned myself, "You're a fool, but que, sera, sera.
	words emphasized	I wanted *three* tickets, not four!
	the names of ships, trains and *airplanes*	*Titanic,* Orient Express,*Constellation,* *Spirit of St. Louis*

4: Useful Spelling Rules

A. If a word ends in **y** preceded by a consonant, change the **y** to an **i** before every suffix except **-ing.**

salary	salaries	copy	copying
marry	married	try	trying
lonely	loneliness	fly	flying
worry	worried	worry	worrying

B. Write **i** before **e**, except after **c** or when sounded like **a,** as in *neighbor* and *weigh.*

i before **e**:   *brief, piece, chief, yield*
e before **i**:   *receive, deceive, ceiling, freight, sleigh*

Exceptions: *either, neither, seize, leisure, weird, species, financier*

C. If a word has only one syllable and ends with a single consonant preceded by a single vowel *(hop, bat)* and you add a suffix beginning with a vowel **(-er, -ed, -ing),** double the final consonant.

stop	stopped	trip	tripped
bat	batter	drop	dropping
rub	rubbing	spin	spinning

If the word has more than one syllable and the final syllable is stressed, double the final consonant.

occur	occurring	confer	conferred
admit	admitted	omit	omitted

D. If a word ends with a silent **e** and you add a suffix,

drop the **e** if the suffix begins with a vowel:

love	lovable	move	moving
desire	desirable	use	usable

but keep the e if the **e** is preceded by **c** or **g** and the suffix begins with **a, o,** or **u:**

notice	noticeable	manage	manageable
courage	courageous		

Exceptions: words ending in **ee** never drop the final **ee**:

agree	agreeing	flee	fleeing	see	seeing

keep the **e** if the suffix begins with a consonant:

use	useful	engage	engagement
love	lovely	move	movement

Exceptions: words that end in **-ple, -ble and -tle,** drop the **-le** before **-ly:**

simple	simply	probable	probably

5: Differences between British/Canadian* and American (U. S.) Spelling

American		British	
e	*anesthesia* *encyclopedia*	ae	*anaesthesia* *encyclopaedia*
-ection	*connection* *reflection*	-exion*	*connexion* *reflexion*
-ed	*burned* *learned* *spelled*	-t*	*burnt* *learnt* *spelt*
-ense	*license* *defense*	-ence	*licence* *defence**
-er	*center* *meter* *theater*	-re	*centre* *metre* *theatre*
-ization	*civilization* *naturalization*	isation*	*civilisation* *naturalisation*
-ize	*criticize* *memorize*	-ise*	*criticise* *memorise*
-ll	*fulfill* *skillful*	-1	*fulfil* *skilful*
-ment	*judgment* *argument*	-ement	*judgement* *arguement**
-or	*color* *neighbor*	-our	*colour* *neighbour*

Note: **In British usage,** words ending in an l preceded by a single vowel usually double the l.

quarrel	quarrelling	model	modelling
travel	travelling	signal	signalling

In American usage, the consonant is doubled only if the last syllable is accented.

signal	signaling	excel	excellent
travel	traveling	propel	propeller

British spelling is often seen in the United States, and in some cases it is quite common; *encyclopaedia, centre, judgement, traveller, theatre,* for example, are frequently encountered. However, these spellings are not the normal, preferred spelling.

* In Canada, British spelling is generally preferred. However, newspapers often use U.S. spelling because it "saves space." In other words, although British spelling is generally considered the norm in Canada, Canadians often use U.S. spellings, particularly in the cases marked with an asterisk (*) above.

6: Some American - British Vocabulary Differences

American*	British
aisle (theater)	gangway (theatre)
apartment	flat
baby carriage	perambulator, pram
bar	pub
bartender	barman
bathtub	bath
battery (automobile)	accumulator
bill (money)	banknote
broiled (meat)	grilled
can	tin
candy	sweets
candy store	sweet shop
checkers (game)	draughts
cookie	biscuit
corn	maize
derby (hat)	bowler
detour	diversion
druggist	chemist
elevator	lift
eraser	rubber
faucet	tap
flashlight	torch
French fries	chips
garbage collector	dustman
gasoline	petrol
generator	dynamo
groceries	stores
hood (automobile)	bonnet
incorporated (Inc.)	limited (Ltd.)

* Canadians generally use U.S. American rather than British vocabulary.

American	British
installment plan	hire-purchase system
internal revenue	inland revenue
janitor	caretaker, porter
john (toilet)	loo
kerosene	paraffin
kindergarten	infant's school
lawyer	barrister
line	queue
living-room	sitting-room
liquor	spirits
long distance(telephone)	trunk
mailman	postman
molasses	treacle
oatmeal	porridge
pants	trousers
paste	gum
period (punctuation)	full stop
phonograph	gramophone
potato chips	crisps
private school	public school
raincoat	waterproof, mackintosh
rooster	cock
second floor	first floor
sedan	saloon car
sidewalk	pavement
soccer	football
subway	tube
suspenders (men's)	braces
taxes	rates
thermos bottle	flask
truck	lorry
underpants	pants
vacation	holiday
vest	waistcoat
windshield	windscreen
wrench	spanner

7: 750 High-Frequency Words:
A Basic Vocabulary List

Nouns

A. action, afternoon, age, amount, animal, answer, arm, art, article, aunt

B. baby, back, bag, ball, bank, bathroom, beauty, bed, bird, blood, boat, body, book, bottom, box, boy, brother, building, business

C. car, center, century, chair, chance, child(ren), church, circle, city, class, clock, clothes, cloud, college, color, company, condition, corner, cost, country, crowd, cup

D. day, date, daughter, deal, death, desk, difference, dinner, direction, distance, doctor, dog, dollar, door, doubt, dream, dress, drink

E. ear, earth, east, edge, effort, egg, end, evening, eye

F. face, fact, fall, family, farm, father, favor, field, finger, fire, fish, floor, flower, fly, food, foot (feet), forest, friend, front, fruit, future

G. game, garden, girl, glass, gold, government, grass, guess

H. hair, hall, hand, hat, head, health, heart, hill, history, hole, home, horse, hour, house, husband

I. ice, idea, inch, interest, island

J. job

K. kitchen, knee

L. lady, land, law, leg, letter, life, light, line, lip, (a) lot (of), love

M. man (men), matter, meat, meeting, member, middle, mile, milk, minute, Miss (Ms.),moment, money, month, moon, morning, mother, mountain, mouth, music, Mr., Mrs. (Ms.)

N. name, nation, nature, neck, neighbor, news, night, north, nose, note, number

O. object, ocean, office

P. page, pain, pair, pants, paper, part, past, peace, people, person, picture, piece, place, plant, pleasure, pound, power, price, president, problem, public, purpose

Q. quarter, question

R. race, rain, reason, report, result, river, road, rock, room, rule

S. salt, school, sea, season, seat, shade, shape, ship, shoe, shop, should, side, sight, sign, sir, sister, size, skin, sky, snow, song, soul, south, space, spot, spring, star, stone, storm, story, street, subject, success, sugar, summer, supply, surprise, system

T. table, tear, thing, thought, time, today, tomorrow, top, town,tree, trip, trouble, truth

U. uncle

V. view, voice

W. wall, war, watch, water, way, weather, week, west, wind, window, winter, woman (women), wood, word

Y. yard, year

Irregular Verbs

(past forms are not counted as separate words)

B. be (was, were), beat (beat), become (became), begin (began), blow (blew), break (broke), bring (brought), build (built), buy (bought)

C. catch (caught), come (came), cost (cost), cut (cut)

D. do (did), draw (drew), drink (drank), drive (drove)

E. eat (ate)

F. fall (fell), feed (fed), feel (felt), fight (fought), find (found), fly (flew), forget (forgot), forgive (forgave)

G. get (got), give (gave), go (went), grow (grew)

H. hang (hung), have (had), hear (heard), hit (hit), hold (held), hurt (hurt)

K. keep (kept), know (knew)

L. lay (laid), lead (led), leave (left), let (let), lie (lay), lose (lost)

M. make (made), mean (meant), meet (met)

P. pay (paid), put (put)

R. read (read), ride (rode), rise (rose), run (run)

S. say (said), see (saw), send (sent), set (set), sing (sang), sleep (slept), speak (spoke), spend (spent), spread (spread), stand (stood)

T. Take (took), teach (taught), tell (told), think (thought)

U. understand (understood)

W. wear (wore), write (wrote)

Regular Verbs

A. accept, act, add, admit, agree,allow, appear, arrive, ask

B. belong, believe, burn

C. call, care, carry, change, clean, close, command, consider, contain, continue, cook, count, cover, cross, cry

D. dance, dare, decide, demand, destroy, discover, doubt, dream, drop

E. enjoy, enter, escape, expect, explain, express

F. fail, fill, finish, force

H. happen, help, hope, hurry

I. increase, include

J. join

K. kill, kiss

L. laugh, learn, like, listen, live, look, love

M. marry, matter, measure, mind, move

N. need, notice

O. offer, open, order

P. pass, pick, plan, plant, play, point, prepare, promise, prove, pull,

R. rain, reach, realize, remain, remember, reply, return

S. save, serve, share, shout, show, smoke, sound, start, stay, step, stop, study, suppose

T. talk, taste, thank, touch, travel, try, turn

U. use

W. wait, walk, want, watch, wish, wonder, work

Conjunctions

A. although, and, as

B. because, both...and, but

E. either...or

H. however

I. if

N. neither...nor

O. or

S. since

T. therefore, though, thus

U. until

W. when, where, whether, while

Y. yet

Adjectives

A. able, alone, afraid

B. bad, beautiful, better, best, big, black, blue, born, bright, brown, bury

C. certain, chief, clean, clear, cold, common, complete, cool

D. dark, dead, deep, different, dry

E. easy

F. fair, famous, fast, fine, foreign, free, fresh, full

G. glad, good, gray, great, green

H. happy, hard, heavy, hot, human, hundred

I. ill, important

L. large, last, late, less, little, long, low

M. million, modern

N. national, natural, new, next, nice

O. old, only

P. plain, pleasant, poor, possible, pretty

Q. quiet

R. ready, real, red, rich, right, round

S. safe, several, short, sick, simple, small, soft, special, square, straight, strong, sure, sweet

T. tall, thin, tired, true

V. various

W. warm, wet, white, whole, wide, wild, wise, wonderful, wrong

Y. yellow, young

Adverbs

A. again, ago, almost, already, also, always, away

C. certainly

E. early, else, especially, even, ever

F. far, finally, forward

H. here, how

I. instead

J. just

M. more

N. nearly, necessary, never, no, not, now

O. often, once, out, outside

P. probably

Q. quickly, quietly

R. rather, really

S. so, sometimes, strange, suddenly

T. then, there, today, tomorrow

U. up, usually

V. very

Y. yes, yet

Prepositions

A. above, about, across, after, against, along, among, around, at

B. before, below, beside, between

D. down, during

F. for, from

I. in, into

L. like

O. of, off, on, over

T. through, to, towards

U. under, until, up, upon

W. with, without, within

Pronouns

A. anyone/body/thing

E. everyone/body/thing

H. he, herself, him, himself

I. I, it, itself

M. mine, myself,

N. none, nothing

O. one, ours, the others

S. she, someone/body/thing

T. them, themselves, they

U. us

W. we

Y. you, yours, yourself

Modal Auxiliaries

can, could, may, might, must, ought to, shall, will, should, would

Determiners

A. a/an, all, any

B. (a little) bit (of)

D. (a great) deal (of)

E. each, every, eight, either

F. first, five, four

H. her, his

M. many, much, my

N. neither, nine

O. one, our

S. second, seven, six

T. that, the, their, these, third, thirty, this, those, thousand, three, twelve, twenty, two

W. what, which, whose

Y. your

8: Measurement Terms and Equivalents

Non-Metric

Linear measure

12 inches	= 1 foot
3 feet	= 1 yard
5 1/2 yards	= 1 rod
40 rods	= 1 furlong
8 furlongs	= 1 mile

Mariner's measure

6 feet	= 1 fathom
1,000 fathoms	= 1 nautical mile
3 nautical miles	= 1 league

Square measure

| 160 square rods | = 1 acre |
| 640 acres | = 1 square mile |

Avoirdupois weight

16 drams	= 1 ounce
16 ounces	= 1 pound
2,000 pounds	= 1 ton

Liquid measure

| 2 pints | = 1 quart |
| 4 quarts | = 1 gallon |

Dry measure

2 pints	= 1 quart
8 quarts	= 1 peck
4 pecks	= 1 bushel

Metric/English Measure Equivalents

Linear and square measure

1 centimeter (cm.)	= .3937 inch (in.)
1 meter (m.)	= 39.37 in.
	or 3.28 feet (ft.)
1 kilometer (km.)	= .62137 mile (mi.)
1,000 m²	= 1 hectare (ha.)
	or 2.471 acres

Liquid measure

1 centiliter (cl.)	= .338 fluid ounces (fl. oz.)
1 liter (l.)	= .9081 dry quart (qt.)
	or 1.0567 liquid quarts

Avoirdupois weight

| 1 gram (g.) | = .03527 ounces (oz.) |
| 1 kilogram (kg.) | = 2.2046 pounds (lb.) |

English/Metric Measure Equivalents

Linear and square measure

1 inch		= 2.54 centimeters
12 in.	= 1 foot	= .3048 meters .
3 ft.	= 1 yard	= .9144 meters
16.5 ft.	= 1 rod	= 5.029 meters
5,280 ft.	= 1 mile	=1.6093 kilometers
4,840 yd	= 1 acre	= .4 hectatres

Avoirdupois weight

| 1 ounce | = 28 grams | |
| 16 oz. | = 1 pound | = .45 kilo (kg.) |

Liquid Measure

1 teaspoon (tsp.)		= 5 milliliters
3 tsp.	= 1 tbs.	= 15 ml.
8 oz.	= 1 cup (c.)	= .24 liters (l.)
2 cups	= 1 pint (pt.)	= .47 l.
2 pints	= 1 quart (qt.)	= .95 l.
4 quarts	= 1 gallon (gal.)	= 3.81 l.

Fahrenheit/Centigrade

$$(°F-32) \times 5 \div 9 = °C$$
$$°C \times 9 \div 5 + 32 = °F$$

Degrees

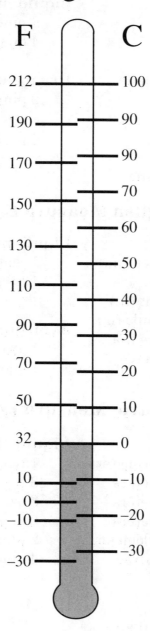

F	C
100°F = 37.8°C	100°C = 212°F
90°F = 32.2°C	40°C = 104°F
80°F = 26.7°C	30°C = 86°F
70°F = 21.1°C	20°C = 68°F
60°F = 15.6°C	10°C = 50°F
50°F = 10.0°C	0°C = 32°F
40°F = 4.4°C	
32°F = 0°C	

9: Common Elements*

Atomic number	Symbol	Element Name	Atomic Number	Symbol	Element Name
1	H	hydrogen	24	Cr	chromium
2	He	helium	25	Mn	manganese
3	Li	lithium	26	Fe	iron
4	Be	beryllium	27	Co	cobalt
5	B	boron	28	Ni	nickel
6	C	carbon	29	Cu	copper
7	N	nitrogen	30	Zn	zinc
8	O	oxygen	33	As	arsenic
9	F	fluoride	47	Ag	silver
10	Ne	neon	50	Sn	tin
11	Na	sodium	51	Sb	antimony
12	Mg	magnesium	53	I	iodine
13	Al	aluminum	56	Ba	barium
14	Si	silicon	78	Pt	platinum
15	P	phosphorous	79	Au	gold
16	S	sulfur	80	Hg	mercury
17	Cl	chlorine	82	Pb	lead
18	Ar	argon	83	Bi	bismuth
19	K	potassium	88	Ra	radium
20	Ca	calcium	92	U	uranium
			94	Pu	plutonium

* This list contains only the commonly known elements.

10: Common Symbols

♂	male		'	foot (6')
♀	female		"	inch (6'2")
			✕	by (2" x 4")
+	plus			
−	minus		$	dollar
✕	times		¢	cent
÷	divided by		£	pound (£ 3)
=	equals		/, s	shilling (5/ or 5s)
>	greater than		d	penny, pence (6d)
<	less than			
≠	not equal to		~	tilde (cañon)
√	square root		^	circumflex (fetê)
π	pi		ͻ	cedilla (Français)
∞	infinity		´	acute accent (passé)
			`	grave accent (à la carte)
°	degree (60°)		¨	dieresis (zoölogy)
'	minute (60° 30')			
"	second (60° 30' 15")		©	copyright
@	at (@ 80¢ per quart)		™	trademark
≈	approximately		&	ampersand (and)
o/a	on or about		*	a hypothetical or wrong form (he *drinked)
%	percent		*	asterisk for note
#	number (#10 nail)		†	dagger for note
#	pounds (80#)		‡	double dagger for note

11: Proofreading and Correction Marks

∧ insert *a word* here	# insert # space
∧ insert comma	.... let it stand
⊙ insert period⊙	STET let it stand STET
℘ delete this	≡ capitalize (washington) CAP
⌒ close up (foot ball)	/ lower case (Ødapital) l.c.
¶ paragraph	Awk awkward construction
No.¶ no paragraph	Frag sentence fragment
∿ transpose (a, b, d, c, e)	Sp spelling error hear *here*

12: Roman Numerals

I, i	1	VI, vi	6	XX	20	CD	400
II, ii	2	VII, vii	7	XL	40	D	500
III, iii	3	VIII, viii	8	L	50	CM	900
IV, iv	4	IX, ix	9	XC	90	M	1000
V, v	5	X, x	10	C	100	MM	2000

MCDXCII	1492
MDCXLVIII	1648
MCMXCIX	1999
MMI	2001

13: Abbreviations (abbr., abbrev.)
A. General (Gen.)

A.A.	Associate of Arts (degree)
A.D.	*anno Domini,* in the year of Our Lord
a.m.	*ante meridiem,* before noon
Amer.	America, American
anon.	anonymous
assn.	association
assoc.	associate(s)
b.	born
B.A.,A.B.	Bachelor of Arts
B.C.	before Christ
B.S.	Bachelor of Science
bibliog.	bibliography
biog.	biography
c.	hundred (4c = 400)
c., ca.	*circa,* about
C.E.	common era = A.D.
cf.	*confer,* compare
ch., chap.	chapter
Co.	Company
Coll.	College
d.	died
D.D.S.	Doctor of Dental Science (Surgery)
dept.	department
E.	east
E., Eng.,	English
ed.	edition, editor, edited by
e.g.	*exempligratia,* for example
esp.	especially
et al	*et alii,* and others
etc.	*et cetera,* and so forth
ex.	example
f.,.ff.	and the following page(s)
Fr.	French
Gr.	German
Gk.	Greek
hist.	history
ibid.	*ibidem,* in the same place
i.e.	*id est.* that is
Inc.	Incorporated
intro.	introduction
It.	Italian
Jr.	junior

K	thousand
lang.	language
L., Lat.	Latin
L.C., LC	Library of Congress
Ltd.	Limited
m	thousand ($55m = $55,000)
M.A.	Master of Arts
M.A.T.	Master of Arts in Teaching
M.B.A.	Master of Business Administration
M.D.	Doctor of Medicine
misc.	miscellaneous
mph, m.p.h.	miles per hour
Mr.	Mister
Mrs.	married woman (Mistress)
Ms.	Miss, Mrs., Woman
ms.	manuscript
M.S.	Master of Science
N.	north
N.B.	*nota bene,* take note, note well
no.	number
p., pp.	page(s)
par.	paragraph
p.c.	politically correct
Ph.D.	Doctor of Philosophy
philos.	philosophy
p.m.	*post meridiem,* afternoon
pub.	published by
q.v.	*quod vide,* which see
rpm, r.p.m.	revolutions per minute
S.	south
Sr.	senior
sic.	thus
Sp.	Spanish
sp.	spelling
St.	Saint
St.	Street
T.M.	trademark
U., Univ.	university
vol.	volume
W.	west

B. Days and Months (Mos.)

Jan.	January	Nov.	November
Feb.	February	Dec.	December
Mar.	March		
Apr.	April	Mon.	Monday
May	May	Tues.	Tuesday
June	June	Wed.	Wednesday
July	July	Thurs.	Thursday
Aug.	August	Fri.	Friday
Sept.	September	Sat.	Saturday
Oct.	October	Sun.	Sunday

Measures

in.	inch	mm.	millimeter
ft.	foot	cm.	centimeter
yd.	yard	m.	meter
mi.	mile	km.	kilometer
oz.	ounce	g., gr.	gram
fl. oz.	fluid ounce	c.	centigram
lb.	pound	kg.	kilo., kilogram
		t.	tonnes
tsp.	teaspoon		
tbs.,tbsp.	tablespoon	ml.	milliliter
		l.	liter
c.	cup		
pt.	pint		
qt.	quart		
gal.	gallon		

Many abbreviations are commonly used like words. There are two kinds: Acronyms are pronounceable words. Alphabetisms are pronounced by saying each letter, but they are usually written in capital letters without periods. Some familiar examples:

Acronyms	**Alphabetisms**
ACTFL	AAA
NASA	ATM
NATO	CBS, NBC, ABC, NPR
PIN	EFL, ESL, ESP
Radar	IRS, INS
TESOL	PC
UNESCO	UN
UNICEF	UPC
WAC	USA
yuppie	Y2K

Postal Abbrs.

State	Traditional	New	State	Traditional	New	State	Traditional	New
Alabama	Ala.	AL	Maine	Me.	ME	Oklahoma	Okla.	OK
Alaska	Alas.	AK	Maryland	Md.	MD	Oregon	Ore.	OR
Arizona	Ariz.	AZ	Massachusetts	Mass.	MA	Pennsylvania	Penn.	PA
Arkansas	Ark.	AR	Michigan	Mich.	MI	Rhode Island	R.I.	RI
California	Cal.	CA	Minnesota	Minn.	MN	South Carolina	S.C.	SC
Colorado	Colo.	CO	Mississippi	Miss.	MS	South Dakota	S.D.	SD
Connecticut	Conn.	CT	Missouri	Mo.	MO	Tennessee	Tenn.	TN
Delaware	Del.	DE	Montana	Mont.	MT	Texas	Tex.	TX
Florida	Fla.	FL	Nebraska	Neb.	NE	Utah	Utah	UT
Georgia	Ga.	GA	Nevada	Nev.	NV	Vermont	Vt.	VT
Hawaii	Ha.	HI	New Hampshire	N.H.	NH	Virginia	Va.	VA
Idaho	Ida.	ID	New Jersey	N.J.	NJ	Washington	Wash.	WA
Illinois	Ill.	IL	New Mexico	N.M.	NM	West Virginia	W.V.	WV
Indiana	Ind.	IN	New York	N.Y.	NY	Wisconsin	Wisc.	WI
Iowa	Ia.	IA	North Carolina	N.C.	NC	Wyoming	Wyo.	WY
Kansas	Kan.	KS	North Dakota	N.D.	ND	Puerto Rico	P.R.	PR
Kentucky	Ky.	KY	Ohio	Ohio	OH	Guam	Guam	GU
Louisiana	La.	LA				Virgin Island	V.I.	VI

North America

United States of America	U.S. U.S.A.	Canada	Can.	Central America	C.A.	
		Mexico	Mex.			

Cities

District of Columbia	D.C., DC	Miami	MIA	San Francisco	S.F., SF
Los Angeles	L.A., LA	New York City	N.Y.C., NYC	Seattle	SEA

Other Postal Abbrs.

APO	Army and Air Force Post Office	Cir.	Circle	Jct.	Junction
FPO	Naval Post Office	Ct.	Court	Ln.	Lane
RFD	Rural Free Delivery	Cres.	Crescent	Pl.	Place
PO Box	Post Office Box	Dr.	Drive	Pt.	Point
		Expy.	Expressway	Rd.	Road
		Ext.	Extension	Rte.	Route
Ave.	Avenue	Fwy.	Freeway	Sq.	Square
Blvd.	Boulevard	Gdns.	Gardens	St.	Street
Byp.	Bypass	Hts.	Heights	Ter.	Terrace
Cswy.	Causeway	Hwy.	Highway	Tpke.	Turnpike
Ctr.	Center				

240

STOP

YIELD

DO NOT ENTER

RAILROAD
ADVANCE CROSSING

NO LEFT TURN

NO RIGHT TURN

NO U TURN

NO PARKING

KEEP LEFT

KEEP RIGHT

LEFT ONLY

RIGHT ONLY

TOW AWAY ZONE

TRUCK WEIGHT LIMIT

SPEED LIMIT

HIKING TRAIL

FOOD

GAS

HOSPITAL

REST AREA

RIGHT TURN　　　LEFT CURVE　　　TWO-WAY TRAFFIC　　　MERGING TRAFFIC

SLIPPERY WHEN WET　　　SIGNAL AHEAD　　　HILL　　　CROSS ROAD

DIVIDED HIGHWAY　　　DIVIDED HIGHWAY ENDS　　　ROAD NARROWS　　　SCHOOL CROSSING

DEER CROSSING　　　PEDESTRIAN CROSSING　　　HANDICAPPED CROSSING　　　FIRE STATION

LOW VERTICAL CLEARANCE　　　NARROW BRIDGE　　　WORKERS AHEAD　　　STOP AHEAD

Pedagogical
Atlas of the World
2000

with keyed outline maps

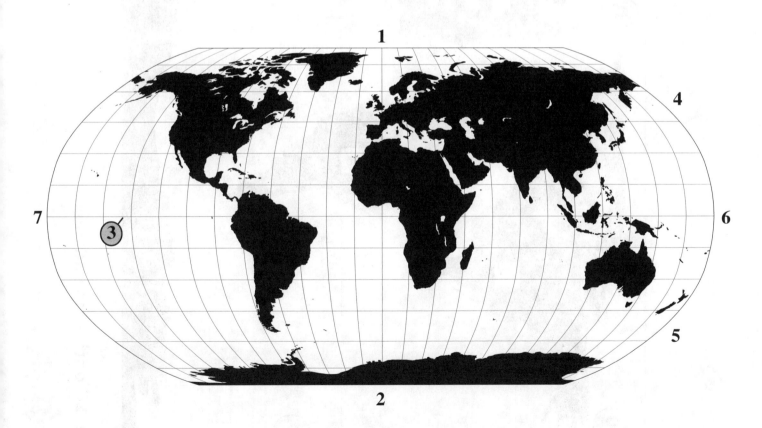

Map 1 World

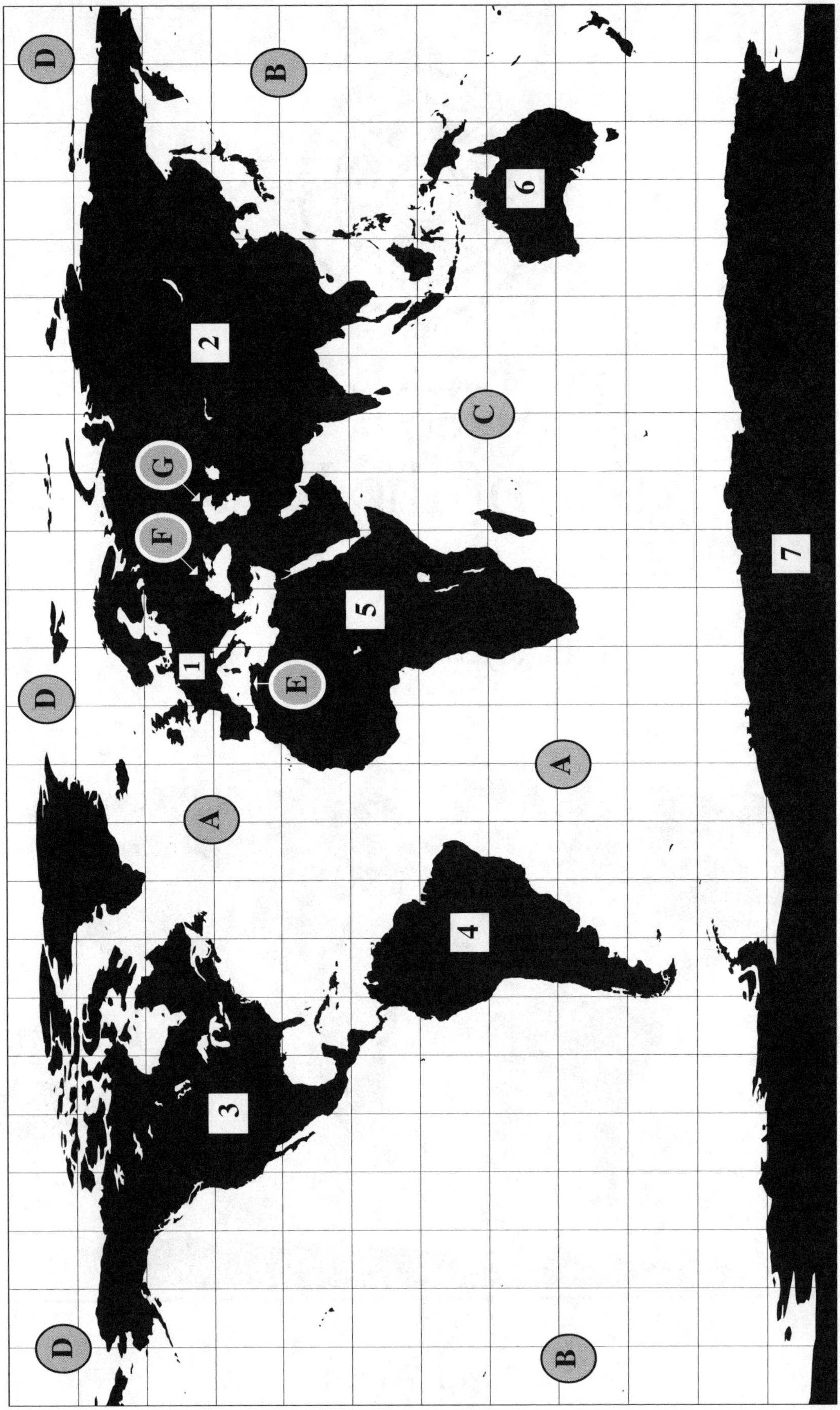

Map 2 Continents and Seas

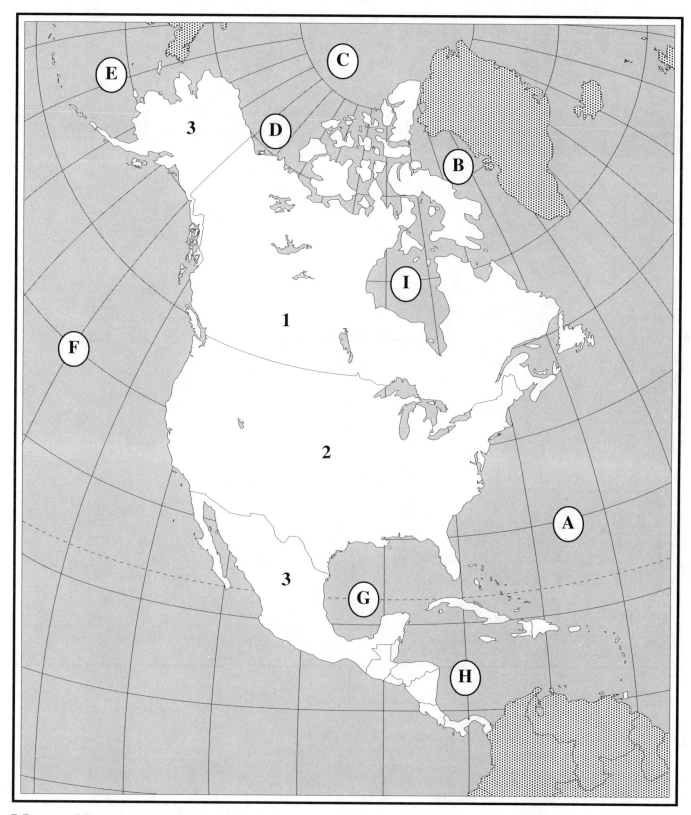

Map 3 North America

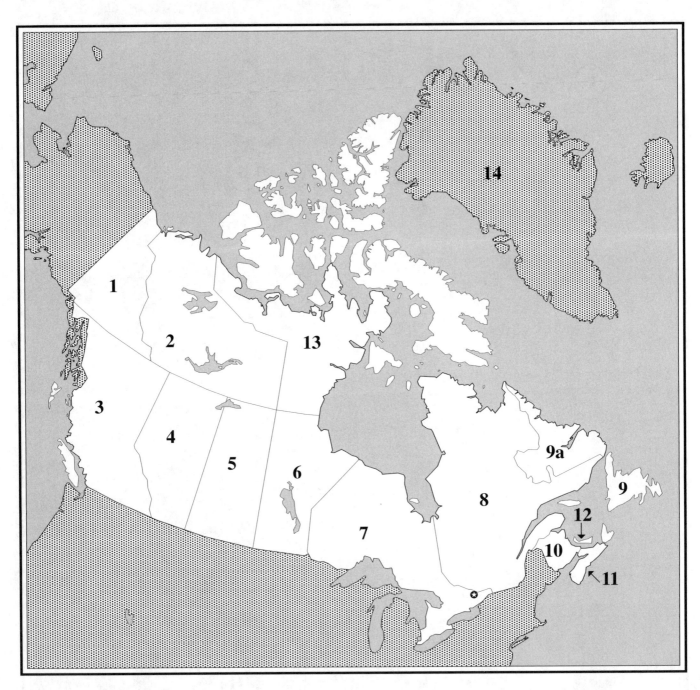

Map 4 Canada

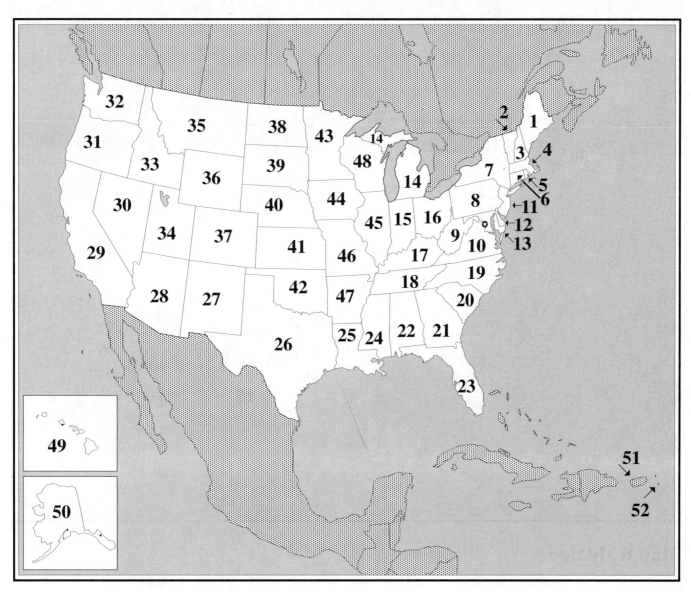

Map 5 United States of America

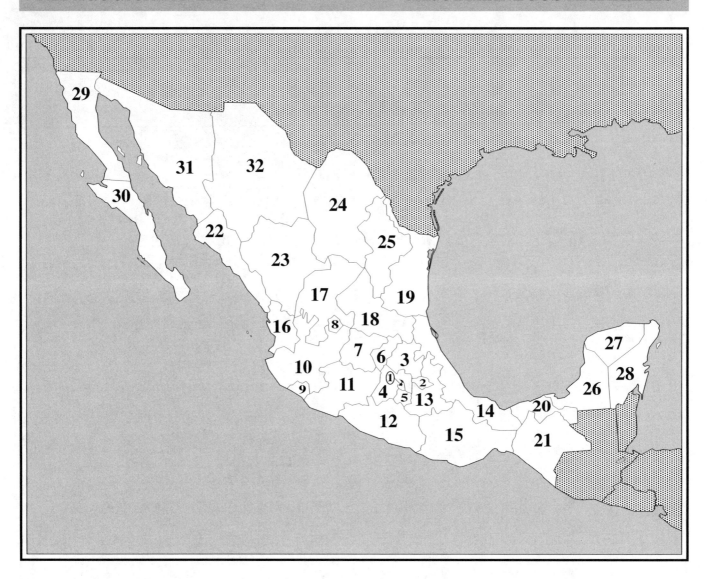

Map 6 Mexico

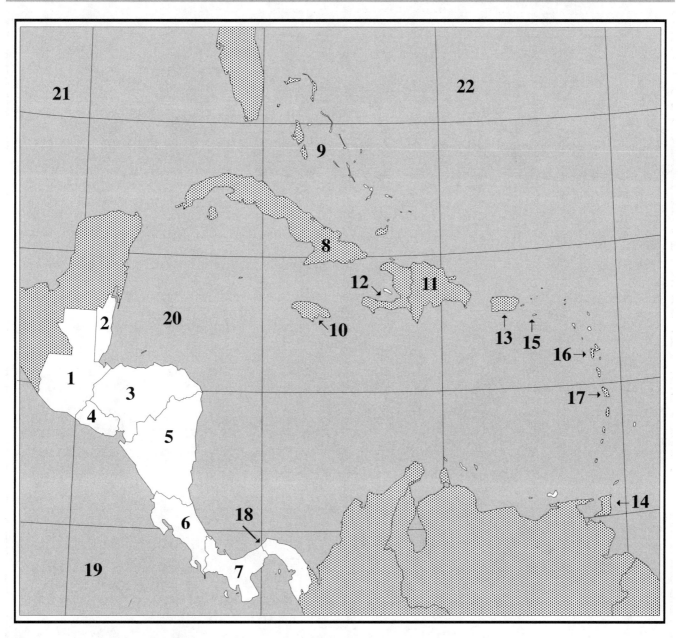

Map 7 Central America and the Caribbean

Map 8 South America

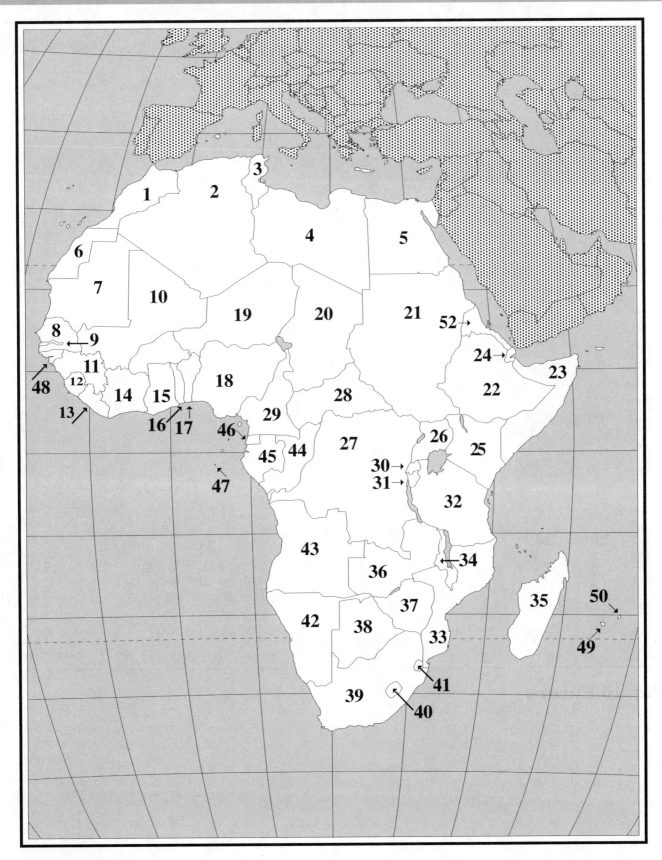

Map 9 Africa

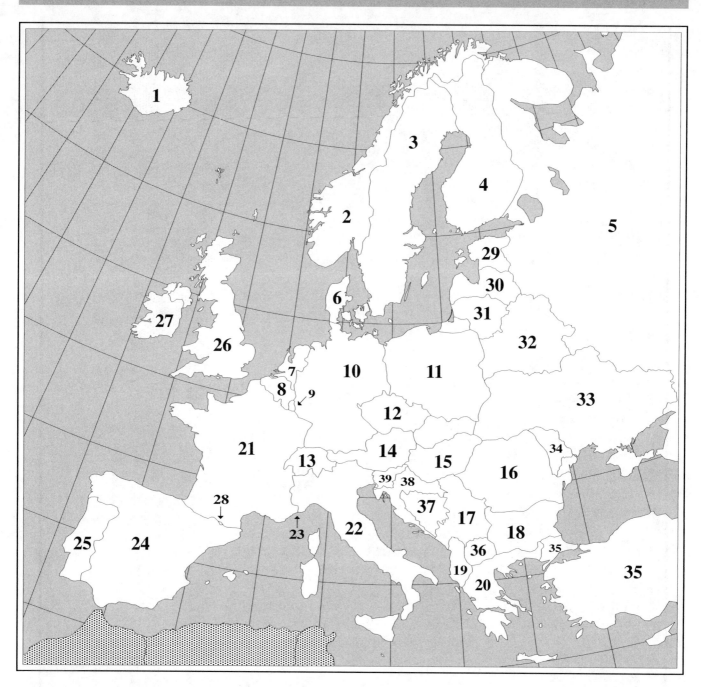

Map 10 Europe

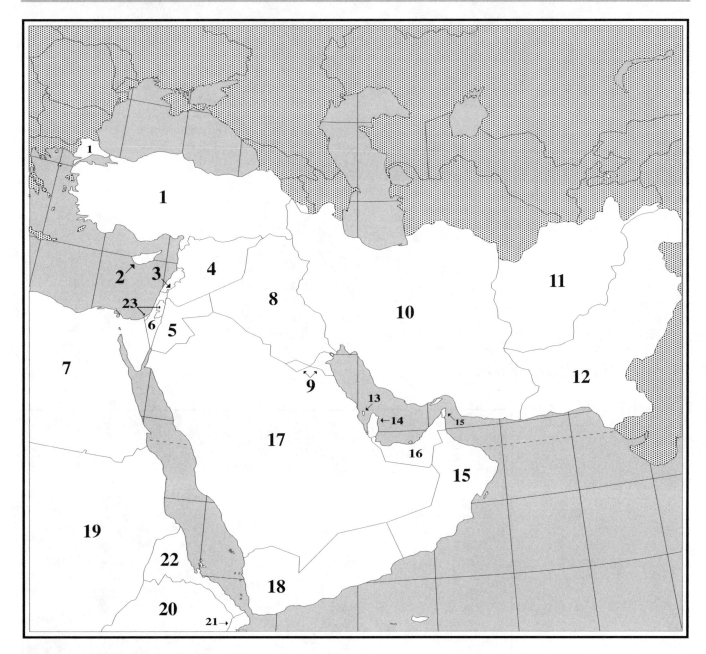

Map 11 Middle East

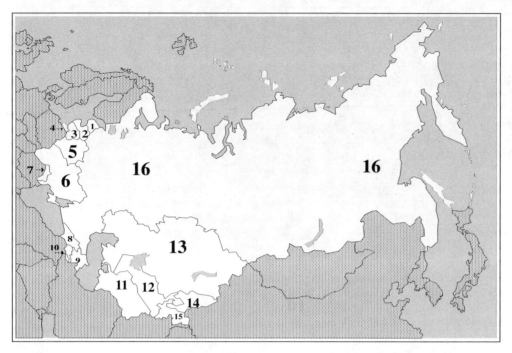

Map 12 Northern Eurasia

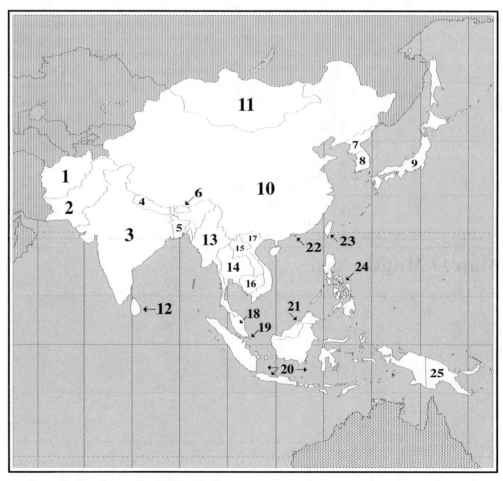

Map 13 Southeast Asia

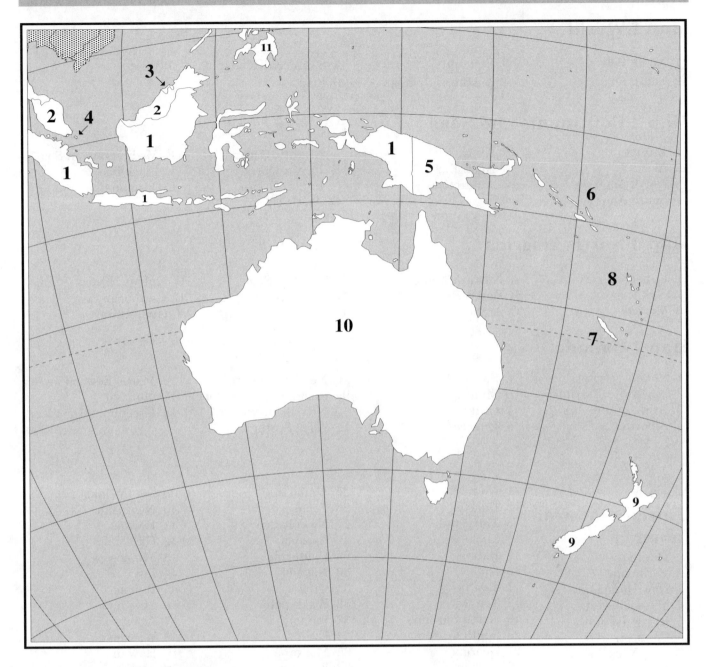

Map 14 South Pacific

Map 1 World

1 North Pole
2 South Pole
3 Equator
4 Northern Hemisphere
5 Southern Hemisphere
6 East
7 West

Map 2 Continents and Seas

1 Europe
2 Asia
3 North America
4 South America
5 Africa
6 Australia
7 Antarctica

A Atlantic Ocean
B Pacific Ocean
C Indian Ocean
D Arctic Ocean

E Mediterranean Sea
F Black Sea
G Caspian Sea

Map 3 North America

1 Canada
2 U.S.A.
3 Mexico

A North Atlantic
B Baffin Bay
C Arctic

D Beaufort Sea
E Bering Sea
F Pacific

G Gulf of Mexico
H Caribbean Sea
I Hudson Bay

Map 4 Canada

1 Yukon Territory
2 Northwest Territories
3 British Columbia
4 Alberta

5 Saskatchewan
6 Manitoba
7 Ontario
8 Quebec

9 Newfoundland
9a (including Labrador)
10 New Brunswick
11 Nova Scotia

12 Prince Edward Island
13 Nunavut
14 Greenland (Denmark)

Map 5 United States of Amenca

1 Maine
2 Vermont
3 New Hampshire
4 Massachusetts
5 Rhode Island
6 Connecticut
7 New York
8 Pennsylvania
9 West Virginia
10 Virginia

11 New Jersey
12 Delaware
13 Maryland
14 Michigan
15 Indiana
16 Ohio
17 Kentucky
18 Tennessee
19 North Carolina
20 South Carolina
21 Georgia
22 Alabama
23 Florida
24 Mississippi

25 Louisiana
26 Texas
27 NewMexico
28 Arizona
29 California
30 Nevada
31 Oregon
32 Washington
33 Idaho
34 Utah
35 Montana
36 Wyoming
37 Colorado
38 North Dakota

39 South Dakota
40 Nebraska
41 Kansas
42 Oklahoma
43 Minnesota
44 Iowa
45 Illinois
46 Missouri
47 Arkansas
48 Wisconsin
49 Hawaii
50 Alaska
51 Puerto Rico
52 Virgin Islands

Map 6 Mexico

1 Distrito Federal
2 Tlaxcala
3 Hidalgo
4 Mexico
5 Morelos
6 Queretaro
7 Guanajuato
8 Aguascalientes

9 Colima
10 Jalisco
11 Michoacan
12 Guerrero
13 Puebla
14 Veracruz
15 Oaxaca
16 Nayarit

17 Zacatecas
18 San Luis Potosi
19 Tamaulipas
20 Villahermosa
21 Chiapas
22 Sinaloa
23 Durango
24 Coahuila

25 Nuevo Leon
26 Campeche
27 Yucatan
28 Quintana Roo
29 Baja California Norte
30 Baja California Sur
31 Sonora
32 Chihuaha

Map 7 Central America and the Caribbean

1 Guatemala	7 Panama	12 Haiti	18 Panama Canal
2 Belize	8 Cuba	13 Puerto Rico	19 Pacific Ocean
3 Honduras	9 The Bahamas	14 Trinidad/Tobago	20 Caribbean Sea
4 El Salvador	10 Jamaica	15 US Virgin Islands	21 Gulf of Mexico
5 Nicaragua	11 Dominican	16 Martinique	22 Atlantic Ocean
6 Costa Rica	Republic	17 Guadeloupe	

Map 8 South America

1 Colombia	5 French Guiana	8 Bolivia	11 Argentina
2 Venezuela	6 Ecuador	9 Chile	12 Uruguay
3 Guyana	7 Peru	10 Paraguay	13 Brazil
4 Suriname			

Map 9 Africa

1 Morocco	14 Ivory Coast	27 Dem. Republic of Congo	40 Lesotho
2 Algeria	15 Ghana	28 Central African Republic	41 Swaziland
3 Tunisia	16 Togo	29 Cameroun	42 Namibia
4 Libya	17 Benin	30 Rwanda	43 Angola
5 Egypt	18 Nigeria	31 Burundi	44 Republic of Congo
6 Western Sahara	19 Niger	32 Tanzania	45 Gabon
7 Mauritania	20 Chad	33 Mozambique	46 Equatorial Guinea
8 Senegal	21 Sudan	34 Malawi	47 Sao Tome/Principe
9 Gambia	22 Ethiopia	35 Madagascar	48 Guinea Bissau
10 Mali	23 Somalia	36 Zambia	49 Reunion
11 Guinea	24 Djibouti	37 Zimbabwe	50 Mauritius
12 Sierra Leone	25 Kenya	38 Botswana	51 Burkina Faso
13 Liberia	26 Uganda	39 South Africa	52 Eritrea

Map 10 Europe

1 Iceland	11 Poland	21 France	31 Lithuania
2 Norway	12 Czech Republic	22 Italy	32 Belarus
3 Sweden	13 Switzerland	23 Monaco	33 Ukraine
4 Finland	14 Austria	24 Spain	34 Moldova
5 Russia	15 Hungary	25 Portugal	35 Turkiye
6 Denmark	16 Romania	26 The United Kingdom	36 Macedonia
7 Netherlands	17 Yugoslavia	27 Ireland	37 Bosnia
8 Belgium	18 Bulgaria	28 Andorra	38 Croatia
9 Luxembourg	19 Albania	29 Estonia	39 Slovenia
10 Germany	20 Greece	30 Latvia	40 Slovakia

Map 11 Middle East

1 Turkiye	7 Egypt	13 Bahrain	19 Sudan
2 Cyprus	8 Iraq	14 Qatar	20 Ethiopia
3 Lebanon	9 Kuwait	15 Oman	21 Djibouti
4 Syria	10 Iran	16 United Arab Emirates	22 Eritrea
5 Jordan	11 Afghanistan	17 Saudi Arabia	23 Occupied Territories
6 Israel	12 Pakistan	18 Yemen	

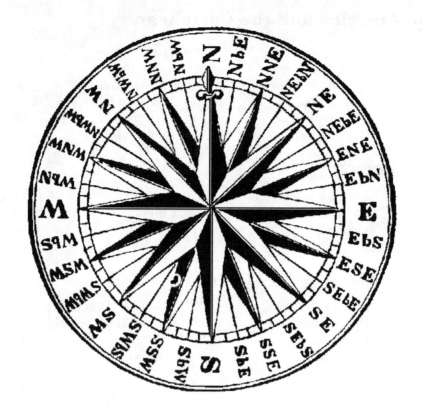

Map 12 Northern Eurasia

1 Estonia	5 Belarus	9 Azerbaijan	13 Kazakhstan
2 Latvia	6 Ukraine	10 Armenia	14 Kyrgystan
3 Lithuania	7 Moldova	11 Turkmenistan	15 Tajikistan
4 Kaliningrad	8 Georgia	12 Uzbekistan	16 Russia

Map 13 Southeast Asia

1 Afghanistan	8 South Korea	15 Laos	22 Hong Kong
2 Pakistan	9 Japan	16 Kampuchea	23 Taiwan
3 India	10 China	17 Vietnam	24 The Philippines
4 Nepal	11 Mongolia	18 Malaysia	25 Papua New Guinea
5 Bangladesh	12 Sri Lanka	19 Singapore	
6 Bhutan	13 Burma/Myanmar	20 Indonesia	
7 North Korea	14 Thailand	21 Brunei	

Map 14 South Pacific

1 Indonesia	4 Singapore	7 New Caledonia	10 Australia
2 Malaysia	5 Papua New Guinea	8 Vanuatu	11 The Philippines
3 Brunei	6 Solomon Islands	9 New Zealand	

The Paralinguistic Aspect

We are using the term paralinguistic to include a variety of acts that accompany language or are used in place of language to communicate a message. Sometimes sound itself is used, e.g. a "wolf whistle;" sometimes the body is used, e.g. a smile. In short, this Aspect is about non-verbal communication. But let us hasten to say, it is not about all kinds of non-verbal communication. Painting and sculpture, for example, could be considered non-verbal forms of communication, but because they are only very distant cousins of language, they are not of primary interest to the language learner and teacher.

We have not dealt with the entire spectrum of non-verbal communication partly because to do so would make the book overly long and partly because paralinguistic communication does not lend itself to exploration in a book such as this one. Such paralinguistic events as a whistle and a smile are not easily classified or captured and catalogued in print, as are nouns, verbs, and topical vocabulary. Paralinguistic communication is very important, however, and we want to give students and teachers a handle on the subject. To do this we have outlined the field of paralinguistics and non-verbal communication. This outline, in checklist form, as usual, is included as a reminder that at some point in the language program it would be useful to discuss and explore the various sounds and actions suggested by the list. Also, as usual, the outline is far from exhaustive; it is suggestive and is intended only as a start.

Because they do fit into the format of this book, we have chosen to present three forms of paralinguistic communication in some detail: the International Sign Alphabet, Classroom Gestures, and a selection or sampling of common American Gestures. The alphabet of the International Sign Language has been included because we feel it is of potential value to language teachers and learners. For example, it can be used in the classroom in instances where a teacher might want to avoid oral spelling. The signs for the vowels might be especially useful because of the discrepancy between the sounds and the names of English vowels (*A, E,* and *I* give students a lot of trouble). And in general, a sign alphabet might be a useful tool for teachers who try to keep their own verbalizations at a minimum.

The Classroom Gestures are included here only to suggest that there can be a pedagogical use for paralinguistic gestures. To a certain extent, such gestures are idiosyncratic, but our brief page of sketches is, we hope, illustrative of some rather widely used classroom gestures. We would like to suggest that teachers and students might be well advised to establish their own system of classroom gestures at the outset of the language program. Our illustration can be used as a starting point.

The sampling of common American Gestures speaks for itself. These gestures have been collected, photographed, labeled, and categorized by Peg Clement in her thesis, *A Handful of English: A Photographic Inventory of Typical American Gestures.* In presenting her pictures, we have used her classification system, with a few minor changes. At the suggestion of Mike Jerald, we added a few photos and gestures to Peg's collection, and we included additional information about the meanings and the sounds that might accompany the gestures. The additional photos were taken by Mike.

Contents

1: An Outline of Paralinguistic Communication

A. Sounds

❏ 1. Individual sounds
   a. Fricatives—Shh!
   b. Nasals— Mmmm.
   c. Trills—Brrr.
   d. Clicks and stops—Tsk, tsk; Pst.

❏ 2. Emotional Intonation
   a. Surprise
   b. Fear
   c. Anger
   d. Irony
   e. Sarcasm
   f. Teasing
   g. Mockery
   h. Complaint
   i. Persuasion
   j. Pleading
   k. Flirtation
   l. Intimacy
   m. Pleasure

❏ 3. Exclamations and Interjections

❏ 4. Voice qualities and styles
   a. Whisper
   b. Baby talk
   c. Falsetto
   d. Command, stern and calm
   e. Command, gruff

❏ 5. Whistling

❏ 6. Humming

❏ 7. Yelling

❏ 8. Laughing

❏ 9. Crying

❏ 10. Coughing and throat clearing

B. Body Language (Kinesics)

❏ 1. Facial expressions

❏ 2. Eye contact

❏ 3. Gestures

❏ 4. Touching (Haptics)

C. Other Areas of Paralinguistic Communication

❏ 1. Silence

❏ 2. Time

❏ 3. Space and distance (Proxemics)

2: International Sign Alphabet

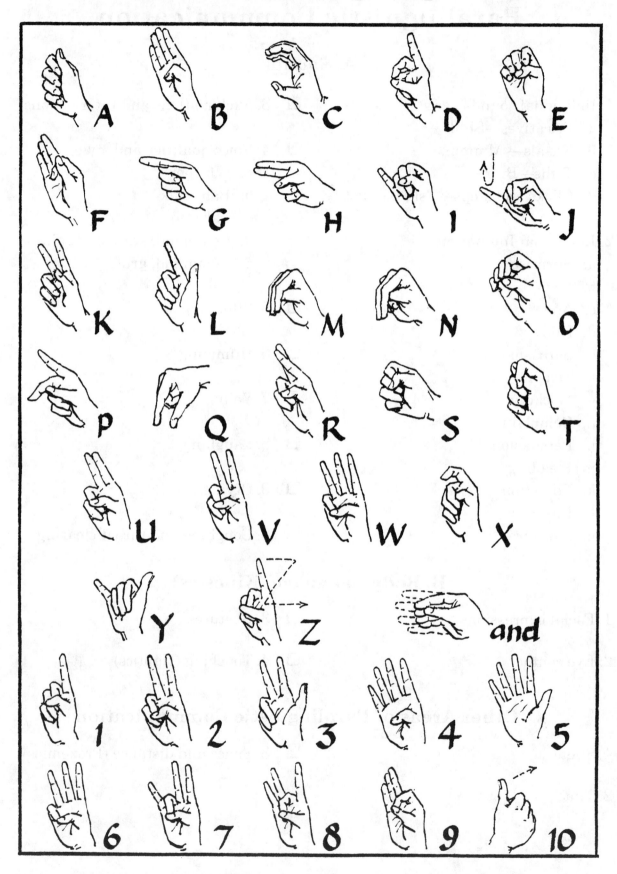

3: Classroom Gestures

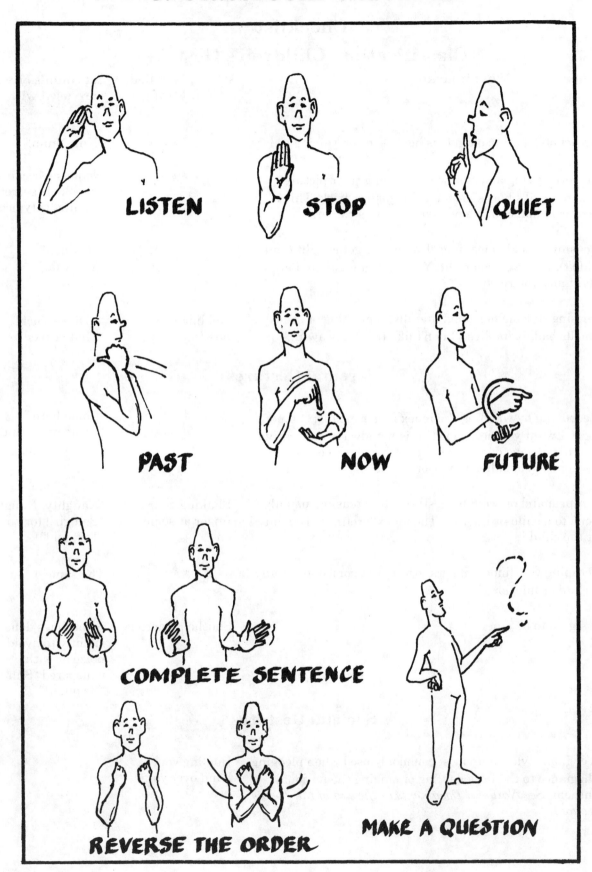

4: Selected American Gestures
Checklist
Classification: Children's Gestures

Number	What it means	What it's called, if anything	What sounds or words are used with it
❏ 1.	An act of defiance, often teasing, to someone giving orders.	* * *	"Nnn Nnnn!"
❏ 2.	Secretly giving a person who is having their picture taken "devil's horns" as a teasing joke or trick. This is very common childish behavior before a camera.	* * *	No noise, because the joke is secret; giggling is typical.
❏ 3.	Teasing ridicule meaning: "Ha ha! you got caught (and I didn't). It serves you right. You made a mistake. I'm right and you're wrong."	* * *	"Naa naa!" "Yaa yaa!"
❏ 4.	Teasing ridicule meaning, literally, something or someone smells bad. It implies, "I don't like that. It is awful!"	Holding your nose.	"PU!" "Yuck!" "That stinks!"

Parental Gestures

Number	What it means	What it's called, if anything	What sounds or words are used with it
❏ 5.	Beckoning by wiggling the index finger means: "Come here. I want you here, now!" It is not always imperative and not always done to a child, although the person beckoned is usually of inferior status.	* * *	"Come here." "Come on."– said encouragingly.
❏ 6.	A reprimand or scolding gesture, often teasing, usually done to a child or inferior. The index/forefinger is pointed at the child.	Shaking your finger at someone.	"Naughty, Naughty!" "Bad girl! (or boy) "Tsk, tsk!"
❏ 7.	Scraping your index fingers together at someone usually a child or inferior.	* * *	The same as 6.
❏ 8.	A signal to be quiet.	Shushing someone.	Sometimes done silently to avoid noise or with whispered "Shh" "Be quiet!"

Societal Gestures

Number	What it means	What it's called, if anything	What sounds or words are used with it
❏ 9.	A civilian style salute most commonly used when pledging allegiance to the national flag or singing the national anthem. *See National Documents at the end of the Topics section.*	Holding your hand over your heart.	* * *

❑ 10. A military salute, a gesture of respect given to a superior or during the pledge of allegiance or the national anthem by military personnel and others in uniform (such as scouts) usually while standing stifffly at formal attention.	Saluting_____. (the flag, an officer, etc.) * * *
❑ 11. The formal stance assumed while taking an oath. This is sometimes done (by those who reject the Bible) by putting a hand over their heart.	Putting your hand on the Bible. "I swear (on the Bible/on my honor) that I will...."
❑ 12. A gesture with several meanings. Here it is shown as a "peace sign" which became popular during the 1960's. It can also mean "victory", either military or political. The gesture must be done carefully with the palm forward, since it resembles an older, traditional vulgar gesture, similar to #22 which is common in other cultures. The context and facial expression are important.	The peace sign. A V for victory. "Peace!" Nothing is usually said with a victory sign.

Gestures of Greeting

❑ 13. A hand shake is commonly exchanged as a form of greeting, particularly between friends and during introductions. There are many variations. In general, a firm hand shake is appreciated. Most people attempt to express their feelings through the touch of the handshake, at least sometimes; they may feel confident, enthusiastic, friendly, gracious, seductive, "in charge," etc. Shaking hands with both hands suggests warmth of feeling. People will sometimes shake hands when parting or as a gesture of having completed an agreement. Hand shakes are more common between men and women, than between adults and children of all ages. People even train their pet dogs to shake hands by offering a paw, a very common trick which amuses animal lovers.	Shaking hands. "Hi." "Hi there." "Good to see you." For introductions: "Hello." "How do you do." "It's nice to meet you."
❑ 14. Between two members of some cultural and ethnic groups, elaborate special hand shakes are popular. Groups which have typically invented and used such rituals include children, athletes, members of secret societies, and people who identify themselves with both a specific ethnic group and a specific social or political philosophy. Knowing and using the ritual gesture is a way of identifying oneself and celebrating one's beliefs or success. Such rituals change constantly. Pictured is a very common hand shake ritual, slap me five, of which there have been thousands of variations. One, a "high five" (simply slapping palms with arms and fingers extended upward, not shown), is the most common gesture of congratulations between successful athletes.	* * * "Slap me five, Brother!"

❑ 15. A wave of the hand with fingers extended is the common form of greeting or saying goodbye from a distance or of getting someone's attention. Emotions or strength of feeling are indicated by the vigor of the gesture.

A wave.

"Hi." "Hello." "Bye." "Yoo hoo." "Here I am."

Gestures of Complicity, Duplicity, Fraternity

❑ 16. A wink is a friendly facial gesture. It may mean many different things depending on the context and the people communicating. It may mean that you are taking someone into your confidence and that you agree with them: Don't let on, but I agree with you. Don't really believe me; I was only kidding. A wink may also be a gesture on quiet con-gratulations: I won't make a fuss, but, between us, you did a great job! Or it may be a gesture of greeting or invitation. A politician may wink to say: I see you are with me and I like you! Others may wink to say: You're attractive to me, Handsome (or Beautiful). Come over and get to know me! People are generally careful who they wink at.

Winking.

Nothing is usually said. Winks are often combined with a slight nod of agreement or encouragement. There is an old saying: "A wink's as good as a nod."

❑ 17. Pointing with one's thumb, while extending the lower lip, and rolling one's eyes upwards, is a gesture of mockery and disapproval shared with someone who will agree with the opinion expressed. It is a common comic gesture.

* * *

"Get a load of this!" This expession is generally thought, not said out loud.

❑ 18. A raised fist is a defiant and often threatening gesture. It typically suggests anger and a willingness to fight. With the palm outward, it is usually a salute of greeting between members of a group or a statement of political solidarity. In the U.S. since the 1960's, it has most often and widely been associated with the "black power" movement among Black Americans, although other ethnic and political groups use it as well.

Often called the "black power salute."

Encouraging expressions such as "OK!" "Right on, Brother!" "Stand firm!" "Give it to 'em." "I'm with you!"

❑ 19. Hitting someone in the ribs with your elbow(usually gently) means that you think what that person or someone else is saying is funny (and is probably meant to be.) The gesture is related to the expression, "He's ribbing you," which means he is teasing or misleading you (usually for the fun of it.)

Poking someone in the ribs.

"Aw, come on." "You're ribbing me." "Ha! You can't fool me!" or "He's kid-ding!" "Don't believe a word of it!

❑ 20. Tapping your temple with your forefinger or making a circular motion around your ear, usually while rolling your eyes towards someone and then pointing at them, means that you disapprove (good naturedly) of that person's behavior or opinions as being abnormal.

* * *

"He's crazy." "...nuts." "...got a screw loose." "...batty." "...loco." "... out of his mind." and other such comic overstatements .

Vulgar and Insulting Gestures

The following gestures should be understood, but non-native "speakers" of American English should avoid either using them or taking serious offense if they are used. "Vulgar" people will often use these gestures and related expressions lightheartedly, being offensive without really intending to give offense. Although these gestures may be expressions of real anger and aggressiveness, they may also be somewhat playful expressions of dramatic humor which may actually be intended to be friendly—children often experiment with such vulgarities among their friends "just for the fun of it." Even native "speakers" generally avoid using such gestures and expressions when they are out of their own cultural and ethnic contexts.

❑ 21. There are several insulting gestures involving the nose. They come from many different cultures, and some have been used for thousands of years. In most of the U.S., the one pictured (touching your nose with your thumb while wiggling your outstretched fingers) is taunting, a comic gesture of defiance and mockery. Flicking the side or bottom of your nose with your index finger is a much stronger, more vulgar insult. Both imply anger and rejection of the person insulted.

Thumbing your nose at someone.

Often done silently, or with provocative noises such as "Yaaa!" "Psss!" "Pppppft!" or almost any vulgar insult.

❑ 22. Jabbing upwards with hand extended, palm inward, and the middle finger extended is the ultimate vulgar gesture in most of the U.S. It is an angry and aggressive gesture, often made with such strongly vulgar expressions as "fuck you!" Although both the gesture and the expressions are commonly sexual in nature, only belligerent anger (real or caricatured for amusement) are intended. In some ethnic groups, this gesture is made with the index and little fingers or the middle and index fingers extended and spread in a V like a pair of raised legs. The intent is the same.

Giving someone "the finger."

Hisses, grunts, or any strongly vulgar expression.

Gestures of Hope or Good Luck

The following gestures were originally magic rituals addressed to the powers of Fate or the goddess Fortune. To some strongly religious people these are gestures of pagan superstition, and some true believers in magic take such rituals very seriously. However, most people practice these gestures, or at least refer to them, as good-natured jokes. Such rituals may amuse people, but they often make them slightly nervous as well. For this reason, some hotels do not have thirteenth floors, and many people will not walk under ladders and they avoid black cats.

❑ 23. A gesture expressing the hope that some specific good thing will happen. This gesture is also sometimes used with arms crossed over the chest (heart), particularly by children, as a pledge of truthfulness: "It's true! Cross my fingers, hope to die, if it's not!"

Crossing your fingers.

"Oh, I hope so!" "I hope, I hope, I hope."

❑ 24. This gesture is done to avoid tempting fate, to avoid bad luck, when someone says something very positive about you or when you or someone else has just predicted some good luck or fortune. Traditionally, the believer looks for something made of wood to knock on. A common joke is to knock on your head, making gentle fun of the ritual and ridiculing yourself as having a wooden head - a block head - stupid enough to go through with the ritual, which, of course, you always do, religiously.

Knocking on wood.

"I hope so— knock on wood."

Gestures of Jubilation and Approval

❑ 25. Gestures of approval and disapproval, dating back to ancient Rome, when "thumbs up" meant 'let the gladiator up; let him live."

* * *

"Thumbs up."
"OK!" "Good work!"
"Thumbs down."
"That's awful!"

❑ 26. Shaking your hands enthusiastically above your head, like pumping a person's hand enthusiastically, is a gesture of enthusiastic approval.

* * *

"You won!"
"You're wonderful!"
"Congratulations!"
"Yea! We did it!"

❑ 27. Shaking your hand with the palm out, thumb and index finger touching, and the rest of the fingers extended is a quiet, happy sign of approval and encouragement. *It should be noted that Americans from some non-U.S. cultural backgrounds may mistake the meaning of this gesture; elsewhere it is a vulgar gesture with strongly sexual implications.*

* * *

"All right!"
"That'a way!"
"That's A OK!"
"Right on!" said with a smile.

Gestures of Congratulations and Self-Congratulation

❑ 28. A gesture meaning that you or someone else has scored a point, either literally, in a game, or figuratively, in a discussion, argument, or some other competitive situation.

Chalking one up.

"OK, that's one for me" (you, him, her, them, etc.)

❑ 29. A comic gesture of self-congratulation. Rubbing your nails on your chest is interpreted variously as polishing an apple, a prize, or a medal.

* * *

The gesture speaks for itself.

❑ 30. Another comic gesture of self-congratulation. You hook your fingers under your suspenders (imaginary or otherwise) and puff out your chest, looking mighty proud! Sometimes you snap your suspenders, particularly if they are real.

* * *

"Well?"
"Don't shout all at once!"
"I'm looking good!"

Gestures of Nervousness, Impatience, Resignation, and Boredom

31. Americans from many ethnic groups chew their fingernails when they are anxious or nervous. This gesture refers to the habit meaning that you are, or should be, nervous. It is often done dramatically for comic effect.

Biting your nails.

"Oh, oh."
"Oh, my gosh!"
"Uuuw!" "Ouch!"

32. A gesture of impatience. When it is done openly while someone is talking, it is rude. It is often done covertly to tell someone that you are bored with what someone else is saying or with the situation you are in. Although it can show real annoyance, it is generally a comic or mocking expression.

Twiddling your thumbs.

"Ho hum!"
"Really!"
"I'm just bored to death!"

33. A gesture of resignation or non-involvement meaning: So, what can I do? It's not my problem. I don't know what to do? I don't know anything about it. Don't ask me.

Shrugging your shoulders.

"Don't ask!"
"Damned if I know!"
"I haven't any idea!"

270

❑ 34. A dramatic stance, leaning back with arms crossed, expressing frustrated boredom and inaction. You are immobile. You have been kept from "going" either because you have been kept waiting or because you disapprove of the direction you are being asked to go in.

* * *

"Where the *** have you been?" This situation is impossible!"

Miscellaneous Gestures Showing Emotion

❑ 35. A gesture of anticipation meaning: that looks good! It is usually made when looking at food, either to show excitement or approval.

Licking your lips.
Licking your chops.

"Mmmm!"
"Yummm!"
"That looks good!"

❑ 36. A gesture meaning "stop" or "slow down." It can be a command or an expression of concern, depending on your facial expression and the authority of your movement.

* * *

"Whoa!"
"Just a minute!"
"Hold it right there!"

❑ 37. A dramatic gesture showing shock or disappointment, particularly with oneself. Variations are clutching your forehead, covering your eyes, or slapping yourself on the forehead. It is often used when you have made a costly mistake.

* * *

"Oh, no!" "Stupid me!"
"How could I?"
"I don't want to look!"

❑ 38. The gesture of covering your mouth, gasping, and staring is one of horror.

***

A quick gasp or sucking sound.

❑ 39. The gesture of snapping your fingers along with an expression of delight and surprise means that you have just thought of or remembered something you have been trying to think of. Snapping your fingers with a stern, impatient, or angry expression generally means that you want someone to do something immediately. Snapping your fingers to get someone's attention (a waiter in a crowded restaurant, for example) is often effective but is considered to be very offensive; it will often get the waiter's attention but bad service as well.

Snapping your fingers.

"I've got it!"
"That's it!"
"Ah, ha!"
"Eureka!"

❑ 40. This comic gesture suggests that you have a good and clever idea for some action. It is sometimes done simply to show anticipation, but when it is exaggerated (often with a grin of evil delight and a low chuckling sound), it suggests that you are being crafty.

Rubbing your hands (in glee).

"Oh, boy!"
"Hee, hee, hee!"
"Oh, just wait 'til I ..."

❑ 41. An expression of puzzlement or bewilderment.

Scratching your head.

"What?" "I don't get it!"
"Huh?" "What's that supposed to mean?"

❑ 42. A gesture of relief after avoiding a serious misfortune. The same gesture is also used to complain about the heat.

Wiping your forehead.
Wiping your brow.

"Phew!" "That was a close call!"
"Oh, that was too close for comfort."

271

❏ 42. A comic gesture meaning: stop doing that, end it, or I disapprove! | Slitting your throat. | "That's it!" "Kill it!" "Wrap it up!" "Cut!" or a sound like "QuekkkkK!"

Miscellaneous Gestures Showing Emotion

❏ 44. Holding your hand out to the side (palm forward, fingers closed in, and thumb extended up) is the signal that you want to be picked up by a passing driver and given a ride. Hitchhikers usually smile and look hopefully at each car while raising their hands slightly or moving them backward and forward as if to get the driver's attention. Long distant hitchhikers often carry a sign announcing their destination. Although the picture shows a lone woman hitching a ride, many women choose not to expose themselves unnecessarily to possible danger or sexual harassment in this way. It is more common to see a woman hitchhiking with a man or another woman for safety and company.

Thumbing a ride. Hitching a ride.

Expressions of thanks are reserved until after the driver has stopped and offered a ride.

❏ 45. This is a "literary" gesture used while a person is speaking before and after expressions which would be in quotation marks were the person's speech to be printed. It may be done in a serious, pedantic way or lightly, for fun. In either case it is a comical, somewhat self-conscious gesture.

* * *

Done either silently, with double funny noises such as "Qurk, qurk" or with the explicit "Quote; Unquote."

❏ 46. Measurement gestures are common to most languages and cultures. The one shown means the object or person was about as high or tall as the woman's hand. Length is shown by holding the thumb and forefinger apart the right distance or by holding the two hands apart with the fingers extended and the palms held inward.

* * *

"Oh, it was about this high (tall, deep)."

❏ 47. Gesturing to get the attention of a waiter is extremely difficult in American English, unless the waiter is attentive. You may wave discreetly or lift your index finger as shown here. You may even say "Excuse me," very softly and politely, as he passes close by. However, these gestures often go unseen in a busy restaurant, and snapping your fingers, clapping your hands, whistling, and shouting out for service are all considered to be very objectionable. They are outdoor behavior, suitable for hailing taxicabs in heavy traffic, an art which may also look like the gesture pictured when practiced by a master.

Catching the waiter's eye.

"um." "oh." "Excuse me, please." "ah. could we please..."

1

2

3

4

5

6

7

8

9

10

11

12

13

14

15

16

17

18

19

20

21

22

23

24

278

25

26

27

28

29

30

31

32

33

34

35

36

37

38

39

40

41

42

43

44

45

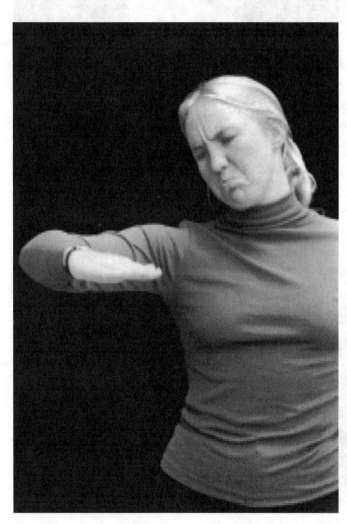

46   47

39

40

41

42

43

44

45

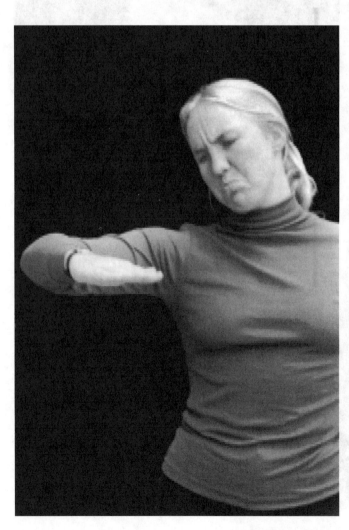

46   47

SOURCES

Allison, Alexander W., Herbert Barrows, et al. *The Norton Anthology of Poetry,* Third Edition. New York, N.Y.: W. W. Norton & Co.,1986

Boone, Eleanor; Rick Gildea, and Pat Moran. *Resources for TESOL Teaching* (Program and Training Journal 26). Washington, D.C.: ACTION/ Peace Corps,1978

Beilenson, Evelyn, and Ann Tenenbaum, eds. *Wit and Wisdom of Famous American Women.* White Plains, N.Y.: Peter Pauper Press, Inc., 1986

Carruth, Gordon, and Eugene Ehrlich, eds. *The Harper Book of American Quotations.* New York, N.Y.: Harper & Row,1988

Celce-Murcia and Diane Larsen-Freeman. *The Grammar Book, 2nd edition.* Boston: Heinle and Heinle, 1999

Chase, William D., and Helen M. Chase. *Chase's Annual Events: Special Days, Weeks, and Months.* Chicago, Ill.: Contemporary Books, Inc.

Clement, Margaret A. *A Handful of English.* Unpublished MAT Thesis, School for International Training, 1978

The Concise Columbia Encyclopedia., New York, N.Y.: Avon Books (Columbia University Press), Hearst Corp.,1983

Crystal, David. *The Cambridge Encyclopedia of Language.* Cambridge: Cambridge University Press, 1987

Dobler, Lavinia. Customs and Holidays Around the World. New York, N.Y.: Fleet Publishing Co.,1962

The Encyclopaedia Britannica. Chicago, Ill.,1990

Encyclopedia of Knowledge. Danbury,CT.: Grolier, 1991

Evans, Bergen. *Dictionary of Quotations.* New York, N.Y.: Delacorte Press, 1968

Evans, Cleveland Kent. Bellevue University, Bellevue, NE

Frank, Marcella. *Modern English: A Practical Reference Guide.* Englewood Cliffs, N.J.: Prentice-Hall, 1972

Gunterman, Gail. "Purposeful Communication Practice: Developing Functional Proficiency in a Foreign Language." *FLAnnals (NI* No.3),1979

Hacker, Andrew. *U.S.:A Statistical Portrait of the American People.* New York, N.Y.: Viking Press,1983

The Hammond Almanac. Maplewood, N.J.: Hammond Almanac, Inc.,1981

Hayden, Rebecca E.; Dorothy Pilgrim and Aurora Quiros Haggard. *Mastering American English.* Englewood Cliffs, N.J.: PrenticeHall, 1956

Indian and northern Affairs Canada website: www.ina.gc.ca 1999

Jacquet, Constant H., ed. *Yearbook of American and Canadian Churches, 1987,* Nashville, Tenn.: Abington Press,1989

Kehoe, Alice B. *North American Indians: A Comprehensive Account.* Englewood Cliffs, N.J.: Prentice-Hall,1981

Keller, Charles. *Tongue Twisters.* New York, N.Y.: Simon and Schuster,1989

Key, Mary Ritchie. *Paralanguage and Kinesics.* Metuchen, N.J.: The Scarecrow Press, 1975

Kin, David. ed. *Dictionary of American Proverbs.* New York, N.Y.: Philosophical Library

Murdock, George P. "The Common Denominators of Culture" in *The Science of Man in the World Crisis,* Ralph Linton, ed. New York, N.Y.: Columbia University Press,1945

Munro, David. *Oxford Dictionary of the World.* New York: Oxford University Press, 1995

The New American Desk Encyclopedia. New York, N.Y.: New American Library (A Signet Book),1989

1996 Census/ Statistics Canada website: www.statcan.ca 1999

Parnwell, E. C. *Oxford Picture Dictionary of American English.* New York: Oxford University Press,1978

Praninskas, Jean. *Rapid Review of English Grammar* (Second Edition). Englewood Cliffs, N.J.: Prentice-Hall,1975

Quirk, Randolph. *A Concise Grammar of Contemporary English.* New York: Harcourt, Brace, 1973

Radford, E. and M.A. *Encyclopaedia of Super stitions.* New York: Philosophical Library,1949

Reader's Digest Almanac, 1987. Pleasantville, N.Y.: The Reader's Digest Association, Inc.,1986

Silber, Irwin and Fred. *The Folksinger's Word Book.* New York: Oak Publications, 1973

The Time Almanac/Information Please. Des Moines, IA, 1999

U. S. Department of State. *Background Notes*

Untermeyer, Louis, ed. *Golden Treasury of Poetry.* New York, N.Y.: Golden Press, 1989

Wallechinsky, David, and Irving Wallace. *The People's Almanac.* Garden City, N.J.: Doubleday & Company, Inc.,1975

Wilkins, D. A. *Notional Syllabuses.* Oxford: Oxford University Press, 1976

Whitford, Harold C. and Robert J. Dixon. Handbook of American Idioms and Idiomatic *Usage.* New York: Regents,1953

The World Almanac and Book of Facts, 1999. Mahwah, NJ: Primedia, 1999

INDEX

Other teacher resources from Pro Lingua Associates:

• **Shenanigames:** Grammar Focused ESL/EFL Activities and Games. A *photocopyable* teacher resource with 49 easy-to-understand-and-play games. These game exercises practice specific, clearly indicated grammar points appropriate for low to high intermediate students at the middle school, high school, university, and adult levels. Everything needed to play the games is provided in 96 pages of photocopyable masters.

• **Play 'n Talk:** Communicative Games for Elementary and Middle School ESL/EFL. A *photocopyable* teacher resource with 61 games to help children build their vocabulary and their grammar, writing, and conversation skills.

• **Index Card Games for ESL, French and Spanish.** The 6 card game techniques explained in each of these handbooks are easy to prepare and play using 3x5 index cards. These are student-centered, group activities which provide practice with vocabulary, structure, spelling, questioning, and conversation. Sample games, given in the target language, are all *photocopyable*. Also available, **More Index Card Games**, with 9 techniques.

• **Families:** 10 card games for language learners. There are 40 comical, full-color, plastic-coated playing cards – 10 families, each with a mother, father, daughter, and son. Each card has 8 features: clothes, hat, shoes, expression, object, cost, transportation, and time. Learning vocabulary and question/answer practice are all part of the game, naturally.

• **Conversation Inspirations.** Over 2,000 conversation topics and 9 distinctive conversation activities. The topics range from lighthearted fun to serious subjects for discussion, from the universal – human nature and interpersonal relationships – to the culturally vital – cutting edge issues in North American society and how people from other cultures feel about them and deal with them. All *photocopyable*.

• **Writing Inspirations:** A Fundex of Individualized Writing Activities for English Language Practice. The book includes 176 *photocopyable* masters for topic cards. Each topic has several variations, so that student have over 600 writing tasks to choose from. This student-centered material is appropriate for students of all ages, interests, and skill levels since students work at their own level. The fundex is ideal for tutorials and for use in learning centers and libraries.

• **The Interactive Tutorial:** An Activity Parade: *Photocopyable* Activities for the Beginning Level Adult ESL/EFL Student. The student and tutor work and play together on these 57 shared activities. Each activity involves developing communicative skills – describing, giving and following directions, guessing, interviewing, asking and answering questions, expressing and explaining opinions, story telling, and narrating. Everything needed for the activities – game forms, boards, cards, and picture cubes – are provided in photocopyable format. The activities are easily adaptable for use with younger students and in classes.

• **Pronunciation Card Games.** 16 pronunciation games are explained in simple terms. They use *photocopyable* sets of illustrated game cards. The games work with the production and discrimination of difficult consonant and vowel sounds and stress and intonation.

• **Solo, Duo, Trio.** 128 *photocopyable* paper and pencil puzzles of 19 different types by Richard Yorkey. Students work on their own, in pairs, or in small groups. The puzzles were developed for adults, but children enjoy them, too. Although each activity gives the student an opportunity to learn vocabulary and strengthen their language skills, the important point is that these puzzles are fun. **"Solo"** makes an appropriate gift for anyone learning English.

American Culture from Pro Lingua Associates:

- **Living in the United States:** How to feel at home, make friends, and enjoy everyday life. This is a brief introduction to the culture of the United States for visitors, students, and business travelers. It is used in cultural orientation programs in high schools, colleges and exchange programs across the country and around the world. In the same series are "Living in" books on Mexico, Italy, France, Spain, Japan, Germany, Greece, and Korea.

- **Celebrating American Heroes:** *13 brief plays* about significant historical figures, American heroes. They are written to be read aloud dramatically. In each play there are a few main characters and a chorus. The heroes are Betsy Ross and George Washington; Dolley Madison; Sacagawea; Harriet Beecher Stowe; Abraham Lincoln; Thomas Alva Edison; John Muir; Jackie Robinson; Jonas Salk; Robert Frost; Cesar Chavez; Astronauts Armstrong, Aldrin, and Collins; and Jaime Escalante. The stories are upbeat and inspiring. Each person has contributed to making this a better nation. The plays are excellent ways to introduce or reinforce specific social studies or history topics. They fit well in citizenship classes. They are also an excellent complement to conversation, pronunciation, and speech classes because the students get the opportunity to practice the natural rhythm, stress, and intonation of the English language. They are well suited to multilevel classes – the more proficient students enjoy the challenge of the speaking roles; the less confident get speaking practice as part of the chorus. Everybody shines. There is a teacher's guide with *photocopyable* masters for exercises and activities.

- **American Holidays**: Exploring Traditions, Customs, and Backgrounds. July 4th, Election Day, Christmas, and New Year's Eve: reading about our American national holidays is not only fun, it is a way of exploring our diverse culture and values. How do we celebrate Memorial Day? What is the history of Thanksgiving? What does "Be my valentine" mean? *Special features:* 4 appendices of typical holiday gifts, traditional holiday songs, readings for the holidays, and a listing of other holidays in the U.S. and the official national holiday of each country in the world. A *cassette tape* of the readings is available.

- **Potluck:** Exploring American Foods and Meals. This reader presents the vocabulary and culture of our North American cooking and dining, typical U.S. foods and meals, regional and specialty foods, tastes, aromas, actions, and implements. This important material is often overlooked in English language texts. **Special features:** for each meal, an illustration showing the way the meal is traditionally served, a list of typical dishes, and a restaurant menu or recipe; a spice and herb chart; a special food index.

- **North American Indian Tales** – *Story Cards.* 48 animal stories collected from American Indian tribes across North America, from Canada, Mexico and the United States. The tales explain how the world came to be as it is—*How Chipmunk Got Her Stripes; Why Dogs Don't Talk; Wind; Bluebird and Coyote; How Fire Came to the Sierras; Butterflies.* The illustrations, by a popular Native American artist and story teller, draw on symbols and motifs from the many cultures represented to impart the wisdom and mystery of the great oral tradition of the "animal people" tales. Other collections of *Story Cards:* **Aesop's Fables** and **Tales of Nasreddin Hodja.**